Jo /
E

(andia U. Husha
Pg. 130

The
Mom Quilt

While each story is filled with hope, some of the stories contain topics that are tough on the heart as they cover things like abuse, loss or illness. We wanted to give you a chance to be aware of potential triggering topics so we have placed a small flower next to the title of these stories. The writers have had to bloom after the hardness in their lives and we are glad that they have shared their endurance and hope with us.

Table of Contents

Introduction

Thank you for purchasing *The Mom Quilt*. This book was a labor and compilation of love, put together by over 60 bloggers, women and moms. We wrote this book because we wanted to be a part of something larger than ourselves. Hours, days, weeks and months of work were put into creating this project but every penny from your purchase will be put towards building a water well in Kenya at *Mercy House*.

Mercy House is a non-profit started by Kristen Welch of *We Are THAT Family* blog. Her story and the story of *Mercy House* is shared in the foreword of this book.

As you read we hope that your heart is encouraged and strengthened by the courage, love and bravery shared in each story.

Most of all, we wanted to thank you. Thank you for supporting this project, for signing on to be a part of something so much larger than any one of us. Our aim is to change one small part of the world through this book. Access to clean water without travel is a life changer for the women of *Mercy House* and we are excited to be able to work towards that together.

You are a part of something that will change lives a world away forever.

Thank you for buying this book and joining with us. May your hearts be encouraged as you read.

If you would like to read more about *Mercy House* visit www.mercyhousekenya.org

If you want to keep tabs on the project and how far along we are towards reaching our goal please visit *www.beautythroughimperfection.com/ the-mom-quilt-well*

That page will be updated regularly with how far we are from reaching our goal of $40,000 for the water well, and the progress of the well when it is built!

Yours,

Paula, Becky & Jodi

Foreword

Kristen Welch, Founder of The Mercy House
wearethatfamily.com

Armed guards walked me, a group of other bloggers, and our guides down a muddy trail into Mathare Valley, one of Kenya's largest slums and most dangerous places in the country. We were observing and writing on behalf of Compassion International who had arranged the trip.

I trembled from more than fear. There was hopelessness everywhere you looked—endless tiny tin shanties where hundreds of thousands of people were crowded, "homes" with no electricity or running water. Plastic bags full of sewage floated in a green stream and the ground wasn't made of dirt at all—it was just a mountain of trampled garbage. The stench was almost unbearable and nearly gagged me.

A majority of the residents were small, unsupervised children. They called out to us, "How are you? How are you?" hoping we would put something in their upturned hands. You could see they were malnourished with swollen bellies. Their faces were filthy with flies covering them and they didn't bother to shoo the insects away.

It was a hellhole, not fit for the living.

I began to cry and couldn't stop. I wanted to shut it all out. I was so angry with God.

Where are you? How can you allow so much suffering?

I stopped and closed my eyes. I saw God's finger pointed at my chest as He asked my spirit the same question: "Kristen, how can you allow this?" In that exact moment, I knew my life would never be the same.

I was a long way from home and my family. I was "just a mom."

– An excerpt from **Rhinestone Jesus: Saying Yes to God When Sparkly Safe Faith Is No Longer Enough**, *by Kristen Welch*

That was the day my life turned upside down. I returned to my comfortable American life and I was a wreck. But I was a mom. What could I really do? Most days my life seemed mundane and messy with sick kids and monotony. I'll admit that when your baby has a fever and you are feverish for something more **it's hard to find God under the laundry pile.** And then a still small voice says, "When you serve the least of these, you are serving Me." I lived in that small, unknown place for more than 30 years.

And all that time, those small yeses and small acts of service to my family were moving me towards a journey I couldn't have fathomed. In 2010, six months after I stood in that hellhole in Kenya, I started Mercy House, a non-profit in America that empowers and disciples marginalized and oppressed women around the globe, providing work for thousands of women in dozens of countries. Our biggest project is maternity homes, overseen by the daughter-of-my-heart, Maureen Owino. I met Maureen in the slum that fateful day. She had grown up in extreme poverty, half-starving, barely surviving until she was accepted into Compassion International's Child Sponsorship Program. When we met in that slum in Kenya, we didn't know that God would graft our futures together in such an unbelievable way.

Neither of us had any idea what we were doing. We've made a lot of mistakes, cried buckets of tears and leaned heavily on Jesus along the way. I continued to blog about the enormous yes to God and moms, a lot like me, continued to give and fund this dream of helping teen moms an ocean away. And somehow, despite our inadequacies and failures, we just celebrated the birth of the 25th baby born in Kenya. 25 rescued pregnant teens. 25 miracles. 25 reasons to give God the glory for what He has done.

Recently, I flew back to Kenya to be with Maureen as she welcomed her first child into the world. We were just two moms again, helping each other, helping moms who couldn't help themselves. While I was there, I learned of an opportunity to provide clean water not only for the homes we've started, but for an entire community of impoverished families who pay for water delivery every week. We knew we had to raise money to drill a borehole to provide water for hundreds of people. Our hope is that it will lead to an opportunity to offer them Living Water.

Most days, I'm still "just a mom." I've got a laundry pile the size of my car and I have no clue what I'm making for dinner. I still write to moms several times a week on my blog; Mercy House is still funded mostly by mothers and I will spend the rest of my life reminding moms around the globe they are not forgotten. Motherhood has shaped me.

If God has taught me anything on this amazing journey, it's this: What we do—however small it may seem—matters. Mom, your small acts of service to God are a fragrant offering to Him. That dollar you give, that prayer you whisper, that chin you wipe, every moment means something. We are all a single thread. At first glance, we may seem weak and insignificant. But when God weaves mothers together, something strong and beautiful is created. Together, we change the world.

My Dirty, Tattered, Ugly Quilt

Angelia J. Griffin
mybestlaidplans.net

I never wanted to be a mom. There, I said it. That is the raw, unfiltered, painful truth. I am about to reveal to you some of the deepest, most painful truths of my life. Things I have never told anyone else. Why? Because I think there is a beautiful woman somewhere out there who needs to know she is not alone—that her pain is real and justified, and that she is more than the culmination of her past.

My childhood was not made of sugar and spice and everything nice. My earliest memories are of huddling under the kitchen table with tears streaming down my cheeks, clinging desperately to a stuffed dog while my parents threw things and screamed profanities at each other. I grew up to a chorus of, "I wish you had never been born," and, "having you ruined my life."

Drugs, alcohol, tobacco, racism, sexual infidelity, and every type of abuse imaginable—physical, emotional, and sexual—these are the tattered, ugly patches that make up my childhood quilt, all bound securely together by threads of pain, hatred, and eventually outright rebellion. It is not pretty or frilly or very nice to look at; nevertheless, it is mine to bear, and I wear it around my shoulders with humble pride. It is a stark reminder of the adversity that I have overcome and the beautiful truth that even the dirtiest, ugliest, most threadbare pieces of our lives can be dismantled, salvaged, and lovingly and painstakingly used to recreate a stunning, priceless masterpiece.

By the time I was in college, I had constructed for myself insurmountable walls utilizing the bricks of distrust and mortar of abandonment that life had so readily furnished. Love was a fraud, people were expendable, and God was a fairytale. So no, I never wanted to get married and I never wanted to be a mom. The circumstances of my life had left me completely and utterly jaded. Why in the world would anyone want to bring children into a world filled with pain? I certainly didn't.

And that is where I was when I met him—my future husband and the father of my children. He was gentle and kind. He laughed easily, waited patiently, loved fiercely, and expected nothing of me in return. He worked hard and spent his spare time helping people in need, and for no apparent reason, certainly nothing in return. He was like a lighthouse, firm and true, sending a brilliant, lifesaving beam of light that sliced through the destructive darkness of my raging storm.

Slowly, my walls began to crumble. He did not try to crush them with a sledgehammer of judgment; rather, he slowly dissolved them with a steady outpouring of love. Two months after we started dating, he decided to take me to meet his family in New Mexico. On a stretch of lonely highway in pea--soup fog, the trajectory of my life would be forever changed. In the dusky hours just before dawn, I fell asleep driving and, at over 80 miles per hour, rolled the small pickup we were in at least six times. The debris from the accident littered the highway for a quarter mile, a perfect picture of the wreckage of my life.

We both should have died that morning, but we didn't. Though I was wheelchair bound for three months, the chains on my heart had finally been broken, and I had been freed. God, in his unprecedented grace, had allotted me an undeserved gift of a second chance, and I was determined to make the best of every single breath that entered my lungs. Just shy of two years later, I would become a willing bride. Though I was still not sure about children, I was certain about him. Two years later, I would bear our firstborn—a beautiful daughter.

If I told you I had been as excited about being pregnant as my husband was, I would be lying. Frankly, more often than not, I was terrified. I wanted to be happy, but the ghosts of my past haunted me. I was afraid I couldn't love my baby enough. I was afraid that the tendency toward anger and abuse had been passed on from my father and woven into my fibers. I was deathly afraid that I would stage a reenactment of my parents' mistakes.

And then she was born—flawless in every way—and my fears were assuaged. I instantly loved her in a way that is utterly inexpressible. In that moment, for the first time in my life, I understood love as it was truly meant to be—a love so pure and intense that you would willingly lay down your life for it. You see, **I never wanted to be a mom, but being a mom saved me.** It taught me that love is real and tangible; not a passing or faux emotion, but a genuine, deep--rooted, core desire to put someone else's needs before your own.

Let me be clear. Being a mom was hard for me, especially in the beginning. I had to struggle against everything I was raised to be and find new and better ways to be a mom. I refused to become the very thing I despised, so I fought with all I had in order to be more—to be better—for my own children. I never had a great role model to show me the ropes. There was no one to call in the middle of the night when the baby was screaming and I felt like I was falling apart. I had to figure this thing out all by myself, working through the beautiful chaos one day at a time the best way I knew how.

Even now, there are some days when I hit the nail right on the head, and there are some days I fail miserably. Sometimes I play too little and work too much.

Sometimes I am too quick to judge, too quick to anger, and too slow to offer grace. Some days I cry myself to sleep and wonder—*Am I a good mom? Do I love them enough? Do I deserve them?*

I have spent my entire life never knowing if my own mother ever, once in her life, actually loved me. I will not inflict that pain upon my children. Do I make mistakes? Of course. That's just life. But I love them fiercely, and they know it. In all my imperfect, struggling, broken glory, I am a good mom.

I have shared this story because it needs to be heard. There are more women than you can imagine walking around with dirty, tattered patches in their own quilt that they do not talk about for fear of judgment and retribution. But we need to talk about it. You need to know that it's okay —that you are okay. I know your pain; I lived your pain.

And I want you to know that you can find healing. You are more than the culmination of your past circumstance. You can overcome the pain and break the cycle of abuse. I am living proof.

Though the ragged patches of my past are still part of my life's quilt, I view them through a different lens now. Instead of seeing them as shameful and dirty, I see them as beautiful reminders of where I have been and how far I have come—that I not only survived, but I overcame and thrived. Though they are still an integral part of my past, they do not define my future. My value is not defined by the circumstances or mistakes of my past, but rather by the direction of my future. Not only am I okay with the tattered patches of my quilt, but I am extremely grateful for them. I now understand that without the dingiest, ugliest, most threadbare patches of my life, I could not fully appreciate the beauty of the new, pretty, frilly ones that are added daily, bound securely by threads of love—the love of a mother for her children.

I never wanted to have children, but I am glad I did.

Ladies, my quilt in all its broken, tattered glory is not ugly; it is unequivocally beautiful. And so is yours.

Unlikely Circumstances
Danielle Agnew
inforlove.wordpress.com

At first, I wasn't even sure I wanted to be a mother. I didn't think I'd be very good at it, but besides that, my education and career goals were my priority at the time.

My husband was ready—beyond ready—to be a father, and I knew he would be amazing at it, so we compromised: as I walked across the university's stage to accept my diploma, my cap and gown could barely hide the glow and emerging baby bump. I was 3 months pregnant.

Two weeks later, I started my career as one of the first Rotational Accountants at a thriving Natural Gas Exploration and Production company in Houston, Texas. And I loved it—loved the company, loved the position, loved the people, and loved my budding career. But as my baby bump grew, so did my excitement to become a mother. And I began to wonder if it would really be possible for me to be away from this little person that was becoming more and more a part of me.

When I held my sweet baby boy for the first time, it was settled, deep in my heart. I was made to be a mother, and I wanted to stay home with him.

Oh, I would have given it all up—my education, my position, my career—to stay home with him. However, going back to work made the most sense for a multitude of reasons, so when he was 8 weeks old, I left him with a nanny and drove away to the office in tears.

It was a struggle. It was a struggle to balance the hormones, lack of sleep and corporate deadlines. It was a struggle to feel my worth while also feeling like I was failing at everything. And it was a struggle to watch other mothers as they chose to stay home with their children.

Most of all, it was a struggle to be grateful in circumstances that I could not change.

As the years went on, I found my rhythm as a working mom. I loved every moment I had with my first son, welcomed another baby boy into our family, continued to enjoy my career, and balanced it all with the help of my amazing husband, who had indeed turned out to be an amazing father. I had excelled in the Rotational Accounting program, been promoted a few times, and worked in a challenging environment with incredible people. Time and time again, both personally and professionally, it had been confirmed that me working was what worked best for our family, and yet deep down I continued to hope for a change in my circumstances... Deep down, I wanted to be home with my boys.

At times, the desire to give it all up and stay home was so strong, I considered doing just that. One day, I even went as far as meeting with my Human Resources Business Partner. She was a working mom like me, and she understood my struggle, but she also saw great potential in my career and negotiated a part-time schedule for me: I worked 30 hours a week and the company cut my pay accordingly but continued all benefits.

It was the perfect compromise.

And it was the closest I ever came to being grateful for my "working mom" circumstances. Because a compromise was still not exactly what I had been hoping for.

During those same years, my husband and I began giving to and volunteering with Compassion International, The Mercy House Kenya, and Child Legacy International, all of which are non-profit organizations that support and empower impoverished and oppressed people in various parts of Africa and throughout the world. As we gave and served, we learned more about the hardships and hopelessness many Africans, especially young girls and mothers, often encounter. We witnessed the impact these organizations were making, and we were compelled to do more. My husband began traveling to Africa each year to visit and work with these organizations and the people there. One year, when my boys were old enough, I was able to join him.

I was beyond excited! Excited to be traveling with him to a place I'd never been before, excited to see the work first hand, and excited to learn more about the work we could do back home to support and advocate for these people and these organizations.

But being excited almost felt strange... Was excitement the right emotion? After all, I was just stuck with needles more than six times for vaccines. They were absolutely necessary to travel to one of the poorest countries of the world, but they had required me to abruptly stop breastfeeding my 18 month old son. Was "excited" the best way to describe my emotions in the midst of the anxiety deep in my gut over leaving two young boys without their parents for over 10 days? Was I really excited at the prospect of encountering extreme poverty and hopelessness face-to-face?

Whether or not it made sense, I was excited. I expected it to be a life changing trip, as such trips often are. I hoped it would be life changing for the people we met, and I hoped it would be life changing for our family.

But I never expected how it would change my life, how it would change me and how I felt about my circumstances.

My first morning in Africa, all my excitement leading up to the trip was justified. What a beautiful and unique continent! The yellowish-orange hazy sky glowed from the sun rising through a long night of smoke from village fires; the deep red earth stood in contrast to the vast horizon; the sounds of roosters signaled waking to work and play, singing and laughter; the eyes and smiles shined bright in the dark faces of the children, and the friendly greetings of grateful new friends echoed... I took it all in and it became a part of me.

Even though I had learned much from my involvement with these organizations in the past, seeing and speaking with the people in Africa taught me so much more. I had known the statistics, but in Africa I met them. I met mothers without children, children without parents, families without much hope for a better life.

I had heard about the obstacles women encountered in obtaining an education and employment, but in Africa, I saw them. As I was kneeling face-to-face with bright, smiling young girls wearing tattered dresses and no shoes, who attended an 876 student, two-room school with a 1 to 120 teacher to student ratio, in a country where over 70% of young people are unemployed, under-employed, or not even in the labor force. There, it hit me: only a handful of these bright, smiling young girls would receive any education past the 3rd or 4th grade.

What would become of these beautiful, lively, smart young girls? What would they do if they were uneducated and unemployed and left with no way of supporting themselves or their families? How would they be exploited? How would they ever break out of the cycle of poverty and oppression in which they currently find themselves?

In that moment, I was suddenly beyond grateful for my education and employment, for my "working mom" circumstances, grateful like I'd never been before!

The opportunity to obtain an education, to have a job, to be able to help put food on the table and reside in a safe and secure home is one that few women in many parts of the world have. In some countries, women are oppressed to such a severe and overt degree that education is forbidden. In others, poverty and the lack of respect for women prevent school attendance and often lead to exploitation. Yet, the opportunity for education and employment was one that was easily afforded to me, comparatively.

That day in Africa, it was once again settled, deep in my heart.

I realized the circumstances I was continually ungrateful for were circumstances many women around the world would be very grateful for. I realized the circumstances I wanted to be different were circumstances many women wanted, even needed. And I realized the circumstances I was hoping would change were the very circumstances that made it possible for me to offer help and hope!

Newfound gratitude motivated me to help impoverished and oppressed young women and mothers with a whole new outlook and renewed passion. Beyond being grateful for my "working mom" arrangement, I began to recognize and be grateful for specific skill sets I've gained in my career, skill sets that allow me to better support and advocate for the organizations that are striving to offer an opportunity for education and employment to those who would otherwise never have it. I've been given so much, and when I am grateful for it, I am able to share it, to give it, to use it to serve others!

When we are grateful right where we are, it opens our eyes and our hearts to see how are circumstances allow us to relate to others in unique ways, and will hopefully impassion us to encourage and help other mothers in their circumstances, whatever those circumstances may be.

Grandma's Legacy
Becky Mansfield
yourmodernfamily.com

Every year, my family and I head to Hilton Head Island. Sure, it's pretty. Sure, it's peaceful. Sure, it's serene... But that's not it. That's not why we go.

Thirty years ago, my Grandma and PapPap moved to Hilton Head Island. Right away, it became our family vacation spot. We drove 12 hours, twice a year, to visit them. It was in Hilton Head that I became so close to my grandma. It was there that she taught me so many things about being a mom.

My grandma had raised four kids: two boys, two girls. She had raised my mom to be just the most wonderful person and probably my very best friend. Whatever she had done with her kids, I had to learn it and do it, too.

My grandma once said to me, "It breaks my heart to see people having kids and then not wanting to really spend time with them. Not wanting to really have fun with them."

This stayed with me forever. Now, even years after my grandmother has passed on, these words ring true when I am playing with our kids. When they bring a book to me while I am working, when they ask me to play with them while I am cleaning, when they ask me to lie down with them at night when I have so much to do... Her words ring in my ears. *Enjoy them.*

My grandma had always wanted me to have many children, especially a daughter. She would talk about it every time that we talked. "When those boys get a sister..." "Oh, Beautiful Beck... The day that you have a daughter..." With every pregnancy, she rejoiced in the news of our sons and would say, "They will certainly love their baby sister."

Let me go back several years... When I met my husband at 13 years of age (and let me tell you that I was hooked from first sight!), I called my Grandma and told her about it. I told her about how cute Mickey was, how funny Mickey was, how smart Mickey was.

When I was engaged to my cute, funny, smart husband at 19 years of age, I called my grandma to tell her about it.

When I had my first son at 23 years of age, I called my grandma right away.

When I lost our fourth child, at 28 years of age, I called her, too.

You see, I had always wanted four kids. My grandma had had four kids, and it just seemed to be so fun. There was always someone there. They went on huge family vacations together. They called each other every day. There wasn't a day that went by when I didn't expect to hear from my aunt. I wanted this.

When I made that painful phone call, she gave me the advice that could only come from experience. She had lost two children: one through miscarriage and one through a still birth. Both times, it was hard. Both times, she felt like she lost a piece of herself. Both times, she remained a good mother to her other children.

A year later, I found out that I was pregnant with our daughter, Allie. By now, my grandma had lost my grandfather and was losing her memory, as well. She wasn't the grandma, the Rosemary, that I knew. She was gone. I could see a glimmer of her now and then, but it wasn't her. She didn't call me twice a day to hear what the kids were doing. She didn't call me on the phone in the morning to say "Good morning, my Beautiful Beck."

No. This time, when I said "Grandma! Guess what?! We're pregnant!" she didn't meet me with a smile or a hug. She didn't respond at all. This time, she was lost in memories of being a child. This time, she thought that I was my mom and she was young. This time, she forgot about babies and pregnancies and enjoying them.

My grandma never did get to meet our beautiful Allie in this world. But because she left us before Allie was born, I have always known that she watches over Allie. She is so much like my sweet grandma—joy-filled, beautiful, funny.

So we carry on our Hilton Head tradition, because this is where my memories were made. This is where I learned that being a mom means stopping everything to pay attention to your child. It means not cleaning up after dinner because you would rather take a walk on the beach with your daughter. It means not worrying about calories when you are eating Oreos with your sons.

Being a mom means not sweating the small stuff because the big things are the things that matter—people, love, friendship.

My grandma didn't live in a fancy house on the island. She didn't have expensive clothing or fancy cars. In fact, she biked almost everywhere on the island until the Alzheimer's became too strong and she forgot how to get home.

For our family, we learned that those things don't matter much at all. Life isn't about impressing other people or having whatever you want. It isn't keeping up with anyone else's dreams or goals. It is just being happy with where you are, in every moment.

She used to say "Aren't we having fun?" with a big smile on her face, several times a day. When we were biking, *Aren't we having fun?* When we were playing cards, *Aren't we having fun?* When we were at the store, *Aren't we having fun?*

You see, a lesson that I learned from her that I carry on forever is this: We have fun with our kids because we choose to have fun. When we are at "grandma's Ocean" and the sand is messy and itchy, we have fun, because these things can be washed away. When we are on a bike ride and our legs get tired, we have fun, because we can rest. When the kids make a mess of toys in the living room and you can't imagine cleaning it all up, we have fun, because as a family, we can do anything together with a smile on our faces.

So, Hilton Head is where we will continue to go. We will lie on the beach. We will build sand castles that are messy and not pretty, but we will take pictures of them like they were made by the greatest architect in the world—because our kids made them. We will swim in the water and teach our kids to do the same, and we will cheer for them, because they need to have their parents in their corner.

And most of all, every night, we will snuggle with our kids while they talk to us about whatever is on their mind, because if we don't listen now, when they are young and these little things are important to them, they won't come to us in a few years, when they are older and they need advice on the big things.

Thank you, Grandma. I love being "Rosemary's Granddaughter" every day. With or without you here on earth, your lessons—the ones that you didn't realize you were teaching—are shaping the way that I raise my kids. And all along the way, I can't help but think, *aren't we having fun?!*

Gracefully Messy Motherhood
Annie Rim
annierim.wordpress.com

The other day, my nearly-three-year-old Bea and I got into it. It was hot, we missed our window to cool off with a post-nap swim, and my husband, Frank, wasn't due to arrive home for at least another 45 minutes. I don't remember what sparked the power struggle, but it was difficult to tell who was three and who was thirty-three.

Realizing that time-out would just frustrate me more, I told Bea I was going upstairs to read and that she had to stay downstairs. Our house has cut-outs on the upper level, so I was able to hear Bea reading in the living room while I was in my bedroom. I have never heard *Hop on Pop* "read" with such vehemence!

Three years in, and I'm slowly learning what seasoned moms told me from the start:

Motherhood is messy.

Before I had Bea and quit my job to stay home with her, I was a second-grade teacher. My classroom was a tightly run operation to the point that we had to have serious discussions about flexibility when I scheduled a substitute. I assumed that when I had my baby, finding a schedule and filling our days with meaningful activities would be a breeze. After all, one child couldn't possibly be more difficult than twenty-six!

And then I had Bea and got my first lessons in the messiness of motherhood. She was a relatively easy baby, and I had no problems achieving my ideals of breastfeeding and baby wearing, though sleep seemed elusive. I even mastered the one-handed read-while-nursing hold so I continued keeping up with my book clubs. What I didn't realize was all the other stuff that surrounds raising newborns.

The inability to get motivated was the biggest. I'd semi-clean, semi-cook, semi-do all the things I assumed would be easily taken care of because I'd have so much time. If I could handle all this with a full-time job, surely I'd have time to do it all and more when I was just staying home all day.

I entered the world of motherhood in the midst of the "embrace your mess" messages. Articles and blogs encouraged moms to let their houses get dusty, to not worry about Pinterest-level activities, and to invite friends over in the midst of the chaos. In many ways, I needed this message. I needed to remember that it's ok to have company, even if I didn't get around to vacuuming. That our friends liked us for us and not the state of the dishes in our sink. I needed to remember that it's ok to buy play-dough from the store rather than making my own—no matter how easy the recipe is.

I learned, too, how to embrace what may look like Pinterest activities to others, but that were really life-giving to our family. Bea started exploring solid foods right as Frank entered into tax season, his busiest time of year as a CPA. Frank loves to cook and so, to compensate for not seeing Bea much during the week, he made all of her baby food. Every Sunday, he'd hold Bea and explain in great detail what he was doing as he mixed kale, squash, blueberries, and quinoa in our blender. They would bond and he would know that she had food for the week that he had made, even if he couldn't be there to feed her. To this day, they still cook together, and some of Bea's first words were "sous chef."

To some, that may look like an insane amount of work—an ideal that would be impossible to achieve. For us, it was a way of bonding our family during a very stressful time of year.

Motherhood—parenthood—is messy, and I need to remember that what works for some may seem out of reach for me, and what works for me may not work for others.

Cooking is life-giving to Frank, but is not one of my passions. During their cooking sessions, I would curl up on the couch and read. Since staying home, non-fiction has become my go-to genre, filling my need to learn and my thirst for critical thinking. In fact, reading and learning became what saved me most as a new mom. I would prioritize and squeeze in time so my brain wouldn't feel like it was turning to mush.

Bea picked up on this. To this day, she meets Frank in the kitchen, where they have important conversations, and she meets me on the couch, a stack of books in hand to read together. Even at three, she understands what brings us joy and responds to it. We, in turn, have embraced the grace in letting some things go and holding tight to the things that make us happy humans, which makes us happy parents.

Maybe, part of embracing the messiness of motherhood, is learning to embrace the grace of our choices.

Life-giving activities aren't confined to hobbies and interests. I was talking with a friend the other day who recently switched from trying and trying to breastfeed to giving her daughter formula. She is so much more relaxed—her days at work aren't spent pumping and worrying—and her daughter is thriving, healthy, and loved. We were talking about how great it is for women who can easily breastfeed and how amazing it is that we live in an era of good, healthy formula.

We pondered the benefits of one over the other and **wondered if, really, babies just needed relaxed, loving parents.** Perhaps that is the true benefit.

Rather than viewing a switch to formula as just the messiness of motherhood, my friend is embracing the grace of options and of choosing what is best for her child and her family.

I have another friend whose philosophy on parenting is "It works until it doesn't." I've tried to embrace this more and more. When Bea was first born, we assumed we'd use our fancy new stroller to take family walks around our park. She absolutely hated everything about that stroller! The most stressful 500 feet I've ever walked were when we tried to go out for the first time. We quickly switched to the baby carrier, where she promptly fell asleep, snuggled against Frank's chest. We didn't necessarily set out to become exclusive baby wearing parents—we just found what worked.

As we left the newborn stage, some things got so much easier, while other challenges arose. Frank and I try to be intentional about raising a strong, opinionated daughter, but that comes with drawbacks of its own. It means a lot of processing and a lot of grace. Grace for myself as I worry about putting in the right amount of boundaries and grace for Bea as she explores and discovers which boundaries she's comfortable with.

In many ways, with this new stage of independence and critical thinking, I've regressed to my idealistic views of parenting: We should be going to more classes; I should buy educational games and activities; maybe subscribing to a monthly science kit would make me a better parent and better fulfill Bea's curiosity.

Instead of embracing the mess of morning meltdowns and days when we just need to hang out and watch a movie, I judge myself. I don't allow for the grace of a child who is very outgoing but also needs her alone time to recharge. I look at other moms who do craft time each afternoon, whose kids are potty trained months before mine, and who make meals from scratch every night. Why is it so hard to remember my own epiphanies?

We are days away from welcoming a new little girl into our family. I know our house will be messy, our schedule will be messy, and emotions will be messy. But this time around, instead of simply embracing the mess alone, I'm looking toward grace. Grace in too much Netflix; grace in setting the baby down so I can still get time in with Bea; grace in accepting help from family and friends; grace in taking time for myself.

When I think of grace, I can all too easily make it into a tame word. It can be lovely or pretty or easy. That is one definition. But grace also means clemency, granting favor, an allowance of debts. I need to remember that type of grace—the grace that still embraces my messiness while simultaneously freeing me from it. The grace that moves beyond simply messiness and into a place of finding beauty in the mess, of asking for help in the mess, and for not settling for that mess while also realizing I'm not here on my own.

Kids watch us. This is something I knew before having my own, but I didn't fully internalize it until the day that Bea plopped down on the couch and chose a book to calm her spirit; it was crystal clear. (Sometimes, this can be amazing. Mostly, it's scarily eye-opening.)

In choosing grace in the messiness, in choosing what is life-giving to me, what I hope to see mimicked is the idea of finding one's own identity. As my girls continue to grow and develop their own personalities, what I most want them to learn from me is that they can be free to find what gives them deep, life-giving joy. What is it that most fills them as humans and makes them better people because of it?

Whether they take on culinary creations or become avid readers or something else entirely, I hope they see how important it is to prioritize that unique thing that fills them with joy.

In the meantime, while I embrace the messy grace to be who I am, I'll be teaching my girls through my actions, with a good book in hand.

The Invisible Disease

Paty Pruet

"Why is he crying?" I turned to my husband in bed and asked in panic. "I don't know," Wes replied in similar fashion. It was probably 3 a.m., and we were revisiting a now common scenario with our newborn.

Newborns cry, of this we were aware, but GW's crying was different. His cry seemed to be desperately trying to tell us something was wrong, as if he was in pain somehow and nothing we did to try to console him worked. He was truly inconsolable—all the time, it seemed.

One thing we were utterly thankful for, though, was that he did not have reflux like our first child. She had been a difficult baby, too. Caroline's reflux led to spitting up thirty to forty times a day—I once counted. Her spit-up caused significant pain until she was prescribed a medicine that helped. She had sleep issues and the loudest cry I had ever heard from a baby. But GW did not have reflux; he rarely spit up... Or so I thought, until one dreary doctor's appointment.

I explained to the pediatrician that GW cried constantly and I could not console him. I had even noticed others avoided holding him, and as painful as that was to witness as his mother, a part of me understood. His crying was relentless. The pediatrician noticed something as I talked and asked me if GW always had a raspy voice. I explained that he did but that I thought it was just a cute little boy voice. The diagnosis followed: GERD.

Instant doubt reeled through my head. *No, no, no. I've already been through that with one baby. GW does not even spit up!* The pediatrician explained that GW did spit up, evidenced by the raspy voice that indicated irritation from the stomach acid. The difference was that GW swallowed the spit-up instead of it exiting through his mouth.

The diagnosis came with another dreaded concern: Caroline had been allergic to cow's milk protein as a baby. An attempt at formula had landed us a scary trip to the ER with her when she was 6 months old. She then associated a bottle with the whole incident that then led to a lot of frustration on my part. So was GW also allergic? I had actually previously wondered the same thing and had eliminated all cow's milk and its derivatives from my diet. The result? No improvement in his crying and milk that resembled white water more than cream. So, the pediatrician instructed me to add cow's milk back into my diet since no improvements were made. *Gladly*, I thought. I felt half-starved from the strenuous diet. GW was prescribed the same medication our daughter had taken, and I left the pediatrician's office feeling discouraged. I had thought he did not have reflux.

If you haven't dealt with reflux before, think of screaming—not me (although it can be so loud and so prolonged that it did make me feel like screaming on more than one occasion) but the baby. And by screaming, I mean ear-piercing screaming; I can hear them in the back yard through the double-paned windows kind of screaming. Reflux was not an ideal scenario, but the scenario I had already lived out with our first baby and the one to which I was apparently returning.

Fast-forward a bit from that 8-week pediatrician visit to the next visit. I reported no improvement with the medication and learned that GW was not gaining weight like he should (my previous trial with eliminating cow's milk and its derivatives had negatively impacted my milk supply).

We began a series of tests. He completed the same barium swallow test as our daughter did to make sure he did not have a rare and scary disorder. Like Caroline, GW's test was clear. However, he continued to not gain weight as he should. By this time, he was also having difficulty nursing. The pediatrician grew more concerned and soon referred us to a pediatric GI specialist.

By the time we saw the specialist, GW had begun refusing to nurse, and we had also learned that in addition to the "severe reflux," he also had colic and Failure to Thrive (FTT). He was only a few months old. My memories during this time are painful. I remember complete strangers commenting on how my baby looked skinny or how he did not look his age. I deemed reflux an invisible disease because GW looked sickly yet did not have a disease or physical abnormality obvious to the general population—they had to ask what was wrong, or worse yet, make some sort of prodding comment such as how he looked young for his age.

Others took the "helpful" approach. Everywhere I turned, someone had a "solution" to GW's reflux or a new technique for me to try, such as eliminating certain foods from my diet or trying something different to soothe him. I even felt some people's resistance toward the idea of him being on medication. While sometimes I sought these tips from others, other times I felt the tips were pushed on me.

Though I whole-heartedly believe people genuinely thought they had good ideas, I often felt my head was spinning from suggestions as I jumped from one solution to another. Worse yet, occasionally the suggestions felt like total insults—as if my mothering were in question.

I like to think people did not intend to hurt me with their off the cuff comments, but oh how they stung. And, oh, how the Lord used this time to reveal to me my own weaknesses and His grace.

Meanwhile, I became aware of a friend whose son had had his own health problems as a baby. He had also had a bad case of colic, and I began asking her for suggestions. She began telling me of the old school tricks of the trade–running water, noisemakers, and the hum of the vacuum cleaner to soothe. By now, I was up for any odd-sounding method. To our great relief, the vacuum cleaner worked! If I sat GW next to the vacuum cleaner, he would stop crying. Running bathwater also helped. Not only did these soothe him (even if the noise did give me a headache sometimes)–they also calmed him enough so that he would nurse. It would still take forty-five minutes or so for him to complete a feeding, but he would eat, and that was a true blessing from the Lord.

Taking GW in public was nearly impossible unless it was a short enough trip that he would not need to nurse. I remember even at church Wes and I would have to pull out the church vacuum cleaner to run while I nursed him.

The Lord's care of GW was becoming evident, as when he provided some dear caregivers to GW during this hard time. Two ladies—sisters, in fact —became what my friend and I called "surrogate grandmothers" to Caroline and GW, and they loved on me and provided me emotional support, as well. Another dear friend who had a child with reflux provided emotional support and practical advice. Family, friends, and church members diligently prayed. Some friends—a chiropractor and his wife—began coming to our house to provide GW adjustments and would not even charge me. After some of the adjustments, GW seemed so relaxed and at ease. It was a special time to see GW look so content.

The Lord also provided some precious girls, also sisters, to babysit for me that summer.

Having the girls babysit provided me mental rest from the stress, and they were even willing to sit by the running bathwater to ensure GW would take a bottle while I was away. I had been instructed by the pediatrician to start supplementing with formula to give GW extra calories, since my own milk had been compromised with the dairy-free trial. Though the formula was good for GW, it was also an added stress. GW now had to nurse first, then take a bottle of formula.

He already did not want to eat, but now he (and I) had to do double duty each feeding. Though it was a measure of grace from the Lord that GW was not allergic to formula, I also found this double duty so exhausting that I seriously pondered stopping nursing and formula feeding him only. That brings us back to our first visit with the pediatric GI.

On our first visit, she was so happy that I was nursing and explained how breast milk is soothing to babies with reflux. I felt deflated again, but I know the Lord was growing me and humbling me. I am thankful he continually teaches me to do things His way and not my own. It felt as if there was no rest for the weary—but if I'm honest, there really was.

Sometimes, they were tiny bits of rest, but they were just enough to sustain me.

To help with the colic, the specialist put GW on some probiotic drops. Wow! After a short period of time on the colic drops, I do not even remember any more colic. She also prescribed a different medication that was specifically compounded for our suffering son. She gave us fair warning that it would take time to kick in—and it did—but slowly and surely GW began eating again.

By the time GW turned six months old, my husband had been hired for a new position with a new company that required us to move to Texas. We found this new venture exciting and looked forward to what the Lord had in store for us. Yet, we also realized we would be 800 miles from our support network. We earnestly prayed to quickly find a church and build a support network in Texas. Oh, how the Lord provided!

We found a church almost instantly that formed an excellent support network—even babysitters (another set of sisters!). Furthermore, our new pediatrician was part of Texas Children's Hospital—the fourth ranked children's hospital in the country. Our son would still be taken care of well.

The new pediatrician spent time reading GW's file, and the transition to the new medical team was excellent. Team? Yes, team; at GW's nine month check up, the pediatrician expressed concern that GW's physical development was not on par with other babies his age. He had just started sitting up and was not crawling yet.

Desperate to be finished with specialists' visits, I explained it was probably because we had moved (which, in hindsight, I recognize makes no sense at all). Reluctantly, she agreed to take a "wait and see" approach, but by the twelve month visit she had a heart-to-heart with me. She was so gentle with me, yet firm that he needed physical therapy and that the longer I waited, the harder it would be to catch him up physically. She explained that the reflux had likely hindered his development because he was so sick as a baby that he did not have the energy to attempt physical activities that promote development.

I dreaded beginning physical therapy. I was weary from his sickness. I did not want to drive to downtown Houston each week for this. I just wanted a normal life back, free from reflux and its complications. And I wanted my baby to be healthy!

Physical therapy turned out to be so good—for both of us. Going to Texas Children's Hospital helped put GW's disease in perspective.

He did not have cancer. He was not an in-patient. He did not have cerebral palsy. At the same time, however, physical therapy was like a support group. There were other children with delays on a similar level of GW's, and I finally realized others were going through the same hard situations. Their children were not deathly ill, but it was still hard. **And I no longer felt the need to justify that it was hard.**

I was grateful that GW did not have a terminal illness, but it was also okay to acknowledge that it is hard to have a sick child. It was okay to need to cry, to need a babysitter, a surrogate grandmother, a chiropractor, a friend, and family members for support. I did not need to write off all our difficulties because his disease was not fatal. For the first time, I felt as if I was around others who understood just how hard it could be.

GW is now two. His tantrums assure us his development is now on par. His impish grin makes us wonder what he has been up to. His "happy dance" makes us laugh. Seeing him run brings joy and thankfulness to our hearts. His love of airplanes thrills my husband. Writing these words makes me want to hold him close and revel in this little life with which the Lord has entrusted us.

I have learned and grown from our experience with GERD. The Lord is faithful, from generation to generation. He provides my every need. He provides our son's every need. I've grown in compassion and tender mercies for the sick—something I never had before. I am grateful for this experience because I can see how the Lord has used it to grow me.

I do not know when the reflux will remit or if it ever will. All attempts thus far to wean GW from the medication has led to a refusal to eat or drink. We will try again in about a month, but this time if it does not go well we will again have to see a specialist.

Do I hope the next attempt will be successful? Yes, with every bone in my body! But will I doubt the Lord's faithfulness if it is not? If I am honest, probably. Thankfully, His faithfulness does not depend on me. He will be faithful still, and I will come to see it in time. And for that, I am eternally grateful.

The Day My 12-Year-Old Got Stabbed

Kelli Pritchard

It started as a normal day in the life of the Pritchard family. My husband David and I were going to see a friend who was recovering from a heart attack. We left the children home to do their chores. They were free to do what they wanted after they finished until we returned for lunch. We had 8 children then, and our daughter, Jordan (17), was the oldest home and in charge of Tana (15), Danielle (14), Keila (12), and Sina, who was 8 years old. I should explain that Keila is my son. He's named after his grandfather, a name that is roughly the Samoan version of Taylor.

The night before, one of Keila's friends had an accident with a knife and nearly severed his finger. More concerning than the cut itself was the babysitter. She was not able to respond calmly and help Keila's friend get to the hospital. That prompted a long and serious conversation with our children regarding medical emergencies and what needed to happen in the event of a serious accident, illness or crisis. We went over what hospital to use, how and when to call 911, and other necessary details that would be useful in an emergency (like who to call and in what order).

The kids asked questions, and we did our best to answer them well. This conversation turned out to be providential.

The ironic thing about this particular morning was everyone was actually doing their chores just like we asked. Keila was loading the dishwasher and not goofing around as he did so. But he somehow slipped on the wet floor and fell onto our 10" melon knife, sticking blade side up in the dishwasher silverware basket. Now, before you think I am a terrible mom, let me just say I had trained my children to *always* lay the sharp knives in the top tray of the dishwasher or blade *down* in the silverware basket. I had been saying this for about 24 years!

Sina saw Keila fall to the floor and begin to bleed from his side. As the youngest, Sina yelled for Danielle, who was next in line. Dani promptly yelled for Tana, and Tana directed someone to go upstairs and get Jordan. When Jordan came down, she found Keila sitting on a kitchen stool with everyone gathered around him.

Danielle had put a kitchen towel (not the most sanitary) on his side to stop the bleeding. Jordan started in with the questions: "What happened?" "Can you talk?" "Does it hurt?" After the assessment, Tana picked up the phone. Jordan said, "Are you calling 911?" Tana replied, "No, mom and dad." Jordan agreed that would be a good idea based on her initial intake of Keila's condition. As far as they knew, the knife cut him as he fell.

David and I were having a lovely visit with our friend and so thankful he was recovering well and would have no ill effects from the heart attack. His outlook was positive, and he had committed to never take life for granted. This had motivated him to live a healthy lifestyle. During this conversation, David took the call from Tana, and I knew immediately that something was terribly wrong.

David is one of the most even-keeled people I know. He is especially calm in the midst of trauma, tension or conflict. So I was surprised when his voice got tense with our children. I heard him ask, "Is he breathing?" Not a good sign. Then I heard him ask, "Is he bleeding out?" He told me calmly, "Keila's been cut." My heart started racing. At this point, I was grabbing for the phone because I couldn't take it anymore. While David was excusing us with our guests, I was grilling the kids with a million questions.

We left with our friends promising to pray for us. We drove towards the kids while instructing them, based on their assessment of Keila, to put him in the car and meet us halfway in the WalMart parking lot. The plan was to go on to the pediatrician's office from there for stitches. I called ahead to say, "Keila has cut himself and might need a few stitches."

It's important for you to know that our doctor is more than just a doctor. Dr. Clapper is our friend who has cared for our children for years. He is also a big supporter of our Young Life ministry. We trust him and he trusts us. We are also a pretty healthy bunch. We try to be low maintenance and tend to see our friend mostly for sports physicals and well-children checks. Therefore, Dr. Clapper knows that when we come in, it is most likely something fairly serious.

The other thing that is characteristic of our family is we always stay together. We are "be withers." Jordan could have brought Keila to us alone, but that would never happen. All five children piled into our small Dodge Neon to transport Keila that day. In the parking lot, Tana put Keila in the van with David and I. The rest of the children followed us to the pediatrician's office. That actually worked out well, because Tana carried Keila each time he needed to be moved.

David and I were feeling pretty calm as we arrived with Keila. Our friend quietly listened as we explained what happened. But as soon as he examined Keila he looked at us and said, "This isn't a cut, it's a stab wound. I'm calling an ambulance. He needs to go the emergency room immediately!" Now my heart started beating hard again. Was my son going to die right here in front of all of us? We asked a few rapid questions, there was a brief exchange between David and Dr. Clapper, and the next thing I knew, we were speeding to the E.R. at Children's Hospital with Keila in my arms!

With my social work background, I began warning David about the line
of questioning I knew would take place when we got there, with the
tamest being, "How exactly did this boy get stabbed?" You see, David is a
big Samoan at 6'1" 250 pounds. If you don't know him, he can easily be
misunderstood, especially when he's focused and driven by love and
concern for his son. He was determined to get Keila there and have
someone tell us he was going to be all right.

I don't think he heard any of my cautionary words.

The nurses led us straight back to a room. It was obvious our friend had
called ahead. The team immediately checked Keila and started him on
morphine as they began to poke and prod his wound. All of our children
were in the room with us. A lot of medical professionals were quickly
coming in and out; there was a lot of activity. I was right at Keila's face
trying to explain what was happening. I could see David listening intently
and processing this whole scene, preparing to respond to decisions we
might need to make. I invited the other children to come around and
explained the issues as best I could.

Keila remained brave during all the commotion (nothing like morphine
to help with courage!). The only time he got teary was when the doctor
determined his spleen had been punctured and told Keila his 7th grade
football season was over.

Our son was a real trooper, and everyone tried to stay strong for him.
Sina had the hardest time, mostly because at 8, she didn't understand
what all this meant. There were a few light moments when we all smiled,
like when Keila looked at the alphabet border and asked, "Do you think
those letters are in any particular order?"

We spent at least 6 hours in ER. I think that was a little long, but I also
think this was an unusual case. We met a very serious, small in stature,
pediatric surgeon who eventually came in with paper, a pen and a plan.
The plan was to take Keila back to surgery and open up his chest to A)
make sure there was no infection brewing, B) check for internal bleeding,
and C) assess the damage the knife had done. Remember that we started
this ordeal expecting stitches and a ticket home. Suddenly, we were
facing much different outcomes.

I took one look at David, and I knew this was not going to fly. I remember
trying to get his attention to remind him we were in a children's hospital.
These people loved and cared for children really well and were really,
really smart and experienced. Before I could get that communicated
respectfully to him, he asked the doctor, "Isn't there anything less
invasive we could try first?"

I was horrified inside but remained steady on the outside. My thoughts
were running rampant. He's challenging the pediatric surgeon! She'll

think we don't care about our son! What if we're wrong and he starts going downhill fast? The surgeon looked sternly at David, held up her pointer finger and said, "Just a minute please" and walked out of the room. We weren't sure what that meant. I didn't know whether to yell, cry or celebrate. She returned with a second plan that was in fact, way less invasive. Rather than surgery, she proposed we use dye, then do a CAT scan to rule out big problems, and then observe him for 24 hours. I fell in love with my husband all over again. I was happy to begin plan B.

We ended up in pediatric ICU, monitored very closely. I stayed with Keila, and David took the rest of the children home. And can you believe it—we never did get stitches!

I know there are families that have experienced way worse than this in the hospital and had outcomes far more devastating. But for us, it was the first time we had been in the ER with any of our eight children. We learned and grew individually and as a family. Keila stayed for two nights under the compassionate and watchful eye of the hospital staff. He was released and put on restricted physical activity for six months so his wounded spleen could fully heal. We were a grateful family.

The full impact of any trauma is often not realized for some time after the event. Here is what deepened in us:

As a wife, my trust and thankfulness for male wiring grew. I sensed a small example of the weight our husbands carry for the protection and provision of their families. I was so glad I had yielded to my husband in that moment of asking for a less invasive plan. We evaded major stomach surgery and the long recovery that would have followed.

Secondly, I was affirmed in our parenting and felt our children exercised the self-control they needed in a very scary situation. They were able to think, act and help each other. I know there will be other times when this won't be the case. But on that day, it was encouraging for them and made a bond and a memory that they've carried into adulthood.

Keila was able to weather the storm of being poked and prodded with great courage. Yes, his family was right there with him, but parents never know how much their children have internalized their character training until the storms of life hit. He was able to respond politely and cooperatively during the exam and the impending procedures that certainly were not pleasant, though they were way better than surgery.

Lastly, the presence of community was comforting and invaluable. We were never meant to go it alone in life. The family, friends, church and community that came around us were amazing. We felt loved, cared for, prayed over and very much covered by many, many people. This changed us forever. It is a transformative thing to know just how much you need each other, not just in the celebrations of life, but also in the storms!

Motherhood –
The Happily Ever After We Didn't Expect

Julie Brasington
happyhomefairy.com

After struggling with infertility for 4 ½ years, I got the surprise of my life one October morning in 2008. With hands shaking and heart pounding, I cut out some paper shaped pumpkins and laid them on the carpet in a trail leading to the kitchen, where the pregnancy test awaited with a note saying, *"Looks like we will be adding a little pumpkin to our family in 9 months!"*

When my husband woke up, he started freaking out and making comments about how he had *thought* my boobs looked larger than usual —ha!

We had to go get blood work done to be sure, but before we left the house, my husband took me in his arms and said with a huge grin, "C'mon, Cinderella, let's get you ready for the ball!"

The blood test results were positive, and our new happily ever after began. For 9 months, I dreamed and dreamed about the perfect birth story. I was determined to have an all-natural, no meds, poop-my-baby-out-like-an-Amazon-woman kind of birth. I envisioned this super worshipful labor where I read Scriptures while enduring contractions, lovingly prayed with my husband through the pain, and shared the Gospel with the nurses in between "hees" and "hoos." And there would be absolutely NO mention of a C-section. No siree-bob.

Then my due date came and went.

And then two more weeks passed without one little contraction. Not even a Braxton Hicks or squeeze of pain.

The doctor ordered an ultrasound, and we discovered that my baby was measuring to be about 10 pounds and needed to be delivered via caesarean right away.

This was not the plan, and definitely not my happily ever after.

I was *petrified*. What if the doctor mixed up my organs when putting them back? Or, worse, what if someone's contact fell into my gaping uterus and they closed me up with it still inside and it would get infected and I would never be able to have a baby again? My husband and I had watched every single episode of Grey's Anatomy, so I knew my fears were perfectly reasonable.

But just as I had to lay down my timeline for getting pregnant, this was another expectation that had to go.

After that, I quickly learned through a baby with colic, nursing issues, reflux, and an almost non-existent desire to sleep, that I had a whole bunch of expectations about motherhood that needed to be tossed into the diaper pail.

I even thought I wouldn't have to deal with pregnancy weight—certainly not for almost 18 full months after giving birth. Just in time to get pregnant with our second son.

On the day of our second son's birth, what was supposed to be a quick and easy C-section I was more mentally prepared for ended in overhearing the doctor's hushed voice to the nurse whispering, "It could go either way..." as they quickly rolled our little baby to the NICU.

You could say that I wasn't exactly feeling like Cinderella at the ball anymore.

Our new baby spent three whole months in the NICU, and we struggled to balance having a two year old at home, full-time jobs, and a sick baby. The doctors told us everything. He had a horrible genetic disease; no, he had an equally awful illness that required six weeks of chemo. One doctor even hugged us and said we better make him comfortable because he wouldn't last long.

This was motherhood?!

This was HARD. In fact, there have been many days where I struggled to not be disappointed with certain aspects of motherhood.

I think it kind of started with those 4+ years of infertility. During that season, I believe I put having children on a bit of a pedestal and conjured up in my head this notion that motherhood was only craft-making and laughter and healthy kids around the dinner table happily eating whatever amazing meal I had all kinds of time to prepare that day.

So, of course when I was given kids who only eat five things and frequently throw up all over the car seat cover that I have no idea how to take off and wash, I have found myself, on occasion, to be a bit disillusioned.

Where were my perfect deliveries and perfectly healthy kids and perfectly easy motherhood and happily ever after?

The answer? NOWHERE.

Because if motherhood were about perfection and ease, it wouldn't be beautiful.

Motherhood involves sacrifice, and sacrifice—no matter what it looks like —is always beautiful.

That body that got stretched for 9 months? It bears the marks of a woman who grew life. That muffin top is a gift and a reminder of what you did for someone else.

That is beautiful.

The birth you planned, down to the candlelit second? It doesn't matter if your baby came out the door or the window—you brought a human being into the world!

That is beautiful.

Those nights where you never slept, and that nursing diet where you could only eat chicken because your baby was allergic to pretty much everything else? It shows a woman giving up her life to serve another.

That is beautiful.

The gentle hands that faithfully wipe bottoms and noses every day?

Beautiful.

The way you still rock your three year old to sleep?

Beautiful.

The hair you held back while your little girl stood over the toilet with a tummy bug?

Beautiful.

The little toy you spent an hour searching for before bed because a little someone would have definitely had a meltdown of epic proportions without it?

Beautiful.

The way you sat and played a video game with your oldest son simply because he invited you to.

The grace you showed them when they colored with red Sharpie on the white fridge. The little love note you slipped in her lunch pail.

All breathtakingly beautiful.

Even those piles of laundry you folded and they just dumped out have beauty to it when you are able to laugh out loud and start a sock ball fight in the middle of the mess.

From the moment we discover there is a little peanut growing in our bellies, we begin to learn about the importance of setting aside what we want in exchange for what's best. It becomes less about getting and more about giving away.

As mothers. we are doing the hard work of serving and loving and raising children who will grow to serve and love and raise another generation. The faithful work and sacrifice and muffin tops make an eternal difference.

It's hard to keep this perspective when they break your favorite plate or rub a booger on your leg, but the seeds are planted with every surrender of your will, your body, your convenience, your comfort, and even, at times, your sanity.

We might have our hands full, but they are full of blessings. And our initial happily-ever-afters get rewritten to tell a much richer story. A story that actually ends up giving back far more joy and beauty than we could have ever imagined.

I remember sitting in the NICU one day, holding my baby and singing worship songs over him, and I felt an overwhelming sense of gratitude that this precious little boy was mine.

I no longer cared that he wasn't "perfect." It didn't bother me that he had a hundred tubes and a diagnosis that seemed to be heading toward us like a freight train.

He is my boy. My blessing. My gift.

And he is worth it.

Cranberried Motherhood

Kate Harden

bellsthatring.blogspot.com

It was midday. The sun was shining through our wide front window, casting beams onto our white rented walls. The house was quiet—a rarity —thanks to the youngest being deep in his daily nap. The oldest boy was immersed in play on the other side of our home. My middle child was in the playroom, most certainly whipping up something fine in her toy kitchen, or mothering her doll babies, or pretending to be a fabulous fairy or something of the like. I was sitting at my narrow oak desk, checking mundane tasks off my to-do list and sending a slew of imminent emails.

Just as I was beginning to get somewhere with my work, my girl walked into my typing space wearing a brightly colored tutu and plastic heels. She was four and half at the time, her round face holding onto a few of her baby features. She shimmied up quietly to my desk with a simple request:

"Mama, can you please get me a cup of cranberry juice?"

In email-mode, I curtly responded with a brash, "In a minute."

With eyes fixed on the lit screen before me, I proceeded for several minutes to answer emails and make way through my agenda list. After a lengthy bit of time had passed, my fancy lady came back to ask again for her cup of liquid fruit. I again scurried her away quickly, assuring her that I would fetch her drink very soon.

After I finally wrapped up my desk work, I went into our kitchen (probably to relieve my own parched throat) and noticed that my girl-child had gotten the cranberry juice out for me and rested it on the counter. My heart started to turn over in guilt at that moment, thinking about her small hands reaching high into the cold refrigerator to grab her drink and prep it for pouring.

Before I could even get over to the juice, however, my girl came in once more and calmly, without any hint of agitation, asked me a third time for a cup of cranberry.

What happened next, has been stamped upon my mother-soul for good. I walked over to the cup cabinet, got a glass, grabbed the juice—and winced. The bottle was warm. Hardly any condensation was left on the container, and its contents were barely chilled at this point. Didn't I tell her twice that I would retrieve her request in only "a minute?" Hadn't I assured her that she would get her drink "soon?"

That room temperature juice highlighted a problem in me: I wasn't keeping my word in the small things.

This was a turning point.

We moms—we will have many of these moments. We will have plenty of opportunities to turn the tide and start anew as we realize shortcomings and slights in ourselves. Over and over again, we will see who we really are—weaknesses, warts, and all—through the varying circumstances and events that fill our in-home parenting years. Having children reveals our honest insides. Our bents and whims and hurts and shortcomings will find their way to the surface as we pour out, and give in, and work to the point of weariness to raise them well. This is normal. And this is good.

What a process parenting enters us into! A mentor of mine once shared that raising children is like peeling an onion. Over the years, and with each new child we birth onto the earth, the layers of selfishness that surrounds our hearts gets stripped away—layer by thick, stubborn layer. While this may not seem like a fun or enjoyable experience at the time, it's molding us into better mothers, better daughters, better wives, better workers, better lovers, better givers, better citizens of our great wide world.

The egocentrism that we inadvertently lug into our child-rearing years begins to show itself. Perhaps you have seen it make an appearance in your own life?

Exhausted from little sleep and no me-time, you melt and snap the moment your crawler wakes up from nap a bit too soon. An elementary-aged child comes home from school with a poor score on a test, and you turn down your eye and devour him with only your facial expression, because you feel like it's a tarnish on your parenting resume. A kid runs through your home, hits the tip of a vase, and causes it to fall and shatter in a million pieces all across the floor, so you do the same. A teenager calls and says she is going to be late with the family vehicle, which means you are going to be late for your appointment, and you lose it right there on the phone line. You have the kids alone *again*, because the husband had to work long hours *again*, and you are sacrificing your time and energy *again*, and you explode in fury because of it. The list of examples could run on and on.

The thing is, all of the above circumstances warrant frustration. They are all events that would naturally cause a human to feel irked and annoyed. And, like the situation I was in with my daughter, we have things we simply have to do. When we are being pulled in yet another direction, our immediate reaction can easily be a scowl and a fit. If you are thinking up all of the parenting situations that you have handled in a similar way, know you have friends who understand. Many of them. We women are human, and life sometimes reminds us of our mortal status.

In those high-pitched moments, however, in those thunderous reminders and revelations of our self-centeredness, we have choices. **We get to decide what happens from there.**

Those occasions lead us to a three-way fork in the road. The first choice is that we can stay where we are, react the way we always have, and mature very little. The second choice is that we can wallow in guilt and condemnation over all the ways we're wrong and weak, and make absolutely no progress. Or, we can choose that third route, and allow the event to be a marker in our minds of what we want to avoid. We can look back and remember those hard instances and allow them to catapult us into being a more mature, and steady, and gracious, and selfless woman.

For me, as I look back in my mind's eye to the moment I saw and touched that cranberry juice—it urges and beckons me to be purposed and present even in the smallest of moments. When I picture her young stubby hands grasping that bottle off the shelf, it makes me want to unravel into a more others-focused mother. At first, it just made me look at myself in disdain and disappointment. Now, it propels me forward.

I've had many about-faces since that moment. I've lashed out and fallen short and shown real immaturity and weakness in my mothering. And every time, I am tempted to wallow in guilt rather than gather the pieces and allow the incident to improve me as a mom and as a person. There is always a split second where I silently scream condemnation at myself. But, most times these days, I'm able to get my wits about me quickly and look out instead of in.

The moment I am able take my eyes off of my failure and onto the ones I've failed, I've successfully turned the tide again. It starts with admitting fault and asking for forgiveness. Going to the child you reacted poorly to, admitting your weakness, and then sincerely asking for forgiveness... Is a beautiful thing. It's a restorative thing. And it's a modeling moment.

What an incredible example we are setting for our children when we go to them and confess wrongdoing! What transparency we are showing when we allow them to see our honest conditions! And what an impact all that must make on their souls! Often, our humbleness and admissions in these situations can overshadow the offense.

And it's this positive impression that ends up being etched on our children's memories and hearts.

There are lessons to be learned in our losses. There are victories to be had when we address those losses correctly. Being purposeful in our quest to improve after each hard situation is certainly a win. Remembering the moments we dropped the ball in our parenting—in a healthy way—makes us purposeful in addressing our actions and behaviors towards those we live with and love.

Parenting our kids in this way sets up an atmosphere of truthfulness, acceptance, and grace in our homes. It teaches our children that none of us are perfect beings, humans fall short sometimes, and truth, openness, and communication are key.

While I, of course, want to avoid handling situations poorly in the first place, I am grateful for the instruction that comes from those unfortunate moments.

That tutu-wearing child of mine unknowingly taught me such a fine lesson that day. And now I'm better for it. And so is she. I hope all of your "warm cranberry juice moments" end up doing the same.

Watching Them Fly
Michelle Recicar
reciteam.blogspot.com

I started my mothering journey 18 years ago. Our family of three became a family of seven in the six and half years that followed.

I am sure, at times, I looked like I was trying to herd cats as I tried to keep track of the little ones at my feet. I am sure, at times, the "bless your heart" comment had more to do with my haggard appearance then a true blessing. And why someone would think I would pick up extra children to take grocery shopping is beyond my understanding, so *yes, they are all mine!* I am a mother with five children—that does not make me crazy... Does it?

As the years have flown by, I no longer have to worry about tripping over little ones at my feet. I now have to try to see around the towering trees they have become.

They no longer have eyes for only me. Sometimes, their eyes are filled with anger towards me. The little hands that were once open and reaching for me are sometimes clenched at their sides in frustration.

During these times—like any good, guilt-ridden parent—I wonder where I messed up, what I did wrong. But here is a thought: **What if it is not what I did wrong, but what I did right?**

Now, do not get me wrong. I am not trying to toot my own horn. I actually think pedestal sitting is for the birds. I have messed up plenty in my parenting and I suspect that I will mess up more in the future. But what if the cause of these tension-filled moments is something I actually did right?

Follow this thought with me.

Remember when they placed your sweet baby or babies in your arms? There is nothing in this world that I have found that can compare. At that moment, I immediately wanted more for that sweet baby. Some were things that I could give them, such as unconditional love, safe shelter, and healthy nourishment. Others were things I could not give them. World peace. Loyal friendships. A struggle-free life. I wanted more for them from the minute they came into the world. What good parent wouldn't?

Soon after I brought my babies home, I not only wanted more for them, but I also wanted more from them. I wanted them to sleep through the night. I wanted them to learn how to crawl. I prayed that my first child would walk before my second child was born because the thought of carrying two children was beyond me. I wanted them to be potty trained. I looked forward to when they could speak.

Even though I wanted these things, I still enjoyed the different stages they went through. I was not trying to rush their childhood. I desired these things because I knew they were good. Good for them and, in a sense, good for me.

Sleep would help them grow strong and help keep me sane. Crawling meant they were developing mentally and physically. Using the potty would save money. When I had three in diapers at one time, my hubby suggested cloth diapers. In my mommy-brain fog, I cried and asked him why he hated me. When they learned to speak, it took the guess work out of what they wanted. It also opened a door for them to tell me how they really felt about a situation.

My children did not always meet the milestones I wanted for them in the time I thought was appropriate. They met them when they were ready physically, mentally and, sometimes, spiritually.

Sometimes, they skinned their knees. Occasionally, a new word came out sounding more like a curse word. (My friend's daughter use to call Snow White, "Snow Wipe.") Sometimes, they peed through all of the extra clothes in the diaper bag. My sister and I used to encourage each other through the hard days by saying, "They're not going to walk down the aisle in a diaper," or "They're not going to walk down the aisle with their bottle," or "They're not going to walk down the aisle _____." (Feel free to fill in the blank).

For every milestone they reached, I wanted more. I encouraged them to be a good friend, to use their words wisely, to problem solve for themselves, to act responsibly, to work hard, and to be more independent. I, as a loving parent, have trained and challenged them to be independent. My children have spent a lifetime learning and exercising independence.

So now, as they approach adulthood, why are we butting heads over their independence?

I believe the way my children and I define independence is part of the problem. This is how Google defines the word independent:

> *Independent:*
> *1. Free from outside control; not depending on another's authority.*
> *2. Not depending on.*

My goal through the years, as I encouraged independence, was that my children would be strong, thoughtful leaders and self-sufficient, responsible, contributing members of society. Clearly, I would align myself with the second definition. But, at this point in my children's lives, they would use the first definition to explain independence. Their goal is to take what they have learned, see if it really works, and buy all the junk food that I never bought while they were at home. They want to test our instruction without having mom or dad looking over their shoulders. They also want to try out some of their own ideas. Who can blame them?

I also believe that part of the problem is timing. Often, my children believe they are ready for more freedom before I am ready to give it to them. As a parent, I have to be wise with the timing of the freedoms I give my children. The stakes are too high to do otherwise. As my children grow, I am no longer dealing with skinned knees and mispronounced words. I could be dealing with underage drinking, teen pregnancy, drug use, and decisions that will affect all of us for a lifetime.

My children may think they are ready for more independence, but it is my job to determine the timing.

My goal in determining the timing of certain freedoms and more independence is not to control them or have them live perfect lives. I am fully aware that my children will "mess up" at some point (or points) in their lives. We will walk through those hardships together. My goal is to make sure that they are as equipped as they can be, based on their own maturity and experience. I should not give in to my child's desire for more independence based on an age or whatever everyone else is doing. It is important for me to remember and remind them that they will meet their own milestones in their own timing.

I want my children to one day fly from our nest, but the truth of the matter is that they are not always ready when they think they are. So what do I do in the meantime? I remember that I have raised yet another who is ready for *livelihood or subsistence, capable of thinking or acting for oneself.* I have conditioned them for independence. This is what I did right. I remember that, even though the battles may feel fierce, they are not always personal. I am the one standing between them and what they believe is their next independence milestone. I remember that I cannot block their way with fear, but guide them away in love. I ask myself, is my roadblock truly for their safety and good, or am I motivated by my desire to keep them close?

In all honesty, mothering is hard on the heart, and sometimes self-preservation is my goal. As my children and I work towards each milestone, I prepare my heart. I prepare my heart to trust my years of instruction and the One who entrusted these children to me. I do this so that, one day, I can lovingly step out of the way... And watch them fly.

Scarred Motherhood
Kara Carrero
allternativelearning.com

Strapped to a table, I heard a doctor say "Here's your little girl dad!" and I watched a nurse walk away with her without ever showing me her face or those little legs I had felt kicking inside of me for many months. It was a moment that haunts me. It was the beginning of motherhood for me; it was marked with feelings of failure that I didn't have the natural birth I wanted and sadness that I somehow seemed to be forgotten in the process.

The next morning, I remember shuffling in pain to the shower and seeing my stitches for the first time. In that moment, I couldn't help but cry. The little stitches that were supposed to hold me together were making me feel like I was falling apart. Those little feelings grew into big emotions over time. Instead of a fresh wound, my cesarean incision quickly became a scar. It was a flaw and imperfection that I chose not to look at and purposefully ignored as much as possible. Because, in the end, that scar was a symbol of failure for me. It was not how I envisioned motherhood, but that's how my journey started.

So for days, weeks, and months, I woke up in the morning already feeling like a failure and feeling so lonely like I had in that first moment of motherhood. Many times, I viewed my days as a mom as something that was difficult and to be dreaded. I still saw the beauty in it, and I still treasured my daughter, but that scar started my mornings. Some days, the ones where I felt particularly big emotions, I found myself staring at my reflection and my scar. And some days, I cried. There was a comfort in seeing myself cry, because then I didn't feel quite so alone.

I really struggled through the first year of motherhood, questioning whether I was fit to be a mom or if I was good enough. The morning after my oldest daughter's first birthday, I had the overwhelming feeling that *today is a new day*. And there was peace in that moment. While I may have never had a toddler before, I had experienced every calendar day as a mother. And there was hope in that. I had survived the first year. Looking back on the year previous, while it had its difficulties, I began realizing just how precious it was to be a mom and how much my daughter had taught me. She had shown me true joy, true happiness, and true determination.

A little over two years after being strapped to a table, feeling empty, I was in my bedroom birthing my second daughter, feeling empowered. I had spent months massaging, looking at, and coming to grips with the "failure scar" in order to know how it felt and prepare myself for a vaginal birth after cesarean. I had confronted my scars to truly overcome them. I had to not only accept them, but embrace them. And I had to realize they were not festering wounds but had, in fact, healed over time.

It had taken many months and even years to realize that just because my initial birth experience had not gone as planned, it did not mean that I was a failure as a mother. It did not mean that I had not tried. It did not mean that I was any less of a person. In two short years, the scar, while initially was one of shame and sadness, turned into a reminder of bravery and perseverance. **The road of motherhood became different as I began to discover the treasure that it is to be a mom, even in the imperfections.** It took looking at the situation from a different perspective to see that I didn't enter into motherhood through failure, but through determination, bravery, and strength, and that we have moments of victory and triumph because of, not in spite of, the scars we bear.

Each hard moment in motherhood is another scar, physical or otherwise. It's not a failure, but something to be celebrated. To rejoice that we have overcome. Of course, the moments that cut deep and leave scars hurt, but they encourage as well. Each scar should encourage us as moms to keep pushing forward and to keep striving to be better. They should remind us of the times we have persevered and given our all. And they prove to us that, as mothers and women, we are not broken. We are strong. And we all find redemption in both big and small ways. The time when a child comes to snuggle even after they have been disciplined is a redeeming moment. The instant when a child says they love you even when it's been a hard day is a victory. And without the hard days—without the scars—we would not be able to feel even the smallest triumphs

Whether it is a traumatic birth, incessant crying, lack of sleep, toddler tantrums, behavior problems, back talk, yelling, or whatever the scenario may be, we all have the days where we start feeling broken down, scarred, or helpless. And those are the days of motherhood we must stand on. The foundation of motherhood is built in those moments that don't go as planned, or when what you expected of motherhood turned out to be the opposite. Those are the instances that build our own character and challenge us to rise up. They challenge us to support our fellow mom and encourage her to embrace the struggles in order to find the true joy that motherhood brings.

So, there are days we feel strapped to a table and overlooked—helpless and alone—but life and joy come even from such adversities.

Our scars are a mosaic of memories and challenges. They are a reminder of the days that are hard, but they also tell us that choosing a scarred motherhood means moving past pain and brokenness toward healing and hope and the strength to overcome.

The Grace of a Milkshake

Sara Reimers
sunshinewhispers.com

It is 9:30 p.m., and I am exhausted. This day has been an utter failure, and I have questioned my sanity as a mom at least a dozen times. Finally. Finally, my daughter has given up and fallen asleep. Sometimes, my precocious (almost) 3-year-old can be a blast. She has enough personality for three kids. She is hilarious, smart, intense, and enthusiastic about everything.

Today was not a blast.

Despite my plans for a brilliant mommy-daughter date day, it was an utter disaster. Today was a day of button pushing, boundary testing, and tantrum throwing. Chicken nuggets were mushed into my face and then followed by a desperate plea for more food (in the form of cookies, of course). Numerous opportunities to go potty like a big girl were refused, in favor of creating a small lake of pee next to the truck (I guess I should be glad it wasn't in her car seat). Then, there was the galactic screaming fit because I didn't guess the correct version of the ABC song to play in the truck. There was no nap. Nope, not today—today, there was hitting and kicking and screaming, but no nap.

But there was also grace. In the form of a milkshake.

A while back, during another day of high emotions, I received encouragement from a mom who had been there and survived (mostly) intact. My friend simply rested her hand on my shoulder and said one of the most profound parenting truths I think I have ever heard:

> *"You are her safe person. The only reason she acts like this is because you are her safe person. She doesn't know where the boundaries are with others, so she doesn't push them. She pushes your buttons because she knows (hopes) that you will love her anyway."*

Wow. I am her safe person. I bet that almost every mom reading this can relate. It doesn't matter if you work inside the home, outside the home, homeschool, public school. It doesn't matter if you have a nanny or if you haven't had an hour of peace in years.

If you are a mom, you are your child's safe person. Isn't that beautiful? If you are a mom, you are the one person your child will look to for validation that they are loved. **You hold the enviable position of being the little voice in their head,** cheering them on, coaching when necessary, but loving—always loving.

Of course, as adults we constantly seek the sanctuary of a safe person. Someone we can just be ourselves with. Someone the house doesn't have to be clean for. Someone we don't have to self-edit around. Someone we don't have to shave our legs for. Granted, it's not like we want to be slovenly, irritable, snarky, and unpolished around the most important people in our lives. However, there is a certain comfort in knowing that if we are having a bad day, month, or year, they won't leave us.

They are our safe person. The ideal would be that we would treat them the best. However, over the course of a life together, the bond of love is strengthened through the hard times as much, if not more, than through the good times. It is easy to love a lovable person. But when you love someone who is being rather unlovable... That is where the true test of love lies.

This is why the concept of marriage is such a big deal.

This is why the concept of love is such a big deal.

This is why being a mom is *such a big deal.*

Think about it—if you, as an adult, seek out a safe person and then proceed to "let it all hang out," why would we expect our kids to be any different? Actually, it makes perfect sense that our kids would push the buttons of their safe person more, not less, than anyone else.

They haven't been around as long as we have. They have little to no perspective on how this thing called life is supposed to turn out. The younger they are, the more their universe will revolve around the people who care for them. I can't speak for school-aged children, tweens, or teens. However, I can speak rather authoritatively about a certain almost-three-year-old.

At three years old, my daughter is just starting to realize she wants friends. At three years old, my daughter is just starting in earnest to find her voice, developing her unique set of personal preferences and passions. It is exciting to be three. But it is also scary.

I can't think of a better way for a three year old to gain the confidence they need to boldly go into the world and be awesome than to know that there will be at least one person who will always have their best interests at heart.

In order to grow, a child needs to know they are loved. More importantly though, they also need to know that they are loved regardless of how unlovable they might become.

So, what about grace and the milkshake?

Well, ever since the friendly pep talk I received a few months ago, I have recited those words to myself as a constant reminder of the important things going on behind the scenes in my daughter's heart and head. Does that mean days like today don't drain every ounce of goodwill out of my already exhausted body?

Nope.

However, when I am in the throngs of the more exhausting episodes of parenting, it does help provide perspective and a glimmer of hope. It's because of love. If there were no love, my daughter would not be comfortable enough to be loud, exciting, tumultuous, passionate— confident, self-assured, joyful, and enthusiastic.

The screaming will make way for giggles.

The hitting will turn into smoochies.

And in the process, our kids will have the space to grow.

Isn't that beautiful? Isn't that miraculous?

There is something else I would like to tell you too. This will not last forever. It never does.

As for me, the utter disaster that was today did end well. Too exhausted to cook, we grabbed dinner at a local restaurant. I ordered a Mint Oreo Cookie milkshake, and as we waited for our dinner to arrive, my daughter and I shared the kind of sweet moment that makes the pain just disappear. We sat next to each other, cheek to cheek, enjoying each other for the first time that day. We didn't really talk. However, I think we both recognized that today—today, our bond of love grew stronger.

Today, my daughter learned that she can be a complete pistol, and I will still accept her.

Today, my daughter learned that even when mommy is at her breaking point, there is still love—there will always be love.

I was my daughter's safe person today. I learned that, even when I am at my breaking point, I am still engaged in a noble cause. My daughter is a spitfire, and I don't want to squelch her spirit. As much as it may pain me now, I want to fan those flames, because they are the kind of flames that will set the world on fire someday.

In the meantime, I will look for the silver linings and sweet nothings of the everyday ordinary. I will embrace the hard days and give thanks for the easy ones. Either way, there is something sweet on the menu that is calling my name. Let's dig in together!

Sharing the Hard
Kelsey Wilkening

As mothers, we are wired to protect our babies. Seamlessly intertwined in our very DNA, it seems, is the insatiable instinct to shield and safeguard those most precious to us from any number of dangers—both perceived and tangible. As we look across the animal kingdom, we see this nature is a part of almost every species. If someone calls you a "Mama Bear," it's not because you seem cute and cuddly. Where in most facets of our motherhood we are often described as gentle and nurturing, we are fierce and strong when our protective drive kicks in. Sometimes, we must act with a moment's notice—grabbing the arm of a toddler before they wander across the street or shooing a child away from a hot stove. But it seems, more often, that we are working to proactively shield our young from harm.

As the culture continues to rattle us into all sorts of new, unchartered territories, we seek to shelter young minds. As hard life circumstances unfold, we strive to guard hearts from what we think will shatter them into irreparable pieces. This instinct has been woven into the very fabric of who we are for a distinct purpose and serves our children well.

But what happens when the inevitable occurs—when our children do get hurt, and there is nothing we can do to stop it? Are we failures as mothers? Our rational minds say, "Of course not! Life happens. Accidents happen. We cannot be everywhere at all times." But when our babies are hurting, rational minds often go by the wayside, and we find ourselves trapped in pain and guilt. It is there that we begin to believe the lie that, somehow, we have failed.

At 29, I had two kids and was in the process of adopting a third. My two biological children were 18 months and 3 years old, and the sweet boy we were bringing home from Ethiopia was 19 months old. Yes, you read that right! The two "littles" as we still call them today, 6 years later, are two weeks apart. I loved my children with a love I never knew existed, and I would do anything to shield them from harm.

My oldest has always been so mature. We have joked since the day he was born that he is a 40 year old man trapped in a child's body. But I hadn't imagined discussing death with him. For most, death is a subject not easily discussed. Our western society doesn't celebrate or honor death the way most other cultures do. When it comes to sharing the realities of death with our kids, there appears to be some unwritten code about how old and mature our children need to be before we even talk about what it means for someone to die. For those of us with a strong faith base, death can be more easily dealt with, but still often makes us uncomfortable and is one of those notions that we think we have to protect our young from.

We love Jesus, and our evangelical faith teaches us to believe that all of those who love Jesus will live forever with Him after they pass away. To me, death is not scary. And while my son, at three, could tell you that there was a Heaven, he couldn't ever tell you why there needed to be one. I didn't discuss death with him; it was unnecessary, in my mind, to "burden" a young mind with the earthly harsh reality of death. I was protecting him.

On August 8, 2009, I was working at a wedding at our church. My husband was home with our two children, and my dad was planting pear trees in our backyard. The wedding was an hour from starting, when I realized my husband was repeatedly calling my cell phone. One phone call I could have easily ignored due to my responsibilities, but multiple calls signaled something desperately needed my attention. The voice on the other end was my husband's, but it was a tone I had never heard before. He implored me to drop everything and come home. My dad was having a massive heart attack in my backyard.

Without hesitation, I kicked off my three inch heels and raced to my car. I drove in a way I hope my children never will and pulled up to my home just in time to see the doors close on the back of the ambulance. I was offered the front seat next to the most patient and gracious driver, and I craned my neck to see through the small viewing window in the partition that separated me from my dad, my biggest cheerleader. There was nothing I could do but cry and pray, and helplessly look through that window at his lifeless body. Fifteen minutes later, while still on the freeway, I heard the flatline. It sounded just like it does on TV, and for months after, I awoke in the middle of the night to that sound in my head. He was gone, and there were no medically heroic acts that could have brought him back.

God had taken him home.

The next few hours are still blurry. But I know that one thing kept going through my mind. *How will I tell Markus?* The only grandson my Dad had ever known (though he had faithfully carried a picture in his wallet of his Ethiopian grandson that he had yet to meet). Markus and his Papa Baber had such a special relationship, and I knew that this was going to crush his little heart. The heart that I had worked so hard to protect from the harsh realities of life.

All of a sudden, I needed to tell my three year old that, on this side of Heaven, he would never see his Papa again. I had to talk about death. I looked up kids' books that might be able to help me, but nothing looked promising. In the end, Mark and I just sat down and told him the truth. His tears flowed, as I expected them to, and I lost all resolve to "stay strong." I cried right along with him, holding him close to me as our tears mixed together in shared sadness.

I could no longer protect my son from the reality of death, and I realized there was another area I had been desperately trying to protect him from, too—seeing me struggling. Seeing me weak. Seeing me vulnerable. Suddenly, my son saw my emotions laid bare, while also processing the loss of his precious grandfather.

I wasn't exactly in a stable place in the weeks following. I was grieving. My kids were grieving. Even Halle Joy, who wasn't young enough to understand that she wouldn't see her Papa again, knew that something was terribly off.

Meanwhile, we were preparing to bring home our Zavion from Ethiopia. We were traveling just six weeks after I said goodbye to my dad. As if the simple reality of losing my dad were not enough, I began feasting on the lies that I had failed my son. That I hadn't protected him from the deep pain that he was experiencing. That I had let him see me, more than once, at my lowest—and that it was a bad thing. I believed that what he was experiencing would damage him, and there was nothing I could do to stop it. I had failed, and the weight of it all was excruciating.

One day, a few weeks after my dad's passing, Markus looked up at me in the kitchen. I was preparing lunch for him, his sister and me. I was tired and weary and overwhelmed. He started to cry, seemingly out of nowhere, and grabbed my leg in a way that only a preschooler does. Knowing that he needed my attention more than he needed lunch, I sat down right there on the cool wood floor and pulled him into my lap.

"I miss Papa," he said in his priceless three year old lispy voice.

"I do, too," I said. This time, I did everything I could to stop the tears from spilling over, determined that I would remain resilient and be the rock he so clearly needed. This time, I would be the strong mom he needed me to be. The mom that protects and shields her young from more pain. But then...

That tender boy of mine reached his fat fingered three year old hand to my cheek, looked up and whispered, "Mommy, where are your tears? Mommy, aren't you sad anymore? Because I'm still sad. I know that Papa lives with Jesus and he isn't sick anymore. But I think it's okay that I'm still sad. Are you?" And there went the tears, streaming down my face, the loss mixed interchangeably with the realization that this boy needed to see my pain. **His heart wanted to know that he was not alone.** He desired the shared experience of grief, and his heartache desperately needed to be validated with mine.

As he often does, my son taught me, the mother, the lesson that day. He taught me that it's not only okay, but empowering to both of us, to be vulnerable with our children. That we are not failures when we can't guard their hearts from every arrow that seeks to pierce them. Markus showed me that the most loving thing I could do with and for him in his struggle was to share mine. Certainly, we must be wise in how much "life" we invite our children into, but more often than not they are more than capable, and their hearts demand to be let into more than we think they are ready for.

It is not a failure when we show our children that we are weak, that we don't always know all the answers, and that we can't safeguard them from every harm that comes barreling their way. To pretend the opposite is to miss out on the sweetness and growth that come from enduring hard things together. I didn't fail Markus because I couldn't protect his little heart from pain. Conversely, in the pain we shared, we were brought together in vulnerability, love and truth, and we were both made better for it.

The Leaf with the Teardrop
Laura Brown

o mother should have to hold an autopsy report for her child. And yet, filed in the very back of my blue file box on the bottom of my bookshelf, is the report for my first child, Toby Matthew Brown.

I remember being ecstatic the day I found out I was pregnant with Toby. My husband and I excitedly drove to my parents' house and announced our news—their first grandchild was on the way! He was the first grandchild on both sides, so naturally, plans for spoiling this baby began right away. The next couple of months were fun times of planning—when I wasn't nauseous, of course!

I remember that I was at work when I got the call. At the time, I was working for a home for adults with mental illness, and due to the demanding routine of my job, I typically could not take calls. But on that day, I happened to have a free moment. My routine blood test had turned up some anomalies, and my doctor wanted to send me into Boston for some further tests. They found indicators that the baby may have Down Syndrome. A deluge of thoughts flooded my mind, but at that moment, I couldn't process any of them. I simply took the appointment information and tried to finish my day at work.

A few days later, my husband and I traveled into Boston, anxious about what we might hear. While in the waiting room, we saw other pregnant women being escorted into exam rooms. Several came out crying. I remember feeling badly for them, and vowing not to cry if we found out the baby had Downs. In my head, I had a plan going. I would talk to my friends who had kids with Downs, and I'd read all that I could to educate myself. It would be challenging, but we could do it.

My turn.

The tech did an ultrasound. This was my first ever ultrasound, and I stared at the screen trying to make sense of the black and white static. The tech was silent. I tried to ask questions about what I was seeing, and got one word responses or nothing back. Measure. Click. Measure. Click. More silence. I so desperately wanted to see my baby and his little forming body and know what was happening, but there was just silence.

Fifteen minutes later, two doctors entered the room. The one who did the talking was Dr. House, and when he told me his name, I almost laughed out loud. Then I heard the words that I never expected to hear: *I'm sorry, but your baby is not going to live.* My brain went into a frenzy. The doctor's words were mixed in with my own thoughts, and I couldn't understand any of it.

Clubbing of both feet... Pleural effusion of the lungs... Don't cry... You can't cry right now... Abnormal umbilical cord... Listen to his words... What am I going to tell my family... No bladder... Abnormal heart... God can do miracles... It might be OK... You could terminate the pregnancy... No way, we are not doing that... Not our life to take... More big medical words...

Ultimately, the diagnosis was Trisomy 21, which is several steps more severe than Down's syndrome. Since we were absolutely not going to terminate the pregnancy, our only option was to schedule weekly ultrasounds to make sure Toby's heart was still beating. We knew that it was likely he would die, but, being people of faith, we also knew God could do a miracle, and so we scheduled the first ultrasound. Despite my best efforts, I couldn't hold back my tears as we rode the subway back to our car. We drove right to my parents' house and broke the news to my family.

It all moved relatively quickly after that. At that first ultrasound, the baby's heart had stopped beating. My Toby had died at 20 weeks. A few days later, I was admitted to the hospital, and, because my body was not ready to have a baby, it took two days to deliver him. The waiting was the hardest, because there was nothing to do except wait. My husband and family were with me round the clock, and my best friend also drove up from Pennsylvania to be with me. Those were the longest days I have ever experienced. Nothing to do but wait to see if the medicine would start to work.

In our hospital, whenever a baby was born, they would play a little lullaby over the speaker system. Never has music been so painful to me as it was then. Our hospital also has a system to let doctors know when it is not a "celebratory" birth, and so, outside my room was a little postcard with a leaf cradling a teardrop. On the back was this explanation,

> *"The leaf with the teardrop reflects both intense suffering and loss and hope for the future. Though fallen, the leaf maintains its vitality, symbolizing hope. It cradles the teardrop with its upturned edges creating a sense of comfort. **As seasons change, so do feelings. Just as there is winter and spring, there is sadness and hope.**" (Copyright 1985, 2004 Gunderson Luthern Medical Foundation, LaCrosse, Wisconsin)*

After two days, Toby was finally born. My husband and I were able to hold him, as was my mom and my best friend, Ruth. As I held him, I wondered what he would have been like and who he would have become. These are things I still think about to this day.

It has been eight years since Toby died. In the time since, we have been blessed with two amazing, precious boys who constantly keep us on our toes. Oh, the stories I could tell you about them! I still think about our first precious baby, and although I try not to, I still cry when I talk about him. The intense pain I felt when he died has diminished, but I think there will always be sadness when I think about losing him. But, like the postcard said, there is hope.

To the precious mommas who have lost a little one or little ones:

You are loved. You are valuable. There are no words that will make it all better. The pain may never go completely away, but it will subside. Cling to your family. Cling to your friends. Let them love you. Let them help you. Cry. Don't be afraid to grieve. You've got to grieve in order to begin healing. The pain will lessen. You may be blessed with other children, but none will replace the one(s) you lost. I remember that some well meaning folks tried to tell me things like, "You can have another one!" "You're young! There is still time to have more." Their hearts were in the right place, but their words were painful. No other children will replace the child you lost, even though they can be added to your heart. It's possible that you may not be able to have other children. I understand that there are no words that would take that pain away. Know though, that you are still valuable, and perhaps there is a little one that is already born, somewhere, who needs the amazing love you have to give. Grieve as you need to, and after the intense grieving has subsided, consider sharing your love and home with a child who desperately wants a forever family.

Know that you are not alone.

I was shocked to learn the number of moms who have lost their babies. There were so many people I knew who had lost a child and I simply didn't know. This does not make it any less painful, but it may provide you with someone you can talk to or meet with to heal. At the very least, there are women who understand your pain in a very real way!

To the friends and family of those who lost little ones (or may in the future):

You are a rock. You are strength. You are needed. There is a great pressure to say and do the right things. You love this hurting mom so much that you want to do anything you can to just make it all better. Please don't worry. All that is needed is you. Your presence. Your hugs. Your tears. Sometimes the best thing you can do is to say nothing, and just cry with your loved one. It's awkward. It's painful. But it is exactly what is needed. If you are a task oriented person like me, then you'll want something you can *do*. Make that momma a meal. If she has other kids, entertain them for a couple hours. The last thing I wanted to do was the mundane things of everyday life. They took energy and mental capacity, neither of which I had in the days and weeks that followed. If you can help your friend or loved one with the little things so they can have space to heal, both mentally and physically, then that is a gift beyond what you will ever know.

Losing a child will always be painful. But there are glimmers of hope, too. I am profoundly grateful for my friends and family who walked beside me at an exceptionally difficult time. I am grateful for a husband who could be my strength. I am grateful that I got to hold my little boy. I am grateful for the surprise of a nurse that my husband knew, who cared for me in the hospital during the night I was the sickest because of one of the medications. I am even more grateful that she was also a massage therapist and could relieve my aching muscles!

I am grateful that I have been able to grieve with others through their own losses.

I am grateful that I am not alone.

Most of all, I am grateful that the winter is over, a new season in my family has begun, and it is beautiful.

Bravery, Birth in Hope
Tiffany Bluhm
learnhowtomom.com

Hope can mean so many things. Hope can invite us to dream past our pain and invite joy into the darkest parts of our heart. Hope isn't always easy to accept, but if we do, in the midst of our struggles, we can make it through hard times with a sweet bravery. Motherhood is laced with times of hope, loss, bravery, and grief.

Hope was hard to come by in the midst of my journey to become a mama. I had always assumed having children would be simple. I know how ridiculous that sounds now, but in my youth it seemed just right. When my husband and I decided to grow our family, we felt prompted to start with adoption. Although many had assumed I was infertile and commented as such, we honestly hadn't even tried to get pregnant. We truly felt a strong sense to bring a son into our home, born to another woman.

We started the adoption process with bright eyes and happy hearts. We were aware there could be hiccups, but none that would mark us so deeply and reshape our understanding of family. We knew the process was a long one. We were told it would be 6-9 months until our son would be in our arms. We would have never foreseen a two-year process. With the plan to empty our bank account, invite our "village" to join us, and pray, we chose to adopt from Uganda. We understood that the process would be a tough road ahead, like a pregnancy, but we were unprepared for the "whatever can go wrong, will go wrong" scenario.

We were elated to receive a picture and information of a sweet boy. His sweet cheeks and big brown eyes made my heart melt. It was the sign of life, like a mother seeing the ultrasound for the first time, we knew we had a long road ahead but one that was all our own. He was 18 months old and had been with our partner baby-home for about a year. As our paperwork progressed, we were eager to prepare the nursery, read all the parenting books, and say goodbye to happy hour in exchange for bedtime stories and play dates.

A year into the adoption process, we got an unexpected e-mail that left us devastated. It detailed how our prospective son's biological father had no interest in raising him, but at the same time refused to sign release papers so we could move forward with the adoption process. We were crushed. The baby showers had been thrown, the nursery was ready, and we were childless. It was painful. We cried ourselves to sleep knowing the little boy we'd grown to love was unadoptable. I had spent my days imagining life with him in our family, giving him a safe space and place, showering him with love and affection, and encouraging him to be the man he was destined to be. All of those daydreams came to a screeching halt. I felt barren. I couldn't hang on to the hope of becoming a mom. I felt like I had done everything right and had come up empty. It sucked the wind out of our sails.

After time had passed, we started the process again. We still felt drawn to Uganda and were encouraged by the directors of the baby home to consider another little boy. His name was Luke. Luke had been strapped to the back of a motorcycle and sent to the police station. The officers had delivered him to a baby home telling them they thought his mother was a teenager with no intent to care for him. He was a year old. He struggled with rage, and his inability to cope left him wailing for hours at a time. He craved love and affection so badly. We felt like we were running on fumes but believed we should move forward to adopt Luke. I'm so glad we did. The curve ball really came, though, when we were asked to adopt two children. So, we had paperwork amended and prepared not only for one, but two in our home. We were a little anxious to go from zero to two, but the anxiety was quickly replaced with excitement and zeal to think we would finally be a family.

When we arrived in Uganda, it was harder than we could have ever expected. Trying to establish a bond with children who have experienced trauma will test every ounce of grace you have. Adoption is born out of loss, and there is no hiding that fact. Day after day, we would prove be a source of food, comfort, and safety that invited our boys to depend on us. Gradually, they softened and saw us a providers. We were building our family trust slowly but surely. Days became sweeter the longer we were there. Wailing and hiding in the corner was replaced with smiles, giggles, and cuddles. It was beautiful to witness two children blossom right before our eyes. **Love is powerful; it can turn orphans into sons.**

Two months into our time in Uganda, we had an unexpected knock at the door. The unexpected knock turned into horrific news. Once again, the father of the younger of the two boys, Moses, decided to reclaim his parental rights. Hopelessness settled into every corner of my heart once again. This time with the loss in my arms, cuddled to my chest. Moses was just three days old when he was left in the orphanage. No one had come for him until we did. I felt like laying in the fetal position as grief welled up in every inch of my soul. Pain swelled up in my heart quicker than I thought was humanly possible. It was tremendous and brought us to our knees in prayer. All I wanted to do was love babies. Why had this been so hard? Every dream of raising Moses was dashed, never to be claimed again.

Our last month in Uganda was bittersweet. We had lost two adoptions and found ourselves fighting for Luke to come home with us. Things kept going wrong, and day by day I felt hopeless thinking the only person coming home on the plane with me was my husband. My tree trunk of hope was whittled down to a slender stick. In the middle of it all I knew I had to keep going. I had to hold onto hope because my other option, disappointment, was too much to bear. Disappointment is inevitable in our lives, but when it commandeers our soul, we lose focus of our future and the precious gifts tucked into each day.

Miraculously, we did come home with Luke, and gave him the name Jericho, a city that was a promise to people who were obedient to God. I could have never imagined the journey it would take to adopt our son and become a mother, but the journey is mine. I can't trade it for anyone else's. Even in the hardest parts, the parts where I felt absolutely defeated, I allowed a glimmer of hope to shine in my soul. I let it happen. We can all let it happen. Life is too hard and too long to live without it.

The best part of hope is that it can lead to bravery. We become the bravest version of ourselves when we believe for goodness in our lives and the lives of our children. Bravery tells disappointment to visit but never set up camp in the crevices of our heart. Bravery, birthed out of hope, can get us up in the morning when all we want to do is lay in bed and pull the covers up over our head.

After we returned home with Jericho, close friends would comment, "I bet you would have never gone through that if you knew that was going to happen," or "I can't imagine you would ever do that again." I would be quick to answer that I would definitely do this even if I knew the heartache involved because I'm a mother and this was my son. Motherhood is no easy road, whether you are biological, step, or adoptive. It's an adventure to become a mother, and it sure is an adventure to stay a mother. Motherhood can cost us our insecurities, comfort, money, tears, and daydreams. Rough waters are inevitable, and we gain strength by navigating them with hope of a brighter, sweeter season ahead. I believe with everything in me that our pain binds us together. No mama escapes pain. We can let it drown us, or let it squeeze out every ounce of bravery we can muster. Seasons of joy will always be sweetly savored when we've braved tough seasons of loss and grief.

Savor the Moments

Marilyn Biddinger

Savor the moments. Let them form deep impressions that will be beautiful memories in the years to come. Be fully present. Immerse yourself in the here and now. Those are the thoughts I heard my brain whispering to my soul as I tied the perfect bow on the sparkling belt that encircled my Sweet Girl's wedding dress. It had been my mantra from the moment she and her Red-haired Boy announced their engagement one year earlier and I came face-to-face with the reality of another new beginning.

The signal that reached my mind as I looked at the train of her dress flowing over the carpet in front of me, however, was not one of drinking in the sights and sounds of these twinkling pieces in time. Rather, the message that filtered through was filled with the very familiar mental checklists that I often carry in my brain. *Would the flowers be right? Did the programs get placed? Was the aisle runner fastened securely? Had they remembered to leave an empty space for Brett's chair? Would it be everything she imagined, and had I put tissues in my purse?*

The lists—old friends that have helped me process things and brought the illusion of a feigned sense of order to my universe. The lists—my steadfast companions and most favored tools for creating pseudo-structure in my very unpredictable world. The lists—faithful colleagues and loyal partners that have been laboring quietly in the background, often without my cognizant participation or full permission, since June 24, 1993.

Over 8,000 calendar squares have been marked off since then, and not one minute has gone by that I have not been acutely aware of the change ushered in by that particular day. It was a Thursday, to be exact. Early morning. The sun had not fully risen, and the knock on the door was the culmination of a night spent pacing the floors as my baby girl alternated her sweet sleep between the little white bassinet and my arms. Something inside me had known throughout that night of worrying and wondering that life was in the balance. I couldn't have articulated it then and I can't bring voice to it now, but something in my soul knew that the mundane and the divine were about to collide and alter my life journey forever. Still, the knock at the door jolted me from the security of instinctual knowing to raw reality. My new life path gained its direction with these words: "There's been an accident."

As my world seemed to spin out of control around me with the news that my husband, Brett, had fallen asleep driving, the lists began to form, grabbing pieces of order for my whirling mind... *I need to get dressed... get bottles made... Get a diaper bag packed... Kiss Brittany—one for me, and one for her Daddy.* Soon my feet and hands were following the mental directory in my brain, and I moved from one task to another until I had each item ticked off and was sitting numbly in the backseat of my in-laws' car, moving toward the hospital and the unknown, 90 miles away.

As the air ambulance helicoptered my husband far above me and the tires of the vehicle I rode in slapped the pavement below, my heart was filled with what-ifs. I knew little about the accident other than Brett had fallen asleep, gone off the road, and been catapulted through the sunroof of his truck. He had been taken to a local hospital where it was determined that his injuries were beyond their capacity and his best chance for survival was transfer to the regional trauma unit. That was my reality—my instinctual knowing taking form—and in the midst of it all, my heart returned to the 8-week-old daughter I had left with a double kiss in the care of her Aunt.

This was not the way it was to begin for her. This upheaval was not welcome in the life Brett and I had mapped out for her, and this kind of uninvited disorder simply would not fit into the charmed existence we had imagined. The jumble of thoughts running through my heart reached out for some semblance of sense to be made of it all... *I'll get there... See what the situation is... Put my head down... And do whatever needs to be done to get things back to normal.* A vague list, but a list nonetheless.

I arrived at the ER prepared to begin checking things off in an orderly fashion... *I'm here—check... Tell me what the situation is...* But rather than receive news about Brett's condition and what would be required to get him better so that my brain could complete the next mental checkmark, I was escorted quickly to the closed door of the triage bay and told by the doctors that nothing more could be done. The door was opened, and I was given a few private moments to say goodbye.

I don't know if any staff were present as I entered, I assume there were, but my heart and my eyes were locked on the disfigured man lying on the table before me, and I knew at that moment that a terrible mistake had been made. The looming checkmark in my mind would be completed as soon as I notified someone about the error. But there was no error. No mistake had been made.

Hard as I try, I don't recall how long I stood there by Brett's swollen body or how many times I touched his face before my private moments were done. I fully confess that I can only revisit that place for a limited time before my heart needs to leave and rejoice in the present day. I do recall the physical ache I had for my little family to be whole... To hold my baby girl, to find comfort in the baby smell that enveloped her and touch the softness of her cheeks. And I can remember all the questions that swam through my mind as I sat in the family waiting room expecting what the doctors had described as "the inevitable." *What would I do without him? How would I survive with only a piece of my heart left? What kind of a life would our Sweet Girl have with only me?*

I cannot pinpoint what occurred to turn the tide from death to life, but the tide did turn, and the "private moments" I was given turned into one miracle moment after another in the weeks that followed. Brett remembers little of this time period other than the sensation of looking at his life through a rotating ceiling fan. My imagination believes this hazy feeling to be some whispered recollection of his helicopter ride toward healing. But that's only my imaginings, and I do not pretend to know how the mundane and the divine collided for him that day, I only know they did.

The days and months that followed were difficult. Brett spent 30 days in ICU and one day in step down at the trauma center. For 31 days, I essentially lived in the family waiting room, watching families come and families go. And nearly every one of those days, Miss Brittany made the 180 mile round trip with family and friends to be with us. Nurse after nurse charted the positive change in Brett when she was there, and I don't feel it is exaggerating to say she was motivating him to live.

My list looked a little different at that time in life... *Chest tubes removed —check, weaned off ventilator—check, femur repaired—check, feeding tube inserted—check, halo attached—check...* Different yes, but still noting progress and bringing order. And with every milestone, the blessing of leaving behind those private goodbye moments washed over me. Life in the shadow of the mundane and the divine would be different, but it would be life, and together we would have a new beginning.

Most people tend to think like I did before a spinal injury touched my family—we believe that being paralyzed simply means one can't walk. In the majority of cases, nothing could be further from the truth. Brett's most severe injury occurred at the C6 level of his spine. He no longer has trunk muscles to support sitting straight, wrist flexion or finger function, and his sensation level stops just below his collar bone. It took much retraining and hard work to begin doing life in his new body.

Four months were spent teaching him and teaching me how to navigate these changes in a spinal rehabilitation facility. Many mental checklists were created, and they involved everything from dealing with insurance companies and securing accessible housing to learning how to dress Brett's uncooperative limbs and get the wheelchair over high curbs. The lists were made, the items checked off, and the rapid fire change of life was ever present. This became our new ordinary, our new mundane, and as is always the case, the mundane of life simply sets the back drop for the divine display of beauty.

I saw the beauty in our baby girl who charmed every therapist and owned every hallway of that treatment center. At 6 months old, she was all about the business of mastering the movement of her little legs, and she was wonder in motion as she pushed her walker over every inch of the tile covered corridors. She was seated in her walker, putting one baby foot after the other and pushing with all her might. She would kick her legs as fast she could and then raise them up to coast with the forward momentum. At 28 years old, Daddy was right beside her, seated in his wheelchair, tucking one foot after the other on his foot pegs, using the palms of his gloved-hands and a father's determination to push with all his might until he could coast with the forward momentum right beside her. At no point in my life journey have I seen such a vivid illustration of the perfect timing of God—the beautiful outcome of the mundane being met by the divine.

The years have passed and the blessings that have flowed from that Thursday so long ago have mounted beyond counting. My mental lists have come and gone and changed with life seasons—little girl lists filled with all manner of finger painting, Big Bird, and the first big girl bed. Preteen lists chocked full of trips to Disneyworld, pretend camping, and overnights with Pop and Gram. Young lady lists made up of homecoming dresses, SAT scores, and leaving for college. Every moment checked off and every moment remembered.

I guess I wear *savoring the moments* differently than most, and full immersion hangs at a different angle from my sleeve. I hadn't realized before I began tying that bow on my Sweet Girl's gown that I am fully engaged when I am about the business of making life and love more accessible, more beautiful, and more attainable for her and her Daddy. It's the tangible expression of my heart toward them. My background labors of love facilitated Daddy and Daughter coasting side-by-side down the corridors, and that same behind the scenes attention to detail, the same full expression of love, was in the background when she walked beside his wheelchair down the aisle. Both of them moving side-by-side toward another new beginning as I sat in the front row, fully present, watching the beauty of the mundane meet the divine.

Is This Love That I'm Feeling?
Aleeca King

I've always wanted to be a mother, for as long as I can remember. But it was never a romantic type of longing. It was more of a fact: You're a girl; you'll grow up to be a wife and mother. I liked that fact. On personality tests, I'm a thinker, not a feeler. That doesn't make me devoid of feelings of course, but I make my decisions based on logic and rules. I could imagine feeling a baby kick in my tummy, but that's as far as my imagination went.

Before motherhood became my role, one of the more profound things I learnt while in Trinidad, attending the University of the West Indies was this: Love is a verb. (I learned it outside of the classroom, though). Unlike what TV taught, love isn't just this thing that you feel and can't control. Instead, love is what you do. That lesson helped me to decide to marry Mario. I knew he loved me. Not because of how he claimed to feel around me (which he did claim, and which I savoured), but because of the way he treated me with respect and wanted to see me be happy and become a better me. I also knew what it felt like to be "in love" – the butterflies at catching him looking at me, or the welling up in my heart when I saw his name in my inbox (the prehistoric era, before Facebook). And mostly, the warm embraces the few times we were reunited during our long distance relationship. He was my best friend, and I was so excited to share the news that we were pregnant just four months into our marriage!

My logical mind went into overdrive. I Googled everything I could about what to expect. The one thing I couldn't Google was what it would feel like to be a mother. I'd read about that overwhelming love the first time you see your baby's face. How "indescribable" it was. Since they couldn't describe it, I'd have to wait.

Feeling the baby kick in my tummy was the closest thing I had to"feeling" that love. My doctor kept bursting my bubble, saying it was probably just gas, that I couldn't feel anything in my first trimester. But that excitement still was not the 'love I hoped to feel. In the meantime, I enjoyed the backflips and inappropriate timing (always at bedtime, baby?), and I still waited for the love.

Judah was born at 11:55pm, five minutes before midnight, after labouring all day and night, by emergency C-section. I felt relief! He was alive; that was the most important thing. They touched his cheek to mine while I was still on the operating table. He was so warm. He was mine. I kept playing the sound of his little cry in my mind after they has whisked him away to make sure everything was fine. Maybe I had read too much, like reading reviews before watching a big movie comes out; you look forward to it so much that the real thing is a little too real. There's no slow motion, no orchestra music crescendo. Just a beautiful baby boy.

Those first months were filled with duty: Get up when he needs you to. Work through the pain and breastfeed him. Watch a million Dr.Newman videos till you get it right. Stop eating cheese and chocolate because it makes him sick. Instead of being washed with love, I was flushed with exhaustion, and sadness. What were all these other women talking about? How did simply seeing his face make the 9 months and labor worth it? I wondered if I was going through PTSD or something after my labor didn't go as planned.

I felt alone. Yes, Mario was there for me, but I was the foreigner in a new land. "Caricom Integration," they call it. I'm Jamaican, and we met in Trinidad, but I agreed to move to his country, Barbados. The culture and expectations were different, and I couldn't just drive over to my mummy or Aunty Hopey's house where my cousins and aunts and uncles would meet. I couldn't feel that familiar love. Skype wasn't enough.

I kept my door locked when Mario was away at work. Just me and this small human that needed me always, even to fall asleep.

My countryman Bob sang: *"Is this love that I'm feeling?"*

My answer was a sharp *No!* There's no love here, just work and tears and puke. My tears mixed with his. You can't feel love, Bob, you just do the work. This was my job. Be a mother. Carry the burden. Smile through it. But *feel* love? I loved my baby more than anything. Nobody could ever say otherwise. I was doing the love by the book (or internet article, I should say).

One of my favourite authors, C.S. Lewis, once said: *If you behave as if you love someone, you will come to feel it.* So I kept loving him, and I waited.

Then one day, it started. He looked up at me and smiled. Just when I was at my breaking point, when I thought it couldn't get any worse. He smiled a real smile. Not gas this time! It was almost as if to say, 'Thank you for holding on, thank you for loving me." No, it wasn't that overwhelming, indescribable sensation. It was more of a light in the distance. Feeling the love was possible.

Maybe it's my personality type, but it seemed that I enjoyed his response to me. Of course, his very existence meant the world to me. I was already giving everything I had in me for him. Maybe it was the baby blues. I don't know. But I do know what I felt when he smiled, because I was his mummy, and I was with him and he with me. Present, together. The more he grew, and the longer I knew him, the more I enjoyed him.

Judah is three years old now. I emerged from the newborn phase and into life; where smiles turned to laughter. Through wet kisses and the offer of half chewed cookies. My heart fills up at bed time when he says "Just hold me, mummy." Most precious of all is when he trusts me enough to obey, even when his little mind can't process why he should. Cause love is a verb, after all.

To be honest, I much prefer this "feeling" of love. It lasts longer and is not blown away by the wind. On bad days, when Murphy and his law try to take over, I know who he is and I know who I am. And I know what I have made it through—no, what we have made it through. **We love each other, even when it doesn't feel that way.** Night will come, and he will need me to *do* the loving, not *feel* it.

So, I love him some more and I love him again. And I bask in the enjoyment of him, and I even dare to try the newborn phase again, for many reasons, but also because I know he will soon enjoy the feeling, and doing, of love that only brothers share.

A Peace and a Purpose

Stefanie Davis

simpleacresblog.com

Do you ever catch yourself searching in life? Searching for something more is a common theme inhumanity. Sometimes, one can search without knowing truly what for and why. I can relate to this.

Before I was a mother, I was searching. As long as I can remember, I have been striving for something to fulfill me. Now, as I reflect back, I'm inclined to say that I wasn't sure what my heart was wandering for. At the time, I understood my searching as a need for something more, for success and achievement. I used to believe that more success in my career meant I had "made it" in life. Making it was my purpose based on a self--imposed perfectionism. To reach peace and purpose in life seemed unachievable, because nothing was ever enough. Success through achievement; more money for things to somehow speak for me, to say I mattered; fitness and health achieved in often unhealthy ways to show I was in control—these were the focuses of my wandering. Yet it was never quenched with contentment. Instead, I felt a bit lost.

Why were success and achievement so important? At the time, I truly wasn't sure I knew the answer to that question. Have you ever found yourself over-valuing things in life that ultimately aren't as important as you had judged them to be? Now, I can clearly see the wandering for "success" according to the standards of today's society to be a search for self-worth, purpose and meaning. Based on these standards, I had it all— college degree, good paying career, home, husband, loving family, a strong foundational faith, and things... Plenty of things. But I did not have contentment and didn't understand why.

Motherhood, on the other hand, offered me something I never knew it would. It was something I wanted but was also afraid of. There were so many unanswered questions about the process of having a baby. During my first experience with pregnancy, it was hard for me to let go of the much needed "control" (or false sense of it) I had always relied on. But then, when my eyes first saw the precious child that I carried for nine months, it was as if I was in heaven. I experienced a peace and an ability to trust the process of life like never before.

This child had given me the greatest gift imaginable. For the first time in my life, I felt contentment. For the first time in my life, there was no more searching! My restless spirit was at peace! I realized that all the years of wandering were for a purpose I had never dreamed of until that moment. The moment I held my first born in my arms, being a mother was instantly real to me. **I realized then that I had been searching for answers in all the wrong places.**

With my firstborn in my arms, I cried with joy and gratitude and sang him a song from my heart. A song of love and blessing poured out of my lips. (Much to my surprise, as singing is not my strength.) Through the first year of his life, this song, would bring forth baby giggles, jiggles and smiles.

Since the treasure chest of motherhood proved so satisfying, I was eager to have more and was blessed with two more beautiful children with my husband. Overcoming the need to control life through my first pregnancy allowed me to truly enjoy my other pregnancies with confidence. I must be honest and say that motherhood is not always easy, beautiful, or fun. Often, it calls for you to sacrifice your time, sleep, hobbies, social life, and so much more. Motherhood pushes one seemingly to the brink of what seems possible. But when those little chubby baby fingers caress your face during snuggle time, your toddler says, "I love you, Mommy," after a public tantrum, or your growing child asks to spend alone time with you —the challenges melt away.

I can remember a most recent night with my children where sleep was an enemy. They were fighting with all the energy they could muster, in an attempt to not go to bed. To be honest, I just wanted some "me" time! I wanted to run away to somewhere quiet and just breathe, but I chose to be calm and lay with my unruly two year old instead (of course). That choice reminded me that even through the exhaustion and loss of me time, it was worth it! My little one finally stopped screaming, grabbed my face with all her might, and gave me the biggest smooch, "Eskimo kiss," and "bear hug" ever! (This is from my most stingy love-offering child!)

These simple love notions reassured me that the new found wrinkles, tired eyes, and messy house were all worth it! These small reciprocations of love have shown me I am doing something right. Even when the days of motherhood are long and tiring and your patience does not endure, the small gestures of love that your children offer provide such a reprieve. After a long day, my children often leave me with an overpowering sense of love and a deep fulfillment.

Ultimately, in the world of motherhood, **success and achievement are measured in love.** My old perfectionist, control freak, ever striving and never contented self would not have fully understood that simple truth. I now know after giving birth to three children in six years that persistent, imperfect, creative, genuine, funny, and stern LOVE is the key to fulfilled mothering—fulfilled life!

I will always cherish the richness each child brought into my life with each new birth. In the worldly sense of rich, I was not. But my children have provided richness to my life that offers more than any amount of money ever could. Motherhood has established richness in my heart. My children have helped me live in the present with more gratitude. I have been able to see the simplicity and adventure of life through their eyes in the way they play and experience new things. The seasons and the changes and the colors in the world around me have intensified. My insight into what really matters has deepened.

Motherhood has brought a deeper level of joy, fun and creativity I didn't know existed. I love living in this place with my children. Stepping into my children's world is freeing and fun and something I have needed for a long time! The joy, peace, and purpose gained from motherhood has been the driving factor that, even after three beautiful children, encourages me to keep the door open for the possibly of another child in the future. Coming from a person who used to believe she would only want two children, this is a lot for me to say. That is how wonderful motherhood is! It can change the very core of who you, if you allow it. To be called "mama" is such a badge of honor that I have been given by grace and will continue to work hard to deserve. Motherhood has given me value, self-worth and love, a purpose for every moment of my life, and inspiration to be the best person I can be. Now, my drive for "better" and "more" is purely to improve my character and make a positive impact in the lives of my family and friends. I strive to model genuine love for others, living in the moment, and gratitude to my children. Often, I fail, and I remind myself that it is not perfection but persistence that makes a difference in life. Even making mistakes provides purpose in motherhood. Where I lack, I can teach my children forgiveness and humility.

Motherhood blessed me with a new purpose: to be a teacher of life and love. My children make me better. Being a mother makes me content. Very little will be remembered in this world, certainly not money, career status, or things—but the heart of a mother always remains as fragments left in the lives of the ones we love. Hold on to this gift of motherhood no matter what. It is the most important calling in life. It is an outflowing of peace. It is true purpose.

Beauty in its Season
Rebecca Linn

For as long as I can remember, I have looked forward to becoming a wife and a mother. I use to dream about the guy that would make me fall head over heels in love. My younger siblings and cousins were forced to play house for hours on end so that I could claim that vision of the future—the title of mom.

Fast-forward two decades, and here I am—a wife and a mother of three. Yet, more than once along the way, I found myself trapped, wishing to be someplace else and doing something else. Somehow, I was missing the beauty in the season of life that I had dreamed of so clearly and for so long.

I remember the day—standing by the kitchen sink, full of dirty dishes, watching the kids run around the backyard. It was probably one of the last nice fall days before winter really set in. We were about three months home with our son Joshua, whom we adopted from Ethiopia. I was tired, and not just physically; I was emotionally and mentally drained, as well. The family adjustment, for all intents and purposes, was going well; the bonds had formed strong quickly among most of the family members. Our youngest, about fifteen months old, was the only one who had not quite accepted her newest brother—the change in birth order seemed to unsettle her significantly. The two of them fought. And when I say fought, I don't just mean yelling and fighting over toys. I mean kicking and screaming, going for the eye sockets and kidneys kind of fighting. On any given day, I could count about ten bite marks on each child. If my neighbors didn't know me so well, they might have turned me into child protective services. Lots of yelling and crying poured from our windows despite my every attempt to make peace.

Our sweet new son brought home from Ethiopia something called Giardia. The little guy probably had this parasite for his entire eighteen months of life; it is very common in the area in which he was born. That parasite must have liked its newly found citizenship in the US and put up a good fight—a really good fight. The docs told us right away that "it is not a major medical issue." It turns out, giardia is a parasite found in water that likes to hang out in the small intestines, usually cleared with a round or so of antibiotics.

Our particular parasite must not have known this, as it took six rounds of antibiotics to see progress.

To avoid spreading the parasite to our other two children, I was bathing our son nightly in a basin by himself on the kitchen floor, flushing the water and then bleaching everything within a few feet radius of the bathing area. I also forgot to mention one side effect of this lovely parasite: explosive diarrhea. You know the kind. It goes up the child's back to their neck line, and you want to toss everything they were wearing because the amount of work it takes to clean it out just doesn't seem worth it. I was changing this kind of mess, no joke, at least ten times a day. The awful smell was so entrenched in my nose that I was becoming paranoid that at least a spot of mess was secretly hiding somewhere on my clothing.

Our oldest, a sweet and sensitive boy of five, loved his new brother—he even came with us to Ethiopia to bring Joshua home and cuddled him to sleep his first night in our family. Still, he was struggling with the family adjustment and was full of emotional fits. He was seeing a counselor, and between all the kids appointments I was at a doctor's office at least every other day. My husband was super busy with work, and the Army used this opportune time to tell us that in three months he was going to deploy to Afghanistan. He would need to leave as soon as his current teaching job was finished. So I would be left to plan and to move our family and everything we owned halfway across the country. To ice this delicious cake of poop and family drama, I learned at this time that I had also caught giardia.

I had been showing symptoms for a few weeks, but the tests were not coming back positive. It was not until four weeks of feeling ill and losing ten pounds that the tests showed giardia in my system. So, not only was I changing a million diapers, but I was also spending my fair share of time in the bathroom.

The stress of these days, along with the knowledge of all that was ahead— doing this alone in a few short weeks—felt overwhelming, exhausting, and as though it would never end. As fall turned to winter, I watched the last autumn leaf drift from the tree to our lawn in the yard behind our home. It was in those quiet moments, tears rolling down my face, that a perspective-altering realization hit me.

The season was changing!

The leaves were done falling, and winter was soon upon me. In that moment of clarity, watching the season transition, I knew that there are things about each season that I love, things that feel life giving, peaceful and beautiful. In spring, with plants budding, new life emerging and the anticipation of the splendor coming forth, my heart is always filled with joy. However, each season also has a list of things that I don't like. I can't stand the cold spring rain. I dislike the dreary clouds and being stuck inside for days on end because it is too much to drag the kids out through the puddles. **But the truth is, without the rain, the loveliness of spring would not exist.** The rain means that the winter's snow is behind me. Thanks to the showers that fall, the plants can begin to wake up and grow. It is the things I don't like in life that often make way for the things that I love. It is in this context that the seasons were the perfect metaphor for my life.

There were hardships, and in this season there seemed to be too many all at once. However, it was through the things I disliked that blessings poured out. I had the family that I dreamed of and prayed so endlessly for. My faith was growing, and I was learning how better to love with unconditional love that came from a source beyond myself. I was being stretched and challenged and left to step up to meet whatever was before me. Family and friends reached out in droves for encouragement and to offer help. Relationships in all areas were deepened, developed and love poured freely. I spent weeks focused on my burdens, and had not paused long enough to find and be thankful for the precious gifts that were mixed into my everyday life.

Within a few days of this pivotal moment at the kitchen sink, I was out running errands and found at a store a small plaque that said, "There is a Special Beauty in each season of our lives." It felt like a confirming gift just waiting for me to find, and it now sits on the windowsill just above my sink, reminding me of the importance of the journey, the struggles, and looking for the positive in everything.

Just the other day, I found myself once again standing at the kitchen sink full of dirty dishes with piles of laundry sitting on a chair, just within my sight, waiting to be folded. In the blink of an eye, my seven-year-old sprinted through the kitchen and up the white carpet stairs with his muddy shoes from the backyard. He was in search of his "bug box," buried somewhere in his messy room. My three-year-olds were wrestling and "loving" each other to literal pieces. In my head, I slowly started to count down from three, knowing what inevitably follows. As if on cue, screams and tears began by the time I reached one. One screaming three year old ran for his cup on the counter and spilled it all over the floor, his second cup of juice (and yet to consume any) in the hour. The other raced to my legs and screamed for a band-aid to cover the small bump she may or may not have had on her head.

I paused just long enough to read the plaque, "There is a Special Beauty in each season of our lives."

Part of me still longs for easier mom-moments or days, but I know that the seasons are changing. In a few years, the dishes and laundry will still be there. However, my seven-year-old will be more interested in hanging out with his buddies than digging up treasures in the backyard mud and bringing them in to show me in his bug box. The laughs and sweet three-year-old giggles of siblings wrestling will fade. I won't be pouring cup after cup of juice to replace the spilled ones. My baby girl will be busy with the millions of things teenage girls do and will not be standing at my feet, vying for my attention and one more Hello Kitty Band-aid. There will still be challenges, but they will be different. I know I will look back fondly on these days and my heart will smile. I am already laughing about the days of smelling like a dirty diaper and will continue to laugh about those hardships for years to come.

Like the beauty of a quiet and untouched morning snow in the midst of a long and cold winter, there is joy amidst the tireless work of being a mom. Sure, there are days where it is hard to appreciate the beauty of the snow because I am longing for summer.

But now, it is those days when I suit up and go play in the snow between the potty breaks and lost mittens, it is in the laughter and squeals of joy, and in the snowmen built and snowball fights fought, that I find beauty in the chaos. Plus, whether I like it or not, spring is just around the corner.

Blessings In Disguise

Laura Falin

peacebutnotquiet.com

My fourth and final baby wasn't supposed to be a c-section.

Rather, my fourth and final baby wasn't supposed to be my *first* c-section.

The minute I discovered I was pregnant with my oldest, I read everything I could get my hands on. I stopped eating sushi. I cut out lunchmeat and red wine. I cut out caffeine. I memorized *What to Expect When You're Expecting* and poured over every book recommended to me by my OB and by my friends with children.

By the time Baby Number Four came along, I was a pro. We didn't even bother with a birth plan. We didn't have the crib set up, and while we had a general idea where the car seat was, in the rafters of the garage, we weren't anywhere close to having it in the car.

I strolled into the maternity ward like it was the first day of senior year. I knew this place. I had this down. Those mamas doing their nervous Lamaze breathing were adorable. My husband and I nudged each other knowingly... And then he headed home to get some sleep.

So it was a jolt when things didn't go according to the script. I was supposed to labor for a few hours, pop out a baby, and be ready to head home in the morning. I earned this. After three long labors, I was due for an easy one.

We mamas worry, and I don't know one who ever stops. Sometimes it's justified. Everyone I know has an Emergency Room Kid that keeps us on our toes (mine started his career yelling, "Hey! I get four stitches like how old I am!" and can now rate urgent care centers based on which ones give out the good popsicles). So I worried, too, about lots of things.

I worried about having a healthy baby. I worried about the emotional health of the other kids. I worried that, with four kids already, one would feel left out or unloved or be forgotten at a gas station in the middle of Nevada on a road trip. I had nightmares where I discovered I'd allowed everyone to swim in a raging river or play in an abandoned quarry (no, really. We don't even have quarries). I even worried she might be born with nine toes instead of the standard ten (the ultrasound was unclear about that one little piggy who doesn't get any roast beef, and when she was born it was a little wonky on her tiny little feet). And I worried about serious complications.

But I never, not once, made any plans to recover from surgery.

As far as birth surprises go, it's not a bad one. It was rushed, but I was healthy, my daughter was healthy, we all recovered just as we should. But I discovered then that I'm a terrible patient. I whine. I get cranky. I want to be out of my bed but I don't want to hurt or be achy and I want to do all the things right now and I do not like this slow recovery business one little bit. I know ladies who fought cancer with more grace and patience than I did my recovery from a c-section.

And I'm terrible at accepting help. I'm a good helper and a people pleaser and I like being The One Who Does the Stuff, but I do not like other people doing the stuff for me. I'm like a three-year-old yelling, "I do it myself!" Besides, other people who do my stuff don't do it exactly like I would. They do things differently, and obviously that's bad even when everyone else likes it better.

And I'm squeamish. I can handle small cuts and bumps, but serious blood and things like stitches or staples in my body... Just... Eugghh. Yuck yuck yuck and also no. No way.

This is what children do, though. They push us, like it or not, to change. They make us physically and emotionally and spiritually uncomfortable, and they make us dependent on other people because we can't do everything for them. We just can't. And ultimately, **despite our intentions, they make us better people for it**. They make us more interesting, because when we'd like to be lying on the couch binge-watching "The Unbreakable Kimmy Schmidt," (You should do this sometimes. Trust me.) we know that we need to get them out of the house. More compassionate, because watching them struggle with friendships and relationships gives us a different perspective on our own. More flexible, because as anyone who's been around a child for more than five minutes can tell you, you have plans and they have plans and it is a rare day on earth when those plans are the same. More creative and relaxed and a hundred other things you didn't know you wanted to be, but now you have no choice.

My recovery was a blessing, really. In a family with three other young children, it allowed me some space and time in the hospital with the newest family member, chilling out, bonding, and warning her that her siblings might be a little much to handle at first but were pretty excited about her. The doctors and I joked about how this would be the child who fell asleep, only to wake up at ballet recitals and piano practices and wherever her siblings were headed next.

It allowed me to talk to the nice older lady who makes rounds every day at 4 p.m., handing out fresh-baked cookies to new moms and nurses (and yes, maybe I briefly thought about faking it for a day or two longer so I could get more cookies. Don't you judge me). And to the other nice lady whose knitting circle makes hats for every single baby born in that hospital. It helped me realize there are a lot of people in this world who are just nice, in all of their unique, beautiful own ways. They really are.

It challenged me to set some goals as well, and in the next eleven months, I went from not being able to walk to the end of the room to running a half marathon. And then a full. And I saw the miracle of these bodies we have and these lives we've been given. That we can be cut open with things taken out of our insides, then heal and thrive and recover.

I like to be in control. I like to know what's coming next, and make a list and have a plan and be ready to go. I don't really like curve balls because I've got all these little people depending on me and I don't want them worrying that I don't know what to do.

But sometimes, life throws you some curves. This was admittedly not a big or bad one, but it did throw me off. And I realized, once again, that Someone knows what I need and what my family needs much better than I do, and He's willing to make me unhappy and uncomfortable if that's necessary. Sometimes it's a spiritual upheaval. Sometimes it's a move across country. Sometimes it's a baby, and a surgery, and the unexpected time to get to know her better while I recovered.

Life with kids is beautiful, and fun, and totally unpredictable, and filled with these blessings in disguise.

I'm in, man. Bring it on.

The Beauty of Losing Control
Caroline Vroustouris

I'm the kind of person you would call analytical. In truth, that's just a nice way of saying that I overthink everything. So, it came as no surprise when, upon learning that I was pregnant on a grey and windy fall evening in October 2012, that I began fixating on the question, "What kind of mother will I be?"

There are a countless number of answers to this question, from the classic "The best mother I can be," to the self-assured "I will be cool/ understanding/supportive," and the self-doubtful "I don't know! I just hope that I can do this!" These and countless other one-off answers that sprang into my mind as I lay in bed next to my newly-minted husband, sleeping soundly next to me after having just learned of his impending fatherhood. I had always marveled at his ability to hold onto joy in any situation without questioning it. Especially when I, now fixated on the question of self-doubt, quickly began to imagine ways that I could screw up being a mother. Since I have a vivid imagination, it was a long night with very little sleep.

As it always does with me, the morning bore a new level of clarity that helped to put my doubts at ease, at least temporarily. In the weeks and months that followed, and as my pregnancy progressed—thankfully, healthy and on track—I tried to practice the mental self-care that every expectant mother should. I focused on being realistic, reminding myself that I was not the first woman to go through this and that is was highly unlikely that I would be the worst mother that ever lived. Reaching out to my own mother, sister, and other family members and friends who were parents helped to reinforce the good things I knew I had to offer this child.

By the time that I was lying in the hospital bed on a beautiful Saturday evening in June, starting the scheduled induction one week before my due date, I was honestly pretty proud of how I felt about my soon-to-be tested abilities as a mother. "I can do this my way," was my mantra through the next 21 hours of labor. I was in control.

Then, all of a sudden, I was a mother. Harrison was born. My world (and the way that I perceive it) was suddenly and irrevocably changed. In an instant, the question of *"What kind of mother will I be?"* was no longer rhetorical. In a haze of love and pain and relief and so many other feelings and emotions that I could not draw upon the words to describe them, I became a mother. A tiny little boy, all perfect with wrinkles and bright pink skin topped with a tiny blue-and-white cap, was laid on my chest and became a part of me.

For an undetermined fragment of time, I reveled in this moment. Maybe it was thirty seconds, maybe it was three minutes. I will never be sure. What I am very sure of, however, is that when the nurse took my sweet boy away to be checked over, weighed and measured, losing control over where he was and what was being done to him rocked me in a way I could not have expected.

It was then that I inherently understood that my pre-birth ideas about being mothering on my own terms and being in control were not going to fly in the real world. As much as I wanted to, I couldn't make the world perfect for Harrison. I could not protect him from everything or be there next to him at every turn. This, unlike any other experience of my life, freed me and frightened me in equal measure.

When I was pregnant, I often heard from people that the moment I met my child would be the moment I felt complete and total love in a way that I never had before. In my experience, that notion was 100% true and opened a space in my heart that freed a hidden love I never knew existed. In that same moment, however, I also was struck by this overwhelming fear of being unable to control the world around my fragile, tiny newborn. Left wondering why no one had ever mentioned this deep rooted super-fear in their discussion of the immediate postpartum experience, I started questioning myself in a way I hadn't since the night in October that I learned I was pregnant. *Was it normal to be afraid that someone would lose my son in the vast expanse of the hospital? Kidnap him when I thought he was in the nursery? Was I experiencing the first stage of postpartum depression? Maybe I was just delirious from not having slept for over 30 hours.* "That's it," I reasoned with myself, "I am afraid the nurse is going to drop my son on the way to the bassinet because I am exhausted. Don't be so hard on yourself, C."

Unfortunately, being hard on myself was not the only cause of the problem.

As soon as we got home with Harrison and I began to settle into the sleepless life of being a new mother, I had an achingly strong realization that my worries and fears were too persistent to brush aside. Some feedings, the bonding times were wrapped in a quiet fear that my baby would choke. Naps were welcome breaks for my boy to rest, but punctuated by so many quiet "visits" on my part that any rest I was supposed to get quickly evaporated. I was anxious. I could not control everything around Harrison all of the time. The anxiety was palpable. Rather than fully enjoying Harrison's first few weeks at home, I plastered on a smile and hid my fears inside. Controlling my emotions was paramount in my mind, as I tried to rationalize my feelings. "What are the chances?" was a phrase I repeated in my head, looking up statistics on how likely it was that my boy would choke, break a limb or even, in the most terrifying case, become a victim of SIDS.

I continued to dwell on all of the terrible possibilities until Harrison was about six months old. While my family and friends were not oblivious to my worry, they seemed to chalk it up to my normal control-freak tendencies, which had been on display for thirty-two years before Harrison came into the picture. Since the feelings were not debilitating, and I was able to work and carry on in a seemingly happy household, there was no intervention or doctor's visit to dig into my feelings. Only my husband knew how deep these feelings really went, and only he knew that I was desperately trying to rationalize every worry-filled thought with the purchase of more books, the reading of more articles and the digestion of more statistics. I could see he was getting weary, because neither his calming words nor the myriad resources that I consulted were helping to ease my anxieties. Something had to change.

Then, at 3 a.m. on a bleary night in December, 2013, the alarm bells went off. Jason and I were awakened in the middle of the night to the sound of Harrison's sleep monitor blaring into the darkness. I had purchased the monitor, which sounds an alarm when your baby isn't producing movement or breathing during sleep, in an effort to calm my nerves about SIDS. I had imagined what would happen if it ever went off. Now, here it was, my worst nightmare come to life. The alarm was beeping with a fierce, unyielding shriek, akin to a fire alarm. My internal house was burning down and I was not even totally awake yet.

As I struggled to get out of bed, my feet hit the floor so hard that I thought Jason would fall onto the floor from the vibration. He was slowly, groggily coming to, as I rounded the bed and yelled, "Jason, wake up, it's Harrison!" His eyes suddenly open and scared, were as wide as I had ever seen them. In about six steps, we were across the short hall to Harrison's room, where it was dark and very apparent that our baby was not crying. That loud, persistent, unbelievably sharp alarm had not awoken my tiny, six-month-old boy. My stomach dropped to the floor and my legs felt like they were melting. I raced toward the crib and peered in, shaking.

"Harrison?" I whispered my voice almost totally absent. Jason picked up our boy, rocking him, saying his name, over and over. Every second seemed like a year. Why wasn't he crying? How could he sleep through an alarm, two frantic parents and a rousing entrance into his room?

Suddenly, without fanfare or fuss, Harrison woke up. Strangely, he didn't cry. He looked up at Jason and then he looked at me, as I tried to keep standing on phantom legs. He scrunched his face and his little tongue peeped out of his mouth. His eyes, big and blue, searched the room for the source of the noise; it was another split second and then his own piercing cries began, rivaling those of the alarm. I quickly took him into my arms as Jason shut off the machine, both of us finally coming to and realizing what had just happened.

We thought we had lost our baby. We thought our boy was gone. For no more than a minute, but a minute that seemed like an eternity, the most terrible outcome that I had ruminated on for six months had almost come to pass. In the moments following the ordeal, while I started to feed Harrison under the light of his star lamp and watched my husband trek wearily back to bed, I had a deeply profound realization: **my anxieties were worse than the real thing**. I was making myself sick with worry, needlessly sick, and it had to stop. Right then, it had to stop.

Now, eighteen months later, I am proud to say that, for the most part, it has. Harrison is now two years old. In the weeks and months since the faulty sleep monitor went off, Harrison has tested my resolve many times.

We have had one emergency room visit and two calls to Poison Control that, if not accurately described as terrifying, were surely harrowing at the least. Beyond that, we've had our fair share of other normal bumps and bruises from the playground and two or three gastrointestinal viruses of various levels of explosiveness. We've had four or five brutal colds to contend with and the new frontiers of teething, vaccinations and making new friends. Before the sleep monitor had signaled my own internal alarms, I used to fear that one or more of these experiences could hurt my son, sending his physical, mental or emotional worlds into orbit. In reality, none of them did. In fact, all of the experiences made him stronger. They made me stronger, too.

What I know today that I could not have possibly known as a brand--new mother was that losing control can be a good thing. In fact, it was the best thing that could happen to both me and my son. Losing control meant being able to take each day as it came and live in the moment. It meant freeing myself from living in fear and pushing myself to live in possibility. It meant, most importantly, becoming a better mother.

I am working toward becoming the kind of self-assured mother that I had dreamed of being the first night I learned I was pregnant. That night, I thought being a good mother meant being in control and doing everything my way. Today, I know that being a good mother means embracing your lack of control. And there's untold beauty in letting go.

Silver Bells
Stephanie Blake

Silver bells, silver bells.... I sang that song over and over again on our trips to and from middle school, for years. My mom would ask me to sing it, and she'd join along. She loved to hear me sing that song, and I loved to sing it to her.

Those moments are precious to me—just her and I, riding along, belting out Silver Bells as though it were our life's anthem. When I sing Silver Bells now, it's just for me. No one begs me to sing it over and over, because now, my mother is gone.

I was 28 when my mother passed away. Due to heavy medication and a worn body from surgery after surgery and a plethora of uncoordinated prescriptions from various doctors, a fall was the last straw. Losing her was so hard in so many ways, but perhaps mostly because I had lost my father at six. When she was gone, I felt like an orphan.

My life with my mother was complicated and hard because her life was complicated and hard. My father was diagnosed with bone cancer just years after they got married. She loved him deeply, nursed him through his illness, and was with him until his last breath. It seemed to many that, when he went, a bit of her sanity went with him. This made for a turbulent childhood. Just as she "found herself" again, she dealt with medical issue after medical issue.

I remember having to hide her keys from her because she wanted to end her pain and anguish by driving her car into a tree. I was 13. I remember her falling asleep with her face in her food at dinner because of her medications. I remember getting my hardship license, taking over grocery shopping and worrying about how to make ends meet. I remember all the conversations that we didn't have. I remember the guilt trips and the yelling. I remember when her anger went too far.

But you know what I remember even stronger than all of those moments? I remember the way it felt and sounded to lay in her lap as she talked. I remember her smile and contagious laughter. I remember how she told me I could do anything I set my mind to. I remember that she always believed in me even if she didn't show up all the time. I remember looking up at her face at church, seeing tears stream down her face as she sang an old hymn.

I remember.

I remember her hugs. I remember her cheese dip. I remember her sassiness and how she stood against injustice as she saw it and always,

always helped the poor. I remember her love for Coke and sweet tea. I remember the sound of her voice. The way she smelled. I would love to smell her again.

Do you know what I mean? It's the small things that you miss when they're gone. Like the fact that you can't just pick up the phone and call (even if it might have been a stressful call...) or just get a hug from your mom.

I've come to terms with the fact that *no one* will ever love me like my mother loved me. No one on this earth wants to protect me with a mother's fierceness. No one wants to see me succeed like my mother. No one loves the features of my face, because they knew my dad, like my mother did. No one wants to hear me sing Silver Bells like my mother did.

My mother is gone, and life continues on, but her absence in my life—as trying as life with her was—has left a hole. That hole has brought clarity into my life and sight that only those who have lost their mother can comprehend.

Mothers are irreplaceable. They make an impact whether present or absent in our lives. The deep connection I feel to my mother even now is so special and unique. The value of my mother in my life is priceless and I treasure it.

So, you see, I have a message for those of you who struggle with your relationship with your mother while she is still alive, as well as for those of you who don't have struggles.

Cherish what you have the best way you know how. That doesn't mean you have to allow boundaries to be crossed—but it does mean that you strive and fight for quality time with your mother while there is still time to be had. Once she is gone... She's just gone.

Breathe her in one more time, listen to her voice with intent, and remember it. Spend time in the kitchen, learning your favorite recipes of hers. Don't hold onto petty arguments. Hug her and try to see her as a woman, not just as your mother. Ask her what she loves to do—what's her favorite music? What are/were her dreams?

Apart from some who have irreparable, abusive relationships with their mother—you will wish that you had taken the time to do these things. Please, take it from me. I was just beginning to be old enough to truly appreciate my mother beyond all the years of pain, frustration and anger. Love her as deeply as you're able while she's here and you won't regret it.

Now, more than ever before, I'm convinced of the great power of a mother's love. I have four children of my own, and when I'm with them, taking in the moment, I ask them to sing to me... And, OH how I love to hear them sing! I look at the features of their faces and I find myself, my husband, my mother and my father there. I tell them that they can do anything they set their mind to. I embrace them and see them breathing in deep, knowing they will remember the way I smell. I believe in them, and I show up. I sing Silver Bells to them and remember her.

Moms, you matter.

Your presence matters. Your absence matters. Even though my mother put me through more than I care to share, I remember her love. If I remember her love through all of that, how much more will your children remember your love more than the way you lose your temper toward the end of the day? They'll remember your love more than all the bedtime snuggles you skipped out on because you were so tired or the short temper on long days.

Mothering is tough, but love them deeply through it all. Loving them doesn't mean you're Pinterest-perfect or that you have it all figured out. It doesn't mean that you are super mom—it means that in the small moments, you tell them you love them, you're present, and when you fail, no matter how big or small, you say you're sorry.

In the end, no one will ever love your children the way *you* love your children. A mother's love is priceless, irreplaceable, and it's yours to give. A mother's work is life-changing, history making, hard, beautiful work. Don't be discouraged. Always show up and give it your best, because they need you... They need you to ask them to sing Silver Bells.

Ezekiel's Story

Nicole Tolosa

In the fall of 2007, my husband, Matt, and I were eagerly anticipating the arrival of our third child, due in April of 2008. Even though this was our fourth pregnancy, due to an early miscarriage during our first pregnancy, we were apprehensive each time I was expecting. We had safely reached twenty weeks, though, and were excited for the ultrasound. We already had a girl and a boy, so we decided to wait to find out the baby's gender.

On the day of the ultrasound appointment, my husband cut his seminary class and met me at the doctor's office. After the ultrasound was completed, the technician told us that she needed to review the ultrasound results with the radiologist. We were told we were free to go and were to wait to hear back from the doctor in a few days. I thought it was rather strange that more wasn't said and that the technician never showed us the pictures of our baby's heart, but it was a new practice, so we just assumed they did things a bit differently. Still, I was concerned as I sat in the room waiting for the doctor.

When she walked through the door, she said, "I think you had better sit down." I knew something was wrong. She proceeded to tell me about the radiologist's concerns in finding fluid around our baby's heart and in the abdominal cavity. More importantly, they could not find our baby's stomach, and the bowels were showing up bright.

The following day, we had a level two ultrasound done, as well as a visit with the perinatologist. They planned an echocardiogram of our baby's heart to get a clearer picture. At this point, I realized I wanted to find out the baby's gender. I felt that I needed our baby to have some kind of identity. The next 24 hours were torture. I was so afraid that we had a partial baby in my womb who had no hope of survival. We knew God had blessed us with this gift of life, but I still wrestled with trusting His sovereignty. I wept and prayed a litany of repetitive prayers and petitions.

The following morning was nerve wracking as we waited for news. In His grace, God answered our prayers as we saw the image of our baby; complete, not partial! Oh, and we were having a boy!

However, we did find out that there was a fair amount of fluid in the abdominal cavity and several calcium deposits on his liver. They were unsure what was causing these issues, but they presumed it was the result of some type of virus. They recommended that we move forward with an amniocentesis to narrow down the cause. There was a risk of premature ruptured membranes if we agreed to the amniocentesis and were told that pinpointing the problem would not "fix" the health risks. Because my previous pregnancy had ended with two weeks of hospital bed rest after my water broke six weeks early, we didn't want to take the chance and risk the life of our son. We knew we were not going to terminate this pregnancy. Our son was given to us by our gracious Heavenly Father, and his life was in God's hands.

Throughout all of this uncertainty, we received numerous emails and phone calls checking in and reminding us of the many prayers on our behalf. We were overwhelmed by the love and encouragement of our brothers and sisters in Christ. Our son was being prayed for by people we didn't even know! We were daily upheld by the strong arms of our Heavenly Father who fearfully and wonderfully knit our son together.

About a week after the initial ultrasound, I tested positive for CMV (Cytomegalovirus). It was discovered that I contracted the virus and passed it to our son during the pregnancy. This was a rare occurrence, and the effects of this virus on our son's health were uncertain. Originally, we were told that the risk was minimal for CMV to cause any permanent damage to our son's health, but two weeks later we learned that the calcifications on his liver and abdomen were where the infection had set in, and that there was really no way of knowing the amount of damage the CMV would cause. The range of physical effects spanned from no health risks at all, to the chance of severe mental retardation, blindness, deafness, and developmental delays. There was also a remote possibility that it could take our son's life. This information weighed heavily upon us throughout the remainder of the pregnancy.

As the weeks went by, I continued with my regular OB checkups as well as appointments with the perinatologist at the hospital. At each appointment, we gained more knowledge concerning the virus, as well as the precautions that would be necessary during his delivery. There would be NICU (Neonatal Intensive Care Unit) nurses present to assess our son after his birth and potentially admit him into the NICU nursery. Because of the CMV, our son would not be kept in the regular infant nursery, to eliminate the potential risk of spreading the virus to other infants.

Because of the circumstances, I was scheduled to be induced on April 2, 2008. The delivery room was filled with doctors and nurses. Following his birth, several tests were done to assess his health, and we began follow up with an infectious disease specialist. We chose the name Ezekiel Simeon. Ezekiel means "God's strengthens," and it was chosen in faith that God would carry this little one through. His middle name, Simeon, meant "to hear, or listen."

While we were in the hospital, Ezekiel had failed his first hearing test. They re-tested him, and he passed. We were told that there are often false positives with this initial hearing test. We also discovered that one the most common health risks with CMV was hearing loss. We had several more hearing tests done with varying results. We had an ABR (Auditory Brain Response) done in July. At that point, it was decided that surgery was necessary to drain the fluid in his ears and that a second ABR test would need to be performed since Ezekiel was still showing signs of hearing loss. We were told by the infectious disease specialist that if the hearing loss was related to the virus, it would be degenerative.

On August 25, 2008, we received confirmation that our son had a 90% hearing loss. During the surgery, they took molds of our son's ears to have him fitted for hearing aids with the desire to move forward as quickly as possible. At this point, Ezekiel had not been hearing for nearly five months. There were many visits to the children's hospital. This was a sobering experience.

My mind was muddled as I processed the many decisions that lay ahead for Ezekiel and our family. Our lives became a whirlwind of questions, doctor's appointments, procedures, research, and a learning curve concerning hearing loss. We were now researching cochlear implants, talking with teachers of the deaf and an interpreter, and checking out sign language books and DVDs from the library.

In mid-September, Ezekiel received his hearing aids—a process that was a bit of roller coaster for all of us. Trying to keep hearing aids in the ears of a six-month-old proved to be a difficult task. What made this more difficult was his lack of progress.

The question we heard almost daily for nearly two months was, "Can you tell if he is responding to any sounds with his hearing aids?" Truthfully, we really had no idea what Ezekiel was hearing. We had only seen small and uncertain signs of his response to sound at all! The ENT (Ear/Nose/Throat) doctor at the University of Minnesota firmly believed that cochlear implants were the best option for Ezekiel considering his profound hearing loss. In the meantime, we were learning American Sign Language while following up with the audiologist and trying to keep up with the unending task of keeping the hearing aids in Ezekiel's ears.

During this time, my husband's company went through a huge lay-off, and he lost his job in the middle of his fall semester of seminary. Our little family of five was being stretched on many levels! Again, we wrestled through trusting God's sovereign hand in our lives. We started speech therapy for Ezekiel at the beginning of November and continued to take him to the University of Minnesota for behavioral analysis and sound field testing. With no real positive results, our audiologist decided to place an order for stronger hearing aids that would allow the volume to be turned up louder, providing greater amplification.

It was about this time that we discovered that the CMV had also caused some developmental delays in Ezekiel's growth and milestones. These findings resulted in physical therapy each week. We had a CAT scan done in December of 2008, to pave the first steps of preparing for cochlear implant surgery. We had another consultation with Ezekiel's ENT doctor at the end of January as we pursued the cochlear implant.

We had reached a point of decision. Ezekiel's hearing aids were not providing enough amplification for speech and language. He was getting sound, but it was simply just noise. With Ezekiel being born into a hearing family and a hearing culture; if we wanted to give Ezekiel the best possibility to learn in school, read well, learn to speak, communicate with his hearing peers, and live with less struggles in his present circumstances, then cochlear implants would give Ezekiel the best chance to be successful. We prayed, sought counsel, and did much research.

We continued to learn and teach him ASL (American Sign Language) in hopes that one day he might be able to communicate with his deaf peers as well. After much prayer, we made plans to have the surgery in May after my husband finished his spring semester of seminary. Many more appointments, behavioral tests, therapy sessions, and another minor surgery would occur in the few months before the cochlear implant surgery.

On May 27, 2009, we woke up at 4:15 in the morning and took Ezekiel to the University of Minnesota for his first cochlear implant surgery. I was flooded with a myriad of emotions and uncertainties. I was still questioning our decision the night before Ezekiel's surgery. But the surgery was a success! Although it was difficult to see our son under the effects of the anesthesia, with a huge bandage wrapped around his head, we were relieved to have this obstacle behind us.

Approximately three weeks later, we returned to the University of Minnesota for Ezekiel's implant activation. There were seven eager individuals in that small audiology booth, all waiting to see his reaction. He was quiet, curious, then cried when the volume was too loud. The audiologist told us his response was quite typical. It was incredible to see Ezekiel not only respond to sound, but look to see where the voices were coming from.

After 14 long and uncertain months, our son heard our voices for the first time!

We are so humbled that He entrusted us with this gift. The journey with Ezekiel was an exhausting and emotional one, but through it all, we saw the providential hand of God along each step of the way. In the midst of our anxiety and uncertainty, God gave us peace.

The Day Super Mom Died

Tabitha Dumas

tabithadumas.com/blog

It was 2008. My husband and I had been married for six years and our first son was three years old when we started talking about having another baby. I started a blog to chronicle our journey, never dreaming that we'd get pregnant on the first try.

We found out on April 21st and enjoyed sharing our good news with friends and family. Our due date was December 28th. A New Year's baby!

After an uneventful first week, I started spotting, then bleeding heavily. Over Mother's Day weekend, we knew it was over. I remember crying in the shower, wondering "Why me?" We didn't even make it past six weeks of pregnancy.

In the weeks that followed, I felt like a cloud of doom was following me. I couldn't understand why God would allow something like that to happen to me, and I wondered if we'd ever be able to have another baby.

Three months later, we decided to start trying again. I was astounded when, yet again, we got a positive pregnancy test on the first try. Just like before, we shared our news right away and asked people to pray for us. After the six week mark, we felt like we could stop holding our breath, and from there, the pregnancy progressed smoothly and was mostly complication-free.

I was about seven months along when the reality started to hit me: we were having another baby!

That vague unsettled feeling turned into full-blown anxiety that I ultimately battled at varying degrees during the rest of the pregnancy, and for many months beyond (and still do, on a much smaller scale). I lost my appetite, my hands and feet would sweat, my heart would race, and there were nights when I was pushed to the brink of what I thought I could handle. I only gained 12 lbs in the whole pregnancy, and it definitely took a toll on me.

Eventually, I was able to overcome my anxiety, but before I tell you more about that, I need to give you some of the back story.

Before the second pregnancy, I was a very busy woman. I was active at our church, teaching classes, overseeing the nursery, serving on the women's ministry team and facilitating the mom's group. I was also managing a direct sales business, running an Etsy shop, blogging regularly, and hosting events in addition to the everyday tasks of raising our son and maintaining our home. My husband and I often passed each other in the evening as he came home from work and I left to go to a meeting or run errands.

What no one could see was that I had grown weary and resentful of the constant busyness and activity. I was irritable and tired, and while venting to a dear friend, she said, "It sounds like you actually resent what you're doing."

That's when I realized that I'd taken on too much and wasn't even enjoying it anymore. I was, without realizing it, trying to prove myself to God and earn grace.

All my life, I'd struggled with feeling inadequate and unworthy. As a worker bee and doer, I was trying to use the teaching, handmade crafts, blog posts and even my sparkling personality as a way to say to God, "See?? I'm earning my keep! I'm doing all of this for You!" Looking like Super Mom had become my attempt to tell God and the world, "I am worthy! I am not a waste of space!"

The miscarriage was a wake-up call. I was trying to please everyone except the very people I loved the most. I was trying to "do" for God and prove my worth to everyone. The anxiety was like a cold sore that festers because you're stressed—it was a manifestation of my inner turmoil.

Losing that pregnancy and realizing that I was wasting my life trying to be Super Mom made me realize how precious life is. It also gave me an opportunity to make a fresh start.

One year to the day after the miscarriage, our second son came home from the hospital. We settled into life with a newborn as we contemplated what to do next. Eventually, we decided to put our house on the market, sell one of our cars and move into a rental just a few miles from my husband's place of work. I stepped down from every leadership position at church, quit my direct sales business, and closed down my Etsy shop so I could focus on my boys, my new home, and my husband.

I can vividly remember after my husband and sons pulled away in the moving truck and I was sitting in the van alone in the driveway after cleaning out our house. I thought about when my sister-in-law had asked me, "Aren't you going to be sad to leave that house?" We'd had it built six years prior and had so many happy memories there. Getting it ready to sell and moving out had been exhausting and I knew we had to do it all over again to move into our rental but as I sat there, all I felt was peace. I made a mental note that I wasn't feeling anxious about it. I knew it was time to move on, both from my house and from my old habits of "try harder" living. That's the day Super Mom died.

The time we spent having one car and living in that rental was one of the best seasons of life we've had so far. Because our rental home was so close to where my husband worked, we often spent his lunch hour together. I had time to craft, read, bake, and play with our boys. And all those activities we walked away from? We weren't missed.

So what did I learn from giving up the Super Mom persona?

As I continued to fully recover from my anxiety and the physical effects of the pregnancy, I had time to contemplate my identity and my purpose. I realized that God doesn't need me *doing* things for Him, He simply wants my attention, my worship and my obedience. For someone like me who actually likes checklists, it's hard to accept love without feeling the need to reciprocate.

The "why me?" aspect of the miscarriage also gave me a chance to really look at the foundations of my faith and what I believed about my identity and worth. Teaching, serving, my businesses, the meetings—going from one activity to another and keeping my mind occupied was easier than looking at the truth: trying to be Super Mom is exhausting. I see busy women around me all the time and wonder, "What is she hiding from?" I was hiding from the truth: God and I were not OK, and I wasn't OK with myself, either.

In the years since, I have been very careful to not take on too many activities or projects. I try to keep our home and family life as quiet and peaceful as possible. I spend quality time with God on a regular basis, I maintain only a few close friendships and I take care of myself so I can better serve others. **I refuse to live a life of constant busyness—I was made for more than that.**

The other hard lesson I learned was that my sons weren't interested so much in play dates, homemade treats or how much I was doing for our church—they just wanted my time and attention. Ultimately, no one wants me to be stressed and resentful, but it's up to me to say "no" and to invest my time and energy into what matters most.

Now my life is very much in harmony, but it takes constant maintenance to keep it that way. It's so easy to slip into old habits but I make a point to assess my busyness levels on a regular basis and I have surrounded myself with people who respect my boundaries. I also take "me time" very seriously. I will never again let people take and take from me without replenishing myself.

The unfortunate truth is that Super Mom is a title and role that women label themselves with. In fact, right after the miscarriage, I grappled with the question of, "What's standing in the way of you and God?" It took me many months to find the answer, and when I did, I stopped dead in my tracks. It was *me*. I was standing in the way. I was placing expectations on myself. I was filling my calendar with activities. I was giving until I had nothing left to give. No one forced the cape on me—I donned it willingly it until it became the very noose that hung me.

I am a very different woman now, seven years later. I write stories like this in an effort to encourage other women not to fall into the same trap what I did. As mothers, it's so easy to let other people tell us how to live our lives. God has plans for us, and they don't include running ourselves ragged until we're of no use to anyone.

I see so many women wearing Super Mom capes. If I can encourage even one mother to remove her cape and embrace her true identity, my journey was well worth it.

The First Time
Kate Skero
nourishinglittlesouls.com

We sat around our dark wood dinner table on a cool July night with the windows open and the lazy wind passing by the ivory lace curtains. Three piles of wedding favors sat in mounds on the table before us, awaiting their assembly. Methodically, my mom placed a packet of sunscreen followed by a pink, yellow or orange flip-flop key chain into each bag, then passed it to me. I put in three Starbursts: one pink, one yellow, and one orange. (In wedding language, those colors are guava, buttercream, and tangerine.) Then, I pulled the ivory ribbon that drew each satchel closed and finally placed it into the basket of finished favors.

The process was time-consuming, though we enjoyed the simplicity of the task. Figuring out how to fit 183 guests into a 160-person reception hall in a comfortable seating arrangement, that was a headache. Designing place cards with an outdated computer, no internet, and no printer, that was frustrating. Figuring out how in the world I will host my fiancé's thirty out of town relatives, that was difficult. Dealing with the bridal shop lady who regretted to inform me, in her thick accent, that my bridesmaids' dresses were not available in the colors I ordered, that was a nightmare. Assembling the wedding favors was one more thing to check off this epic wedding to--do list, and it was easy. No headaches, no difficulties—just take the time to put everything in the bags. My mom and I could have it done in one night.

After five months of wedding planning on overdrive, our relationship needed an easy night as well. My mom and I had been bickering since I came home from college in the middle of May. She thought I wasn't doing enough for my own wedding, and I thought she was doing too much for my wedding. This struggle reached its peak when we were arguing about who was doing more work for the wedding in the car about a month before the wedding. She was so frustrated with my sharp words and snarky attitude that she slammed on her brakes and demanded, with coarse language, that I get out of her car. I was happy to get out, and I slammed the door behind me. I stomped into the nearby Wendy's, knowing that she couldn't leave me there with my fiancé in the car and her on the way to drop him off in Chicago. My dad drove to the scene after work to talk to my mom; my fiancé chased me into the Wendy's, and some forced, pride-filled peace was made between my mom and me. We drove to Chicago in an unquiet silence that said, *we'll agree not to argue for our own sanity and for the sake of this wedding, but I still have plenty of problems with you.*

It was clear that our problems ran deeper than surface-level wedding disputes. We were becoming new people. I was on the verge of beginning a new kind of life, free from the yoke of parental supervision, while she was on the verge of losing the last of her children: the last of the ones who depended on her for everything. At the core, I think we were both afraid of losing intimacy with each other, and we expressed it in different ways. We struggled against each other, my young adult ego often getting the best of me, and her fear of the future proving the worst of her.

After filling our first fifty bags and feeling satisfied with our accomplishment, my mom went out to the porch to sip water and smoke cigarettes. I sat back in my chair, eating the red Starbursts that were restricted from joining the rest of the wedding favors because red was not one of my wedding colors. I chewed, enjoying the bursts of flavor and wondering how many Starbursts were too many. My wedding dress made me stop after three. I saw it down the hallway, hanging on the hooks by the front door in its safe plastic bag, altered to fit me perfectly—so long as I didn't eat one more Starburst. It was the first dress I tried on, at the first bridal shop we stopped at.

I remembered pulling up to the run-down, out-dated bridal shop and whining to my mom. "Why are we stopping here, Mom? We're going dress shopping tomorrow in New York!"

"We have some time before we have to meet with the florist. Let's just see what we can see," she persuaded.

"Okay, but there is no way I'm getting my wedding dress at a place with a broken neon sign in the window."

The first one I tried on was exactly what I wanted. It was a shimmering ivory color with a halter top style; it was tight enough to show my figure but it flared out enough to make me feel like a princess. The quirky Asian owner of the shop, named Connie, shoved a veil into my hair without permission, and it looked perfect. My mom cried. I told her to stop crying. Connie said, "Look good," and she was ready to ring us up.

My mom thought it best for me to try on more dresses. The next five were simply let-downs. So, Connie put pins in the spots in need of alterations, my mom pulled $400 out of her wallet, and the dress would be mine to take home in a few days.

I thought back to less than a year ago, how I had so similarly picked the man I would marry. After two weeks at college, against all of my desires to remain boyfriend-free for a portion of my college career, David took me on a cheesecake picnic overlooking the Chicago skyline at night, then asked me if I thought I could be his girlfriend. He was just what I wanted: godly, strong in leadership, hilarious, and handsome as all get-out. It wasn't difficult to see that God had designed this man for me and me for him. I loved him. My mom thought I should date other boys before I set my mind on this one, but my mind was already set. Five months later, he asked me to marry him in that same cheesecake spot. Five months after that, he would make me his wife while I wore the first dress I tried on at the first shop I stopped at.

I straightened my Starburst wrappers against the table, folding them and stacking them in compulsive ways, wondering when my mom would return. I heard the flicker of her lighter again. Wafts of smoke came in through the screen door, and I turned so I didn't have to breathe it. The usual questions filtered through my mind.

When will she ever stop this disgusting habit? Doesn't she realize that this will kill her if she keeps it up? She doesn't want to hear it. She rolls her eyes if I even mention it. I should just be happy that she stopped smoking inside the house.

"Alright, let's get back to work," she said with a clap of her hands. She set down her ice water that was more ice than water. The glass sweat rolled onto her napkin coaster. Open the satchel: one sunscreen, one key chain, three Starbursts—draw it closed, and done. We did this over and over, concentrated and quiet.

"Katie, do you have any questions about your wedding night?" she glanced up at me as she untangled some of the key chains.

"Umm, nope. I think I have an idea of how it works," I said. Her untangling stopped up the workflow, so I rested my hands. Though I wasn't embarrassed to talk about wedding night details, I honestly didn't have any questions. I think I knew more than she thought I knew, and I didn't feel like telling her that. Friends, movies and too many crossed boundaries with boyfriends past, I guess. But I could tell that she wanted me to ask questions.

She finished untangling and resumed filling the satchels. "You may want to lay a towel on the bed, sweetheart, you know, for the blood," she paused, "And be sure to pack some pads in your wedding night bag." Too personal. Too detailed. Maybe I'm embarrassed now. I desperately wanted to change the topic, but I could only think to redirect it. "Really, Mom? Is that what you did? Did you lay out a towel in the heat of the moment?" I asked incredulously.

"My first time was different from how yours will be."

"Well, what did you do? Did you and Jason plan it out? With a towel?" Jason was her high school boyfriend whom she married and divorced within the two years that followed her graduation. That failed marriage is the reason she didn't initially support my marriage at such a young age. She thought she saw history repeating itself. She didn't, and the difference is Christ. Maybe she realized that her stubborn daughter wasn't changing her mind or maybe she truly saw the difference in our relationship, but she came around. She and my dad drove me out to the site of my dream beach wedding and booked the place before David even put a ring on my finger.

"My first time was different, Katie," her tone changed. "You want to talk about my first time! Let's talk about your first time!" She looked down.

"Come on, Mom, I can handle it. I'm getting married in two weeks for goodness sake!" She lifted her eyes in line with mine. "Oh Mom, I know you had sex before you were married. I'm not stupid."

"I was raped, Katie."

Silence. I couldn't believe her words "What? What do you mean, Mom? What happened?" "When I was thirteen years old, I babysat for this family," she took a deep breath and looked hard into my eyes. "It was just a little baby, and the parents would leave but the dad would always come home first. And he was always drunk." I felt darkness set into my heart. A hard mass of pain settled in the back of my throat. "I didn't know what to do," she said. "So I just let him. And there was blood everywhere the first time."

"It was more than once?" My eyes filled with tears.

"Yes," she said calmly. "It happened several times. After a while, he started bringing his drunk buddies, too."

"But Mom, why did you let them? Why didn't you tell Grandpa? Why did you keep babysitting?" I couldn't stop the questions.

"I was scared, Katie. And naive and young. It was the seventies. I didn't know what I should do. He told me if I ever told anyone, he would kill me. I didn't think anyone would believe me anyway. So, it just kept happening." I was weeping, but through my blurred vision I could see that she was not. She told her story like a brave soldier. "It gets worse, Katie," she reached over and grabbed my hand. "Three months after it started, I wasn't feeling so well. Grandma brought me to the doctor and they figured out that I was pregnant," she squeezed my hand. My mind went in so many directions. *Do I have an older sibling somewhere in the world? What happened? Who is it? Why don't I know her?*

"The doctor said that I was too little to have a baby. He said that I could die if I went through with having it," she took a sip of water. "My parents knew I wasn't into boys yet. So, they finally got me to tell them what

96

happened. And they decided to abort the baby." My stomach was sick with grief. My mind flashed back to all of my passionate anti-abortion speeches in high school, the posters—and here in my home was a woman who had experienced the pain of abortion first hand.

"Do you think about the baby?" I finally asked.

"Not a day goes by that I don't think about that baby." I paused to process, then asked, "What did Grandpa do about that, that man?"

"He was livid, Katie, let me tell you. He would've killed him if it was legal," she smiled pathetically. "But we couldn't prove that it was him after the abortion, and of course he denied it.

The police didn't do anything of worth. His wife called me a whore. I couldn't go out of the house for a while because the stupid hillbilly would try to run me down in his pickup truck. He threw bricks at our house," she was still speaking in an even-tone. "So I took some time off from school until I finally transferred to a another school district. Janesville. That's where I met Cindy," she smiled and I thought about her best friend, the one who would be honored as a mother at my wedding in a few weeks. The one whose daughter, Courtney, would stand up as my maid of honor on my wedding day. "You see, God has a way of working things out for our good, Katie."

I sat there, digesting the story, drinking the details down into the pit of my soul, then spitting them back up again because I hated them so much. Fresh tears continued to pour. I hated the injustice. *Why did she have such a terrible childhood while mine was so easy? No wonder she can't stop smoking. No wonder she can't handle the idea of her youngest child leaving the safe and loving home that she has fostered all these years.*

She embraced me and I cried into her hair. "I'm so sorry, Mom. I'm so sorry." It was all I could say. It was all I could say for all of the years that I didn't know who she was because I didn't know this one thing about her. For all of the years that I judged her flaws while I stood on her broken shoulders. I thought about my white dress hanging in the hallway, and I thought about the blood she wasn't ready to shed. And I was so sorry.

"Katie, it's okay. That was a long time ago. You're hearing this for the first time now, but this was a very long time ago." Her dry eyes told me that this was true. "I have Jesus now. And I have your dad, and your dad is so good to me, Katie. And I have you and your brothers," she paused to assemble some strength, "That hillbilly has no power over me. He can't take away the wonderful love I have in my life. My daughter is going to college and she is going to be a journalist and she is going to do great things for Jesus and she is getting married in two weeks!" she held my face in her soft, motherly hands. "He can't take away how proud I am of you, Katie. I hope you can forgive him the way I have forgiven him."

My wedding day did not come quietly. We set the white tents and chairs up lakeside in the morning, but a severe thunderstorm struck before the ceremony, devastating my dreams in just one violent hour. The storm passed into a peaceful lull with just enough time to set everything back up.

Twenty minutes before my walk down the wet sand aisle, my mom brought me up to my dressing room, prayed with me, and told me to take the next few moments for myself, she would come to get me when it was time. I needed those quiet moments after that storm of a day, that storm of wedding planning. I sat there in my wedding dress gazing out the window, down at the beach and the guests trudging through the sand in their pretty clothes. I thought about my husband-to-be, wondering what he was doing or how he was feeling. I was excited to spend the rest of the day with him, the rest of the night with him—the rest of my life. Then I thought about my parents. Oh, how I would miss them every day.

My mom returned with a little knock. "Katie, it's time!" I met her at the door. She handed me my bouquet and wrapped her great-grandmother's handkerchief around the stems. "Just in case," she said as she closed my hands around the little embroidered cloth. I hugged her, hugged all of her. I hugged everything I knew about her. I loved her for who she was, for all that she had been through, and for all that she had done to bring me to this day. And my love for her ran deeper than it ever did before this whole wedding ordeal. It was more mature, more tested, more full. **It was love that had survived through a thunderstorm and saw catharsis at the end.**

"I'll see you at the end of the aisle," she said with a wink as she handed me off to my dad.

"I'll see you there, Mom."

Each Child is Unique
Janet Kirk

I am a mom to two children, a boy and a girl. I am also a step-mom to three, and I now have seven grandchildren. Each child is unique in every way. Not only do they look different, but they have very different interests. Their personalities are different. They like different colors. Some children are loud; some are quiet. There are so many ways they are different. No two are exactly alike, like snowflakes. I believe they are born this way.

The two children I gave birth to were different even before they were born. My daughter was quiet and moved slowly in my womb, and she was in no hurry to be born. It was a struggle to give birth to her. It took many hours, even with drugs to quicken the labor. Today, she remains an introvert. She talks quietly. She is a nurse, who loves taking care of people and truly cares about her patients.

My son was active, kicking all the time in my womb. We joked about him being a soccer player, and he is! He played soccer from age five through his first year of college. It is his first love in life. When he was born, he was in a hurry. He did not wait for the hospital to decide to let me come in for labor and delivery, but I could tell he was ready, so my husband and I went to the hospital anyway. It was a good thing, because they did not have time to give me any drugs, no enema, no episiotomy. We went straight to delivery. The next day, the nurses told me that he was the most active and aware newborn they had ever seen! When he was little, he learned to run before he ever walked. He was always full steam ahead. He has always been loud, very active, and loves to be around people—a total extrovert.

As a mother, it was my job to raise our children with love, and to recognize each child's uniqueness. As their mother, I helped them learn to grow up well, teaching them what to eat, how to get dressed, how to bathe and how to comb their hair. I also helped them find out how they are unique. **I believe that children will enjoy life more, if they can enjoy and express their uniqueness,** so I did not try to make my children be the same as other children, or each other, not even like me. I allowed them to try different activities, in order to find what they liked best. My daughter loved art and music and softball and had one good friend; my son loved soccer, and spending time with many friends at parties.

Because of my son's hyperactivity and need to move and talk loudly, he got in trouble in school a lot. I knew he needed my support so he could express his exuberant personality. I told him that I would always love him and encourage him, no matter what. Some people call this unconditional love. He knew I always had his back, and I always loved him. I felt this was very important in order for him to grow up happy, and proud of his unique abilities, even if other people did not always appreciate his energetic and loud personality.

In school, some subjects were difficult for my son, although my daughter found school to be easy, and always did well. My son had to work hard to do well in school. Spelling was one subject that was especially difficult for him. To help him, I recorded his spelling words on a tape recorder. I said a word, and spelled it, and repeated it, and used it in a sentence. I went through all his spelling words this way. He would listen to the recording, and try to spell the words along with the recording. The whole time he was listening to the tape, he would be running around the room, jumping, and going in circles. I did not make him sit and be still, like they do in school. He learned better when he was actively moving, and his spelling grades improved as a result. Years later, I found out that researchers discovered that some children learn better when they are moving, or doing hands on activities. My instincts as a mom found this out years before. Although it took extra work for me, I wanted to help my son find ways to succeed at school. Later, he learned to adjust his own study habits so that he was able to graduate from college. I am very proud of him, because I know he worked hard to achieve this. He has been working for the government and is successful in his career.

Now that I have grandchildren, I can enjoy the uniqueness of each one, but I don't have to raise them. As a grandmother, I can understand the difficulties of raising them, but it is not my responsibility. I just enjoy watching them grow up and have fun watching them express themselves each in their own unique way. We have one granddaughter who is very feminine. We have another granddaughter who is very active in sports. We have a quiet grandson who prefers video games. We have a grandson who is very energetic, but has not found what he is interested in yet. One grandson is tall for his age; another is short. With seven grandchildren, the differences are many!

It is not unusual for a family to have children who are very different from each other. As mothers, we love each one. This may be different with twins. I will find out soon, since my oldest step-son and his wife are expecting twins in a few months! We love watching unique personalities develop and can't wait to meet the newest members of our varied little family.

Finding What Matters Most
Priscilla McConnell

I used to live in chaos. This chaos translated into every area of my life. My finances, my three seemingly way-wilder-than-any-other-boys-on-the-planet sons, my messed up self-imposed out of whack sleep schedule, my always a mess house, and my time management (or non-management I should say). I truly felt like I was flying on the coattails of my life circumstances. Not only was I not in the driver's seat, but I was being dragged from the back bumper of the vehicle. I don't think I felt I had one thing in order.

The laundry would be in a heaping pile—and not for just for a few days or even weeks. I had piles for months. No one had clothes in their dressers. It was out of control. I was out of control. Why couldn't I spring into action? I didn't have the boys on a routine, and they just would make a mess before we had a chance to clean up the one before. After a while, I just gave up on cleaning up after everyone. I had my oldest son in preschool at the time and forgot to bring him to class for a whole week because I forgot what day it was. I would procrastinate for hours until it was 3 a.m., and then I would finally get up from researching something to finish washing the dishes. My head was in the clouds.

My husband would work nights and sleep during the day, so I felt I was doing life alone, and I was very good at convincing myself that I wasn't cut out for this. Obviously I wasn't, or else it would come a little bit more naturally. I was a mess. I would wonder, *How did I get here? Who am I? Why can't I keep up with life like everyone else? What's wrong with me? Is there something more? Is there a purpose for me besides cleaning up after everyone and breaking up fights? Do my circumstances really have to dictate my life?* Well, it took a few years, but I'm so grateful I found out the answers to these hard and soul bearing questions.

The truth is, I loved my family. My boys were my life, and even though I wrestled with my use of time and my extremely horrible domesticating skills, I enjoyed them the best way I knew how to. I would sit and play right in the midst of the chaos. I would block out the beckoning of the laundry pile, dirty dishes and clutter, and I would hold their hands and dance with them in the kitchen.

I would try to be present, but in my heart I knew I was falling apart. There was this uneasiness inside of me that I couldn't shake. It was a feeling that I wasn't doing what I was created to do, even though I had always wanted to be a mom. I had a lot of guilt. I felt guilty about yelling at them because of my own short comings. I felt guilty about our finances and that we weren't in any position to give generously to others. We qualified for WIC, Medicaid and other government assistance programs, and even though my husband was risking his life every night as a police officer, we were literally counting our coins to go buy food for the next few days before payday. We had moved to a bad part of town in his mother's house, and we still didn't have enough money to last us to the next payday. It was a depressing time, but I would look at my little studs and they had no clue of our struggles. I was so busy keeping up with the urgent that I didn't stop to think about the important. We were living the daily grind, and I didn't stop, even for a minute, to think about my purpose.

It was a true miracle that we were able to move out of my mother-in-law's house after several years of living in survival mode. My husband left law enforcement, and all of a sudden we found we could pay all our bills between paychecks! We were able to move to a safer part of town. We had more than doubled our square footage and even had completely empty rooms that we didn't know what to do with. We had lots of space where the boys could actually ride their bikes and run around. We were so grateful for a seemingly fresh start at life. Now, things were surely going to get better.

What I noticed, though, was that I still had the tendency to feel like a victim. I was still inclined to blame others to deflect the emptiness I felt inside. I had changed my environment, but those deep seeded questions remained unanswered. The chaos followed me, and I suddenly realized it really wasn't about my life circumstances—it was me.

I still had a hard time keeping up with the house. I still was surviving the day, dealing with whatever came my way. I still wasn't in charge of my life. I was simply going through the motions and dealing with issues as they came up. Then one day, on a whim, I picked up a book to escape the chaos in my soul. This book changed my paradigm and in a lot of ways changed the trajectory of my life. The book was called *Visionary Parenting* by Dr. Rob Rienow.

In this book, he challenges readers to answer the question, "Are you missing what matters most?" To answer that, I needed to take a few steps back, sit in solitude and contemplate what my ultimate dreams were for my life. After thinking about this question for weeks, I swallowed my pride and finally answered a resounding, *Yes, I am missing it.*

I thought about why I was on this planet. I thought about what I would want my children to be like as adults. I thought about what in my life I would be proud of years later, lying on my death bed. This completely changed my everyday thinking.

The "something" that was missing from my life was my purpose! I learned that thinking about what you want your children to look like in 20-30 years really shapes how you raise them today. If I want them to be smart then, I have to focus on academics today. If I want them to be athletic and value being part of a team later, I should put them in sports today. If I want them to be confident as adults, I need to encourage them and give them opportunities to practice standing up in uncomfortable situations today. There are so many character traits I want them to have—but if I'm not careful, I can raise my children to be smart, athletic and confident and still miss what matters most.

I want my children to know God. I want them to love Him above all else. I want them to seek Him and when they have a victory I want their first response to kneel down in thanks. When they have a failure I want them to seek God's comfort and wisdom. I want them to be leaders and do the hard things that so many others are too apathetic to do. I want them to be visionaries themselves; to see the big picture and make good choices that will get them to where they want to go. I want them to be intentional and recognize their need for a Savior every single day. This, and a thousand other values, I wish for my young boys.

Ministry to me was something you did through the church organization, like serving in the children's ministry, the sound system ministry, or the feeding the homeless ministry. I never saw motherhood as a ministry, but it's the number one ministry God has called me to. Before, motherhood was something I was thrown into. Now, I've awakened to a new way of seeing myself. No longer do I see all the disruptions as an inconvenience, but rather multiple opportunities to influence and teach.

Discipline comes from *disciple*. A disciple is a student of a teacher. When I discipline my children they should be learning something. Consequences should be a means of teaching a lesson, not an angry expression of annoyance (which so often it was). Conflict resolution is so important. Gone are the days I force one son to just say "sorry" to the other just to hurry up and move on without any thought into it. Now, it's an event. We hash it out. We look at our hearts and we go through a process in our apologies. Forgiveness is every day, multiple times a day. My husband and I model forgiveness. We also go through the process with them, and to each other. If in the heat of the moment I say a disingenuous, "sorry," they call me out and I go through the process with them. They want to know I've dealt with my heart and are sincere—the same say I expect them too.

Now, when I hear an attitude, it's an opportunity to dive into the feelings behind it. We apologize for harsh tones and bad attitudes as much as we do for hitting and pushing. We practice kindness and patience. This is our classroom; this is our safe place to fail and try again.

When I see my role as mother as a personal ministry, I change from life juggler to intentional teacher. My ministry is instilling these difficult values into my children while at the same time seeking God to refine these same values in me. I refuse to delegate these life lessons for others to teach. I want to teach them about Jesus and not leave it solely up to the children's church ministry. I want to talk about these values when I sit at home and when I walk along the road, when I lie down and when I get up. I want to tie them as symbols on my hands and bind them on my forehead. I want to write them on the doorframes of my house and on my gates. (Deuteronomy 6:7).

You see, I have come to realize that I was made for this. **I'm no longer feeling like a victim of my circumstances but an intentional consistent presence** to bring the ultimate love and light to my children.

My children are getting a bit older now. They see my effort. They see how I've found my grit. They see that it doesn't come easy to me, but I wake up and try every day. They see me make mistakes. They see my struggles and how I don't give up. They see that anything worth having is worth fighting for. They see the value in consistent effort and how hard work trumps perfection every time. They see me fighting for them, for their souls. They are learning it's not about tidy homes, well behaved children who make all the right decisions, being a sports star, or getting straight As. Family is the teaching ground for how to love God, apologize well, and how to utilize our God given gifts to be the best version of ourselves we can be.

This chaotic inconvenienced life has turned into something I'm proud of. I'm not proud because of where we are or that I've arrived. I'm proud that I'm living my ministry every day with intention and purpose, regardless of my life circumstances. I'm starting to believe the lessons I'm teaching my sons—to be empowered by the process, to find your grit in life, to live a life of purpose no matter what the situation.

Making Room for His Grief

Megan George

The last year has been a bit of a doozie for my nine year old son, Ramsey, the eldest of our four. He had an especially difficult year at school. He was, finally, thankfully, diagnosed with dyslexia after getting progressively more frustrated with school for several years. His two best friends moved away, and he has had a hard time making new ones. We finalized the adoption of our beautiful, spunky daughter from China, after months of grueling fundraising and paperwork that stretched my husband and I incredibly thin. Nine days before we left for China, we had to put our dog to sleep. Two hours later, while we sat at dinner, we got a phone call that would shake our family's very foundation.

I knew, from hearing my husband's side of the conversation, that my dad had died, but I refused to let him tell me right then, because I was already so weary and overwhelmed that I did not want to hear him say it out loud. I told him we needed to just put the kids to bed, and we quickly did. He went to my dad and stepmother's house to help her talk to the relevant officials and doctors, while a dear friend came to sit with me. We told the kids the next evening, and their reactions were quiet and understated. I do not even remember any tears. We were all numb with everything that was going on, and the next eight days were a blur of extended family, funeral arrangements, packing, last-minute details, and getting on a 14-hour plane ride to go meet our little girl.

The first few weeks home from China were triage. Our lives completely revolved around jetlag, doctor appointments, attachment, sleep deprivation, and adjusting to being a family of six. I vaguely wondered if I would grieve at some point, and I wondered if the kids were doing okay—but honestly, I was just getting through the days awake and with my teeth brushed. If everyone was fed and had clean clothes to wear, it was a victory. Then one day, I started crying and couldn't stop. I was getting about two hours of sleep, my typically rock-solid marriage was strained like it had never been before, my faith was tested, and I was overwhelmed with the heaviness of all of my responsibilities. I was still attaching, feeding people, washing clothes, and keeping the house passably clean, but I first had to talk myself into getting out of bed in the mornings.

Right then, when I was at my lowest, grief also swallowed Ramsey.

He and his Grand Dad had been incredibly close, sharing their love of history, adventure, and sports. We were fortunate to live close to my dad and got together about once a week for lunch or fun outings. My dad called these outings, "skulking," and they included anything from exploring every last corner of the zoo to finding out where the circus animals were staying when they came to town and getting special permission to go visit them, to special art events at museums.

Ramsey was heartbroken and furious. He picked fights with his five-year-old brother about every little thing. He started screaming at his beloved three-year-old sister, after she misplaced a photo of my dad, saying that she must have wanted Grand Dad to die. He asked me dozens of difficult, deeply personal questions, and wanted endless stories of my dad's life and my childhood. He would start crying during everyday tasks. Some days I handled it okay, and others I miserably failed. Once I snapped at him to go back to sleep when he came into my room crying after a particularly hard bedtime. I later apologized to him, but still struggled, in my exhaustion and selfishness, with wanting to grieve alone. I didn't know how to make room in my own head and heart to mother him through this shared grief.

My sweet husband encouraged me to figure out how to find a little bit of myself in these crazy weeks, and always pushed me to lean on our shared faith in God. With his help, I took one day, sometimes one hour, at a time, read novels voraciously to have a little time to myself, and tried to get some exercise. We made a relaxed schedule for the summer months, and tried to find a new normal that included less busyness and more time with people who love us unconditionally and let us just be in this hard place however we needed to be. Ramsey sometimes embraced these changes, and other times lashed out in anger. I knew he was struggling, and I tried to figure out how to reach him.

Slowly, I started to get through. When he would walk past me or come to talk to me, I would whisper to myself inside my head to pick up my arms and hug him or tickle him, even if I felt like I desperately needed space. If he asked me a question or for a story and I could not think of something, I made a note in my calendar so that I would remember to get back to him. One night, when he came out crying after bedtime, we sat together with hot chocolate and talked about some of our favorite memories with Grand Dad. Another afternoon, while the younger kids were napping, we talked about some ways for all of them to remember Grand Dad. We printed pictures of him to put in laminated magnets on the fridge, so they can see them every day and handle them as they want to. We each carefully picked out a few hats from his extensive collection to keep at our house to wear and display. We planned to go to some of his favorite places over the next few months to show our newly adopted daughter and sister some of the adventures we loved to take with him. We laughed about funny things that my character of a dad had said and done to keep everyone in stitches. We talked about writing letters to him to say the things we wish we could have said to him and to say goodbye.

Doing this grieving with him, in many ways, also finally allowed me to grieve. It made me remember some things about my dad that I had forgotten, and it let me see him again through the eyes of a child. I considered how he had always been fiercely loyal to the underdog when Ramsey was asked to watch out for another child at children's camp, and I made a mental note to share that part of him with my kids. When the manager of one of his favorite restaurants saw my family and asked where my dad had been, then began to weep along with us, confiding that my dad had always remembered her name, made time to ask how she was really doing, and brightened even the worst of days when he came in, I realized I needed to encourage them to be like him in that way. To take the time to notice and love people who may often be overlooked and under-appreciated. As an adult, my relationship with my dad was sometimes complicated, and it's easy to look at everything through the filter of the difficult parts, but finally making room within myself to grieve together with Ramsey helped me to see the full picture of my dad for the first time in many years, which was so much more multifaceted and beautiful than just the difficult parts.

Our family still has an enormous amount of healing and growing to do. Both the loss of my dad and the addition of our fourth child will change everything from this point forward, and we are only beginning to assimilate to those changes. I am grateful that Ramsey was able to be gracious with me, and I hope that he will feel empowered and encouraged to bravely step forward to future challenges in school, in relationships, and in life, knowing that his thoughts and emotions are deeply valued and respected, however imperfectly I show it sometimes. I pray that as an adult he will remember that I did not handle it wonderfully every day, but that I was able to open up and allow him into my grief process so that he did not have to grieve alone.

I cannot promise my eldest that the next year will not be just as hard, and with just as many changes. His learning disability will always be part of who he is, relationships will always be in flux, and challenges and loss are permanent fixtures of life. My wish for him is that he will lean hard on his faith and his family in those times, taking one day, sometimes one hour, at a time, refuse to give up, and allow himself to be in the trenches with the people he loves, so that when each trial is over, he will look up and see that his relationships are stronger, and so is he. Just like he has done for me.

Dear Daughter

Casey Snyder

gracefaithcompassion.com

I first became a mother on a very hot day in North Carolina, in August of 2006, to a 9 lb. 7 oz. girl. We moved to Texas when she was seven months old and have lived here ever since; except for the six months we lived in Canada during the winter. It was a great experience living there, but it made me very grateful for Texas winters.

Flash forward to now, and I am a single mother of two strong-willed girls —one almost nine, and the other recently turned five. I have been a single mom for almost three years now, and the job is every bit as gratifying as it is exhausting. It has not been easy or simple, but I love the little family we have made. I have found an incredible source of independence and strength through being a single mom. I decided right after my divorce that I would accept it. This is not what I wanted for myself or my daughters; but this is my reality now. I can't go back in time and change anything, so I am accepting the situation for what it is and moving forward.

My own mother was a single mom through part of my childhood. My teenage years were sometimes difficult because I didn't always have what other kids had. She worked hard for what we had and taught me to do the same. She made sure I had clothes every year for school. Sometimes, it was from the mall, though maybe not the latest fashion, or sometimes it was even from a yard sale. She taught me the value of hard work. My first job was as a babysitter, and then when I was 15 I went on to become a waitress throughout high school. I worked to have my own gas money and help pay for my car payment. It was in the lessons I learned from her that I received what I needed the most: how to be independent, strong in faith, compassionate, and an overcomer.

"Being a single mother is twice the stress and twice the tears, but also twice the hugs, twice the love and twice the pride." – Unknown

The biggest thing I have learned on this journey is the power of friendship. As a single mom, you sometimes have to put aside your pride and ask for help. It's ok to outsource and let others help you. I have some amazing friends who have been there for me. I firmly believe God puts people in your life when—and how—you need them.

Another thing I have had to learn is that co-parenting is hard. I cannot control what they do or watch at their dad's house. It is really hard to let go sometimes. They have a teenage stepbrother so they are sometimes exposed to shows I would never let them see. There are situations that come up where my oldest daughter will say they are allowed to do this or watch this at dad's house. I just remind her that we have different rules in my house, and when she is at my house she needs to follow those rules. We both have different ways of parenting, and that is ok.

I do remember my 4-year-old coming home and having nightmares because they let her watch Chucky. They are not the ones that have to deal with her having the bad dreams from watching a scary movie, so I think are times when you have to step in and talk to the other parent.

Even so, I have always made sure to never say anything negative about him or their stepmom in front of my daughters. He has shown the same respect by not saying negative things about me. Yes, there are times when I call my friends and vent about his parenting decisions that I don't agree with. But it is very important that the kids never hear me say anything negative about their father in front of them. When children hear bad things about one parent, they hear bad things about half of themselves. If they hear bad things about both their parents, they feel that both halves of themselves must be of little worth.

An upside I have found being a single mom is that I can recharge while they are away at their dads. Even though it is only eight days of the month, I cherish that time I can get rest and renewal!

Many of us arrive to motherhood in different ways, but no matter how you became a mom, the fact remains that motherhood is hard. Whether you are a single mother or not, motherhood can be frustrating and exhausting, and it can be equally fulfilling and rewarding. I read an article the other day called "The one thing you must tell your child" from thebettermom.com. There were a couple of things that stood out to me:

- Our children need to hear us say, "I will always love you. Nothing you do will make me stop loving you."

- Just like God loves us, we will always love them. God never gives up on us and we will never give up on them.

I agree that we should remind our children of our love often, even when we are angry with them. Not long ago, I had an opportunity to exercise this with my daughter.

My oldest is turning nine in a couple of months. The last year has been challenging with her attitude and behavior as she is approaching the "tween" years. Our weeks are full of practices and trying to squeeze in some fun after a long day of work. On Saturdays and Sundays, though, we have quiet time. My youngest takes a good nap and it's a chance for me to sneak in a short nap or work on some things on my to-do list. This is a challenging time for her; she struggles with just taking an hour to have some quiet time to herself without coming into my room to ask a question or tell me she is bored. We have had several talks about it—

about how I need to have some quiet time and how she needs to have the quiet time for herself as well. They share a room, so I think it is good for them to take some time apart from each other.

The other day, after getting in trouble, she came into my room while we were having quiet time. She had made me a sandwich and brought it to me with a note.

Dear mommy,

I have not listened to you here lately. I am going to change that now. I hope you can forgive me. I love you with all my heart. I will respect you I'm not just saying that. I am going to show you that I do. Know that I love you.

So, I wrote a letter back to her. I wanted her to be able to read how much her words mean to me. She had taken the time to think about what she has done and the choices she was making.

Dear Daughter,

Thank you for your letter. I am sorry I have not listened to you lately. I'm sorry that I told you just one more minute and let me finish what I am working on and then I will listen to you. I am going to change that now. I will take the time to stop what I am doing and listen. I hope you can forgive me. I love you with all my heart. I will respect you, and I'm not just saying that, I will show you that I do. Please know that I will always love you and nothing you can do will ever make me stop loving you.

I wish I could freeze these moments like this. Record them so I could play the over and over again. To me, this is what motherhood is all about. We have the hope that the good moments outweigh the bad ones; but sometimes we have to have the hard moments in order to have the good ones.

Sometimes it's in the trenches, through the hard moments of parenting, that we learn the most. You learn a lot about yourself, and I've found that it's the act of prevailing through the hard times that define us.

I read a quote somewhere that said, *"I don't want to survive motherhood, I want to thrive in motherhood."* I don't want to just go through the motions of parenting; I want to be present in each moment for my girls. I want to teach them to be strong, independent, and compassionate women when they grow up. It's not what you do for your children, but what you teach them to do for themselves—often, by modeling it through your own challenges—that will make them successful human beings.

Grieving Gumdrops
Daphne Greer
grievinggumdrops.com

At 31 years old, I was confident and strong, taking the world by the reins, believing I could conquer anything. I was a working mom with a challenging and exciting career in law enforcement. I had two wonderful children and a fabulous husband, but something was lacking. I had an uneasy feeling and a sense of discontent bubbling ferociously inside me. Who would have imagined that a routine drive to work would be devastating and life changing one summer day, taking my anxiousness to a whole new level? It was beyond my comprehension just how much my life would change and the different path it would take.

One hot July morning, my daughter, son and I loaded up in our little commuter car and headed to daycare. Just a few short minutes later, after saying goodbye and telling her daddy she loved him, my healthy and vivacious first born girl on the verge of entering kindergarten, would leave this earth.

The accident happened in a blink of an eye. Just seconds before, my little darling was brushing her strawberry blonde hair in the backseat as she sang her favorite tune from the movie Annie. "The Sun Will Come Out Tomorrow."

And then.

The deafening sounds of clashing metal and screeching tires combined with a young child's screams haunted me for years and is something I will never forget.

What had just happened? I did my best to stop in time but it wasn't enough. As I sat in the borrow ditch among the tumbleweeds and gravel clinging to my son waiting for help as my daughter lay lifeless in her car seat, my life flashed before my eyes. It was an accident—but what had I done?

My daughter wouldn't survive, and my life would be forever different. Guilt ridden and shameful, I avoided everyone and everything, yet somehow had to plan a memorial for my little girl when I should have been planning a birthday party.

I looked into the mirror days after the accident and didn't recognize the woman staring back at me. She was a stranger. Who was I? A terrible mother? All sense of identity and normalcy was stripped away instantly, leaving me just a shell of a person with nothing left inside. The thought of drinking myself into oblivion to escape my new reality was very appealing, I have to admit. However, I was terribly fearful I would lose control and wouldn't be able to stop.

Regret remained in the forefront of my mind for quite some time. The record of my last moments with her, the trip to Disneyland we never took, the vivid yet suffocating reality of having no first day of school, no more dance recitals, no proms, no wedding... The No's were endless.

My future had been destroyed.

Suddenly, nothing mattered anymore. I had failed. Failed to protect my most prized possession. Failed horribly as a mother. I was at the bottom of the food chain.

As if that weren't enough.

I had to relearn to parent my only living child, which at the time, proved to be the most difficult thing I had ever done. I couldn't take care of myself, yet I was expected to take care of my son, too. The thought was overwhelming. Taking him to preschool, I would cry every morning on the way there and on the way back home, sobbing at the wheel as I felt the eeriness of an empty car seat behind me, saying softly to myself "I'm sorry, I'm so sorry."

I had to learn to live again, yet life as I knew it had ended. The darkness surrounded me, the trauma and flashbacks consumed me, haunting me for years. Every breath was a challenge. Perspectives changed. Getting up off the couch to get a glass of water was monumental, and eventually, not burning the toast or sleeping for more than three hours straight became something to celebrate.

I couldn't make sense of it. Why did this happen to my family? Things like this never happened to people I know, let alone my family. It wasn't supposed to be this way. This wasn't how I pictured my life.

After college, I got married and became a mother at the age of 26. When I learned I was expecting, I was full of nervousness, yet overflowing with joy knowing the incredible miracle that would be arriving in a few short months. The day finally arrived, and after 24 hours of grueling labor, my little girl made her entrance into the world. Complete with a full head of dark hair, she was perfect in every way. Full of peace, I experienced a fullness deep within my heart that I never knew existed. I was bursting at the seams with love for this little gift from above, fantasizing about all the things we would and how marvelous our life together would be.

At that time, I didn't realize that being a mom would be the toughest thing I had ever done, yet the most rewarding and fulfilling.

I was living the American dream—a magnificent husband, two beautiful children, and challenging yet amazing careers. Our life was what others only dreamed of. Yet, I didn't grasp the value of what I really had.

And now, for the rest of my life, I will be a grieving mother. A tough pill to swallow and a frightening journey to be thrown into.

Over the years, I have learned so much. I was forced to grow up before my time, facing my fears and tragedies head on. Diving deep into my faith was the only answer. No one could help me and give me the magic potion to fix this, though, despite my longing to do so. My eyes were opened to this whole new, dark world that I had never known. I was desperate to fast forward through this horrifying tragedy.

My first months—well, my first entire year, pretty much—I lived in darkness and hiding. The back corner of my closet became my safe place. A place where tears could fall in the blackness and loneliness would encompass me. I was able to let go of my emotions and conceal my grief in a place where no one could see me.

Grief. It was real and so very debilitating in the first years, causing physical ailments and poor self-worth. Yet as time went on, it presented me with an incredible sense of humility and breathed new life into me.

I was different. Different than I was before it happened and ever so different than my friends whom I had known for years. I now attended support group meetings for bereaved parents and found comfort knowing that these mothers understood what I was going through. We gained our strength together by sharing our stories and our children, the happy and the sad, the good and the bad. They had been there. They got it. They appeared so strong but were also weak like me. And for the first time, I felt a tiny shimmer of hope igniting inside me.

I would have given anything to trade places with her that day, but God had other plans. Since she passed away, He has given me three new children to love. I never knew my heart was capable of so much love, exploding and unique for every one of my children. I am ecstatic at the opportunity to start again, a sort of do-over. I am wiser beyond my years and know the possibilities of how life could be—the good and the bad.

Receiving a new outlook on life, I came to a place of acceptance and understanding that accidents happen. Bad things do happen to good people. They happen to all of us when we least expect it. No one is exempt, and we can't control everything. Our reactions to these unfortunate circumstances make all the difference. Attitude really is everything. I came to a crossroads and had to make a choice to change how I was going to live the rest of my life. Wallowing in self-pity and darkness was not going to benefit me or my family.

Throughout it all, I have been blessed. Blessed with knowing and understanding the grieving process, knowing the value of the gifts I have been given in life. Feeling the immense pain of my brokenness, being disrobed of my ego and having my world come crashing down brought me to a place of complete helplessness where I had no choice but to embrace the pain and realize just how fortunate I have been in life, careful not to take anything for granted.

I have been restored and have learned to live with gratitude, being thankful for what I have been given, never wanting for more. Most importantly, I learned to appreciate the moments. The loud boisterous kids, the messy house with a sink full of dirty dishes, dirty hand prints on the white doorframes, stickers on the light switches and the physical exhaustion that accompanies the role of mother.

Braving the storms, I now have a purpose, a passion to help others and provide them with a sense of hope. If I can survive this, anyone can.

And although my life has been full of pain and sorrow, I know it could be worse. A lot worse. This eventually became my silent mantra, which made everything else small in comparison. By finding the bright side and focusing on the positives, I can take steps forward.

Despite it all, I wouldn't hesitate to do it all over again in a second, even if I knew what was to come. We mothers never forget that first moment that we became "moms." The instant our hearts tripled in size, we were forever changed. The challenges of motherhood and unspeakable sacrifices we make on a daily basis connect us all. Although things may not go as planned, we are equipped with resilience and are stronger than we know. The bonds we create with our children and the unconditional love we share will last for all eternity.

The Hardest Thing

Randomly Fascinated

domesticrandomness.blogspot.com

One of the hardest things that I've had to do for my children was to breastfeed them. When you're pregnant and you read all of the information about how to take care of a newborn, they tell you all about breastfeeding. They make it sound so easy. But that wasn't the case for me.

When my first was born, I was surprised at how awkward it was to try to hold the baby and feed him. I had been holding babies most of my life, so I thought I knew what to do. But to nurse the baby, I felt like I needed three hands, maybe more. And none of the nurses offered to help me—I actually had to ask for help, which was also awkward. I thought the lactation consultant was supposed to come and help too, but I found out she wasn't coming until the next day. **I remember wondering what I was supposed to do and how I was supposed to know how to do it.** And of course I had lots of family that wanted to see the baby, so I didn't feel like I had time to figure it out. I just felt so *awkward*.

When I did finally get my baby to my breast, he had no idea what to do, either. It seemed like he would try to latch but not quite get there and then fall off again. The few times he did latch, he would fall asleep almost immediately. I didn't know what to do, but I kept trying. After trying several times, I felt like I had some idea of what I was supposed to be doing. But I was still struggling because it hurt really badly. I asked the lactation consultant to come in and see if he was latching properly. I assumed he wasn't because everything said if he's latching properly it won't hurt. The lactation consultant watched and said that everything looked OK. What I learned from that is that even if you're doing everything right. breastfeeding can still hurt a lot.

That was in the hospital—when I went home, everything got worse. I no longer had a team of people bringing me food and water 24 hours a day and checking on me to make sure that everything was OK. I had to do everything myself. Of course, my husband tried to help, but he didn't really know what to do either. I did have some family and friends to help, but I didn't really know what to ask for. And none of them could help me with the hardest parts.

The pain was horrible. I wanted to squirm away from this pain but I couldn't because it was my baby and he needed to eat. It would take me over an hour and a half to try and get in one feeding. And since we were on a three hour schedule, I only had about an hour and a half or less in between feedings. I would be bruised and hurting from one feeding, and my body would have no time to heal before I had to start all over again. It seemed the pain would never end.

I was so conflicted. I believed that breastfeeding was the best thing for my baby. But I didn't know if I could keep doing it. I daydreamed daily, hourly, sometimes minutely of switching to formula. Every feeding, every time I thought about feeding my baby, I daydreamed about giving him a bottle. I would think about how much easier it would be, and how much happier I would be. I even went so far as to wish that he had a medical reason to switch to formula. If he had a medical reason then it wouldn't be my fault, it wouldn't be my choice, I wouldn't be doing it to him. And I felt like a horrible mother for feeling that way.

After a couple weeks of agonizing, I knew I couldn't keep going like this. I had done some research and found out about something called a nipple shield. I had also read that it wasn't best to use, that you would have to wean off of it eventually or it would hurt your milk supply. But I didn't know what else to do. I had to do something or I wouldn't be able to continue breastfeeding. So I bought one and tried it. And it worked! It wasn't perfect, it didn't take away all of the pain, but it dulled it enough that I could handle it.

I was so thankful that I had found the nipple shield, but I knew I would need to wean off of it. So I decided to go back to see the lactation consultant. I had avoided going to her because I hadn't found the lactation consultant in the hospital to be very helpful and I didn't have any time to waste. But I'm glad I went in. She did help me nurse without the nipple shield and without pain. My one and only time. I discovered upon getting home that the techniques she showed me only worked with the chair that she had and the pillows and the extra hands she lent me. But the best thing I learned from her was that I could keep using the nipple shield as long as I pumped to keep my supply up.

Honestly, that set me free. I didn't have to worry about being a bad mom anymore because I didn't want to feed my baby. And I didn't have to worry that eventually I wouldn't be able to feed him. I could just feed him. It made a huge difference. The daydreams about switching to formula slowed. It was no longer every feeding, it dropped to once a day, then once a week, then stopped altogether. By the time he reached six months old, I wondered why I would consider stopping. We had fought so hard, and it had finally become easy! We then made it to a year, and it was kind of a mutual weaning. It was the right time for both of us.

When I found out I was pregnant with my second a week after my first turned one, I was a little worried about the pregnancy but a lot worried about breastfeeding again. I dreaded breastfeeding even more than I dreaded the morning sickness and other pregnancy discomforts. But it turned out my fears were unwarranted. My second was an excellent nurser. And I knew what I was doing, and I knew that I could use the nipple shield, so it was comparatively easy.

When I found out I was pregnant with my third, I didn't know what to expect. I knew it could be extremely hard or fairly easy. So I tried not to think about it too much and just went with the flow. It turns out my third was both harder and easier to nurse than the other two. He had severe tongue-tie, which made nursing practically impossible.

Before I found that out, I thought by now I should know what I am doing. But I had no idea how to feed this kid. He would try to eat, but he didn't seem to get anything. That happened every time I tried to feed him. And he was so sleepy. And I was in excruciating pain even though I was using the nipple shield. I am pretty sure he did not get very much food the first two days of his life. I didn't know how to give him food, and I felt like a failure again.

Fortunately, this time the lactation consultant was the hero. She noticed his tongue-tie when she saw him crying and got right to work. She got the doctor to give a referral, and then she got the specialist who was already there to go ahead and clip his tongue. The difference was night and day. Although it wasn't immediate, it took him a couple days to figure out how to use his tongue again. But nursing went from excruciating pain even with the nipple shield to normal, low pain, bearable with the nipple shield.

I suppose nursing will always be somewhat painful for me. I have learned a lot from my experiences—and I'm sure I have plenty more to learn. But now I have several tricks up my sleeve and a whole lot more confidence!

Finding Happy

Lorie Huneycutt
loriehuneycutt.wordpress.com

Motherhood has been nothing short of an adventure for me—and it has been nothing that I had anticipated or expected. It has been full of challenges that I had to face alone, figuring out on my own how to navigate them. It has been full of emotion in every way imaginable, forcing me to pull strength from places I did not know existed within me. But I am grateful for it because I would not be the person I am now without having walked through it. Still, if I could go back in time and give myself one bit of wisdom, it would be to focus on what I am thankful for, and not on the challenges and difficulties.

I became a mother when my daughter Rylie entered the world four months early, at 1 lb. 9 oz. Our family began in a place of confusion and stress as she was quickly whisked away to a hospital an hour away that could better care for her. My husband and I temporarily moved in with my parents because they lived much closer to the hospital, and we could visit her every day.

Her first weeks and months of life were nothing like I imagined they would be. She spent them literally fighting for her life, instead of resting at home. Her first sounds were those of beeps and dings of the machines that were keeping her alive and monitoring her every move. Her first meals were drops of milk through a tube down her nose and fluids through a tiny IV. Instead of sleeping in her crib in her nursery at home, she slept completely enclosed in an incubator type bed, as though she were in some sort of institutionalized display case. She shared her room with at least 10 other babies, all in the same types of beds. Her first sensations were those of pain and discomfort, as her body and skin were so fragile that human touch was initially painful. Instead of holding my daughter after she was born, I had to wait two weeks before she was stable enough to hold her for just brief periods. This was not at all what I pictured as my first weeks as a new mom.

The day in, day out of driving up to visit to mostly just sit beside her bed became the routine. It was just what we did. Time seemed to almost stand still, and all I could do was sit and wonder when we could actually take her home. Anger began to grow within my heart, on top of hurt and discouragement. I was also full of sorrow. *Why did this happen? How could this possibly work out well?* Ninety percent of my thoughts were consumed with how hard this was and what else could possibly go wrong. There were glimpses of joy, when we saw Rylie's tiny legs kick, or when she could finally turn her head. And it always made me happy to hear the nurses describe her as the "feisty one" in the nursery. Even when she made small progress, my thankful thoughts were few and far between.

After 123 days in the Neonatal Intensive Care Unit, she was discharged to go home. I had spent so much time consumed with how difficult and stressful the whole ordeal was that I never really took time to fully rejoice in the fact that she could come home, and without any medications or machines. Her first days home were spent focused on taking care of her instead of enjoying her. It seemed I was not capable of finding joy in having her home. I am not sure if it was from spending the first four months of her life in the hospital or that my heart was just hard, but after a few months of having her home, I realized I acted more like a caretaker instead of her mother. I realized I was not even sure what being a mother looked or felt like. I felt like I did not have the natural instinct that other women have when they have children, and I allowed these thoughts to consume me for a while as I battled depression on and off.

At 1 1/2 years old, Rylie's development was nowhere near where it should be, so we took her to see a specialist. She was diagnosed with Cerebral Palsy. All was silent in my head. I was not even sure how to begin to process this diagnosis, and what it would mean for the rest of our lives. I could only see the negative once again, and my heart ached as to how something like this could happen to my daughter. My husband and I had dreams of going overseas to live and work, and this diagnosis would mean that dream would never come true. Anger continued to grow in my heart as I could only see it for what it was, and not for what good could possibly come from it.

At this point, my husband had taken a job across the other side of the U.S. and we were nowhere near our family. It was a lonely space in time. Not only were we 1500 miles from our families, but I was suddenly thrust into a world of special needs and caretaking, though I had not the first idea on what to do next. I felt like no one on earth could possibly understand what I was going though. I felt that even if I were able to verbalize all of the emotions and thoughts racing through my mind, it still would not be relatable to anyone. People would constantly question how she was doing, but I never felt like I could give a full answer because who would understand all of the medical jargon I had just recently become versed in? It was like learning a whole new language, except very few people spoke it, and I had yet to meet anyone in person who actually understood at that point. Over the next few years, therapies, doctors, and medications became an everyday way of life. She spent her days in a wheelchair. completely dependent on me for her every need.

I spent the next few years striving for joy and peace, but mostly just struggling to not be negative. As the years went on, her disability faded into who she was as a person. Her personality began to shine. and she became one of the happiest kids I've known. To be wheelchair bound and completely dependent on me for her every need, she is amazingly resilient, joyful, and laid back. Her disability was not defining her, but her determination and joy for life was flowing out of her.

Over time, she began to pick up social cues and hear the ways we would respond to other people. She began to say *thank you* to me and anyone else who would help her or give her something. Her brother who was born two years after her, has become her source of motivation and encouragement, and ultimately is her favorite person. Both of my kids are amazingly positive and upbeat, which completely boggles my mind, as I am naturally pessimistic! I began to actually be influenced by them and their joy for life, realizing how much I really have to be thankful for.

Over time, I began to climb out of depression and see the positive aspects of our situation and the ways in which Rylie's disability was forever molding my heart and our family. I began to find pockets of thankfulness, and when things were going really well, I could see how she impacted the lives of others in a positive way.

Recently, she had an emergency with her medical pump, sending her to the hospital for six days in the Pediatric ICU. It was completely unexpected and required yet another surgery to resolve the problem. After five sleepless nights, and undergoing an extreme amount of stress there with her in the hospital, by the sixth night I felt like I could not hold on anymore. I felt as though at any moment I was going to have an emotional breakdown. As a friend was messaging me that evening, she told me to try to be thankful. She advised me to just start thinking of everything I was thankful for and see if it began to change my attitude. My first thought was of angst, as I could not possibly imagine what I could be thankful for in this extremely traumatic situation. I eventually decided to try it, and start small. **I was thankful for... Earplugs!**

Earplugs? Yes, earplugs as the last night we had been moved to a room with a roommate whose mother described her as "a screamer." I was thankful for the decent food they had at the hospital. I was thankful for the amazing care she was receiving at the hospital. I was thankful it was not more serious and that we would be able to go home soon... Sure enough, the more I began to try to think of things I was thankful for, the easier it became to be thankful! Not only that, but my mind was suddenly focused on something else entirely rather than focusing on the misery of yet another sleepless night in the hospital, with our new roommate "the screamer." I could not believe it was actually working! Why had I not tried this a long time ago?

You would think that as positive, upbeat, and happy as Rylie is naturally, that it would have rubbed off on me. She is the child thanking the doctors and nurses when they come and poke and prod her. She thanks me when

I change her or when I help her eat. She thanks me for taking her to the library. She thanks her brother when he helps her play, and her daddy he helps her in the van. She is so quick to say thank you because she is so quick to see the positive in any situation. She knows that we want what is ultimately best for her and trusts us when we take her to doctors, even if the process is unpleasant.

I may never understand why my daughter has the blessing of such a happy attitude toward life in general. She has every right to be irritable, and you would think she would scream every time we even get in the vicinity of a doctor's office. But she has the most amazing demeanor and attitude of anyone I have ever seen. How ironic is it that I am learning to be thankful, through the one person who has been the center of most of the trials in my life?

It will be a learning curve for sure, and it will take some time to create better habits, but in time I hope I can focus on what I am thankful for before I complain or stress. It is one small choice at a time. In time, I hope my natural inclination to be negative will become an old nature, and that as I make the small choices to think about what I am thankful for, that it will create a new thankful nature within me! Even though I wish I could go back and tell myself to think this way ten years ago, I'm *thankful* that it's never too late to create new habits!

The Ugly Elephant in the Room with the Adorable Baby

Charisse Segee

Every mother that receives prenatal medical care is given a brief speech by their OBGYN at some point about Postpartum Mood Disorders–Baby Blues & Depression. Everyone naturally assumes that this does not apply to them. I was that mom, with my first pregnancy and again with my second pregnancy. I was confident that I had what it took to raise, love and support my children, and I wasn't concerned. But no one told me I would fall prey to this medical condition, against my own will, or that there were different variations of Postpartum Depression. I was educated in my Master's program for social work about Postpartum Mood Disorders; and that's it. I wasn't aware that there were other forms of PPD.

My pregnancy went smoothly, and my epidural was magical. I know this drug choice is not for every mother, but I have a low threshold for pain and thought I was dying at 2 cm with my son and at 4cm with my daughter. In order to get to 10cm, I needed help or someone else to push my kids out! As soon as I was told to push, nurses and doctors came running in and threw the oxygen mask on my face. I immediately pulled it off and asked what was wrong. I was told that the baby's heart rate dropped and she needed to be vacuumed out. I instantly threw the oxygen mask back on! All we want as mothers are healthy and happy babies and children, and I am fairly confident I started praying in that instant for just that.

My daughter, Savannah, was born unharmed shortly after, and we bonded with ease. Michael, my husband, had to leave the hospital for about two hours to care for our son Parker, and our special needs son Daniel (from my husband's previous relationship and was visiting from out of state). Before leaving, Michael made sure my friend, Francesca, was going to be joining me so that I would not be alone. So in she came and out he went. While I was speaking with Francesca, my baby was across the room being looked over by a nurse. I noticed the nurse and casually asked, "What are you doing with the baby?" The reply was that she was bathing the baby and giving her "meds." This aligned with my expressed written birth plan, as well as written on the baby care board, and as verbally expressed to the hospital staff upon entry. As I was being wheeled out of the labor room towards the post-delivery wing, the nurse handed me a vaccine sheet. I told her we didn't need it because the baby was not going to get it. The nurse replied, "Oh, I just gave it to her."

This was the beginning of that downward spiral I mentioned.

When the nurse relayed this mind blowing news that my newborn infant was vaccinated against my expressed written and verbal consent, I was flooded with emotions. The nurse apologized, and when I asked her where my birth plan was, she said she did not know. Once I made it into my new room, I immediately asked Francesca to hold the baby, I didn't want my negative energy to affect her. My mom arrived at that moment, wearing her supervisor hat because she was just as upset as me. Michael entered shortly after. We met with the heads of departments, and I was immediately questioned with "Well, why didn't you want it?" That was not the point. The nurse was wrong for not following a choice that my husband and I agreed to. We were told that there was no harm in her receiving the vaccine, but that a special report would be filed and we would receive a call in a few days. Well, I never got that call—ever.

My first night in the hospital, I was a nervous wreck. I was upset that Michael had to return home to be with Daniel. I understood why he would need to go, but for some reason I did not want to be left alone with our daughter that night, and was I unable to explain it. Michael eventually agreed to stay the night with me, and I seemed to be fine. I would nurse and comfort my daughter as needed, change diapers that were pee. I delegated the poop to Michael since that black tar stuff was too much for me!

Michael returned home in the morning, and I was doing fine, although I had to relive that night throughout the day. Every nurse that I worked with heard the news before they entered my room and wanted to gossip. It wasn't until nightfall when a nurse came in to tell me she needed to take the baby out of the room later to get bathed and weighed that I went spiraling. As soon as the nurse left the room, I started bawling and could not stop. I got on the phone with my mom and my friend Francesca and they were able to eventually calm me down. When the nurse returned I told her I was not comfortable with her taking the baby out of the room since I was unable to physically follow her. I told the nurse my story, and she replied she only knew to give me "Extra TLC." The nurse agreed to bathe and weigh Savannah in the room later that night. Needless to say, my daily hospital care goal was to go home.

This spiral continued for about six months and life was tough. Parker, my two year old son, just started preschool and would bring home a world of germs for us all to catch. Anytime Parker and Savannah got sick, I was left feeling crappy both physically and mentally because I couldn't protect my kids. Every little thing would cause me to think and feel helpless, hopeless, incompetent, guilty, and shameful. I wasn't able to protect my child while I was in the same room as her! If I couldn't protect her while we were in the same freaking room, then what good am I?! You name any negative self-thought, and I felt it. Life hit me with every curve ball imaginable at the time and would leave me frazzled. I knew all these thoughts were crazy, but they would consume me daily and leave me in tears at least weekly. It was a battle of common sense vs. poor coping skills.

This quickly spilled into my marriage, and it was probably our roughest year. I often refer to it as Year 5 on my blog for opmrc.com (a unique alternative to couples counseling). I was aware that my thoughts were all over the place, but I had no clue I had postpartum problems or that it was affecting everything in my life. My marriage was at its darkest. It wasn't until my husband and I had a major hiccup that summer that we both went into individual counseling. I quickly learned the madness had a name—Postpartum Anxiety—and that my anxiety was causing my husband anxiety! So two spouse/parents are suffering from anxiety trying to raise a two year old and a newborn. That was a recipe for disaster and explained why marriage and motherhood sucked for those six months!

In therapy, I was able to put things into perspective about what happened to Savannah and myself on the day of her birth. I thought about Restorative Justice and how an offender takes accountability for their actions and the harm that was caused—which hadn't happened. So, I filed a legal claim to hold them accountable. The hospital was wrong and never owned up to it. I would have been fine with a simple apology, but that didn't happen. So I put on my lawyer hat and filed the claim.

When the claim was denied because it didn't show in the records that this incident happened, oh I was mad. You mean to tell me my life has been hellish because of something I imagined? When I called to question the decision, I learned the representative hadn't checked my mental health records—a big chunk of the claim. So he was going to reopen the claim and do his homework. At this point I didn't trust him to do his job, so I put my lawyer hat back on and pulled every medical record there was— "legal" and "non-legal." I was in every hospital office that allowed patients access, from actual records departments to the labor and delivery wing.

At this point, **I just wanted my experience to be acknowledged**. An extreme example of how this felt: that's like telling a rape victim they weren't raped! Bullpuckey, right? So I racked my brain, poured over hundreds of records trying to find how my reality was not recorded, especially after all of those nurses knew of my story before entering my room. And then I met a woman who mentioned, "What is the 'Standard of Care'?" It was a week or two before I actually understood this. But somehow I managed to put two and two together and discovered the *federal law* that requires parents are given a VIS (Vaccine Information Sheet) *prior* to a vaccine being administered. My golden ticket!

Thanks to my newfound knowledge, I was able to successfully win my claim with perseverance, faith, and my family by my side. At the end of the day, any day and situation, I want my family to know that I tried my very best. I take peace and comfort in knowing that and hope to pass this down to my kids. I share this story with my children, not for the golden ticket but because this was my bad, ugly story that transformed into something beautiful. I was once consumed in a whirlpool of guilt, shame, hopelessness, and helplessness, but I came through it even stronger than before. That is what transforms my story into beauty.

I share this story with you, because as much as I wish that no mother experiences this, you could. Educate yourself, not just about the topics here (postpartum & VIS), but any hurdle you encounter. As mothers we are wired to do any and everything for our families, so why shouldn't we be educated and empowered? Put on whatever hat you are called to wear, and wear it proudly. Everyone has the good, the bad, and the ugly in their life. It's how you overcome the bad and the ugly that can transform your story into a beautiful one.

I Often Wonder What She Was Thinking

Kari Scott

lanternno7.blogspot.com

A 17-year-old sitting next to her mother-in-law in the church pew of a Southern Baptist Church on a cold Sunday night in November. Was she ignoring the pressure on her pelvic floor as this little mess of cherub chubbiness and red hair decided to make her way in to her world and her heart? Was she even aware of the duties before her? That she would become the eternal worrier, guardian, and biggest fan of this sweet baby girl?

My mom, 17, dropping out of high school and chasing stability that would not come for many years. As I now raise a precious 15-year-old daughter at the age of 39 and counting, I am in awe of the courage my own mother must have mustered to decide to be an adult rather than an adolescent. Having a newborn in a stable marriage at 25 rocked my world, but at 17, she was just a baby herself. And I completely and totally lose my moxie imagining my own daughter becoming a mother at 17. I mean, really. Who is ready to be a mother at 17? I am a first-time mom every day, and ready for the teenage years, I am not; ready to be a grandmother, I am not...

My parents divorced after a year of marriage, which I imagine is an accurate statistic for the manner in which I kicked my way into the world. At the age of 20, another marriage and a new little brother were on their way to enter my little life. I was still too young to really remember anything of much significance from that time in my life and my mother's, but my mom says it probably wouldn't have lasted—too much secrecy.

Instead, that marriage ended accidentally on a snowy road when a semi-truck jack knifed and sent our single cab truck, no seat-belts, three-year-old standing up, into oblivion. My mom says we had never gone to work with him, but that morning when he went to check oil wells, he wanted to show me the deer.

This is what I remember in my mind from that morning, how my three-year-old brain retained the after-accident:

Two men on either side of me in white uniforms, I am laying on my back looking up and everything is bright. I am crying and telling them I want my mommy, and they say "we have your mommy." That is it. Crying, wanting my mom, bright lights. I have no idea when I learned that my head was full of staples and stiches or that my stepdad hadn't survived the crash. But my mom was spared with broken ribs and six months to wait to bring my fatherless brother into the world.

Now, my brother is approaching two and I am approaching five and ready to go in to Kindergarten. My mom is remarried... To a man that beats her and my little brother. Somehow, she always knew when it was going to be a bad night. I had a secret drawer that my mom had shared with me that had phone numbers in it, and she taught me how to use the rotary phone. I felt very important. If I heard her scream, I was to immediately get to the phone and call the first person on the list. Twenty-two. She was twenty-two and dealing with two kids under five and an impossible relationship.

I played the mother role several times during the year—or was it two?—of that relationship. I would grab my brother and hide him in the dryer or under the bed in an effort to protect him from the tide turning. Mom always said that the reason he never hit me was because I was in school and they would call the authorities. She finally got brave enough to leave for good, brave enough to love herself, brave enough to get us out of the recurring nightmare, although her shoulder became a constant look-over. He later died in a motorcycle accident. We did not attend his services.

Seventeen, putting one foot in front of the other to keep moving. Twenty, widowed. Twenty-two, gathering two toddlers and moving to another state without any help from family and few friends. Twenty-four, entering into a fourth marriage and blending two families, finally fully committing to "for better or for worse."

I can't help but compare the composure and maturity she had at her various stages to that of my own. At age 17, I was a cheerleader, student-council representative, national-honor society inductee, driving a 1989 Buick Regal that I paid for myself, working at Dairy Queen for my third summer. A snotty, teenage kid. I could not fathom, nor did I want the responsibility of a child. My meager wages sure could not have supported a baby.

At age 20, I was finishing my second year of college and planning a wedding to a man that promised to never lay a hand on me. I had attended college on a full scholarship, was in a sorority and was an officer for our Campus Leadership group. I had big career dreams to go to graduate school, become a Hospital Administrator, and of course, make lots of money.

Twenty-four, I had finished my undergraduate degree, put my graduate degree on hold, been married three years, I was traveling and recruiting for my *alma mater*, had bought my first home, and was trying to start a family.

Two lives, a mom and a daughter, although sometimes it was more like sisters, completely devoted to each other and bound by a rocky start, finding its way to a paved road free of snow. A 34-year old woman determined that I would not make the same mistakes she did and sacrificing daily luxuries to ensure that I chose living-in-the-moment over searching for commitment.

She told me every day that I could be anything that I wanted to be. I was told how and where she went wrong and how it did not to be a history-repeating event for our family. I was told that the only thing she didn't regret was having her kids, but she would do it all over again in a much different way if she could.

So, taking on the mother role again, I did everything I could to make her proud. Proud that she had decided not only to give birth to me, but to raise me and make every day her best effort to make a life for me. Proud that I hadn't followed in her footsteps. Proud that I had a high-school diploma, proud that I had a college degree, proud that I married after four years of dating, and proud again, when we welcomed the first grandchild after four years of marriage.

A beautiful daughter to carry on the bond of mother and child. A beautiful being to share the amazing story of how rock solid her Nanny was when it would have been very easy to let it all crumble to dust. The vow that she thought she was making to men, all along, she was making to a legacy of women. **A pledge to be a mother above all else, for richer or poorer, in sickness and in health.** To unconditionally seek out opportunities to provide a better and safer life for them. To sacrifice new clothes, nice cars, nice vacations, and social circles so that your daughter could go to gymnastics lessons, have new cheer shoes, have gas in her car to get to work. To cry in private early on so that the wall would not be broken. To cry in public later so that the wall would be adequately reinforced.

My favorite thing to do is watch my mom with my daughter. For my mom, there is an enjoyment there that is not bound by the stress of being her sole provider and protector. With all of us kids grown and out on our own, we now have time to completely enjoy girl-time and stolen moments to stop and take a deep breath, and realize that we survived. Not only did we survive, but we kicked much booty along the way. We lived a hundred lifetimes in my first seven years, and I am sure that we were frequently doubted. My childhood has made me live by the motto "be kind, for everyone you meet is fighting a hard battle."

I think somewhere it should be carved in marble that being a mom is the ultimate commitment. A desire so deeply imbedded in my heart to make a positive impact on another creature in order to multiply all the blessings that I have had or dreamed of having. To not be ashamed of life lessons that made me better, in order to make her better. To know that in that church service on a cold Sunday night, on that snowy road on a cold morning, and within that cold third marriage, someone was keeping vigil over my mom and me. And I know in my heart, as I look at my teenage daughter, that it was to keep her warm. She is going to do far greater things than me because of the wall she sits on, built brick by brick by a legacy of mothers who never gave up.

Queen Anne's Lace
Candra Fisher

The flowers, light and soft
As they sway in the wind
Remind me...
Remind me of you
My first born child
Child of wonder and grace
Of my younger days

Queen Anne's Lace
A faint memory of your
Childhood days

Anne... Anne of Green Gables
The "depths of despair" Anne
The Queen Anne's Lace Anne

Now as I watch the sea of Lace
Move in step to the wind
I say a prayer for you
Each flower–hundreds of
Wispy cream colored souls

Lift up prayers for you...
My prayers quicken to match
Their rhythmic movement

And then I say
With all my heart
On the tender flowers of grace
"Give her peace"

The peace of the gentle moving Spirit
As the lace bends
So does life...

Oh God, give her peace.

The Job
Jodi Durr
meaningfulmama.com

I was perfect for the job. If you read my resume, you'd agree. I have a degree in education, years of experience working with youth, teaching experience and was a camp counselor. If you read my cover letter, it would mention that I'm full of joy and a kid at heart. I was the perfect applicant and without hesitation was given the job the moment I applied.

But the job didn't turn out quite like I expected. All of my experience did not prepare me. I had so much wisdom going into the position and was pretty sure the job was made for me. It was all I ever wanted. Instead of feeling like I had arrived, I felt confused, frustrated and inadequate. I really wasn't sure I was cut out for this.

The position I had received was titled "Mom."

I should have been thankful for that title, but instead I struggled. I didn't find joy in the struggle. I just tried to survive the day in front of me.

Again. A spill that needs to be wiped off the floor.

Again. A child who seems completely out of control with her emotions.

Again. Sharpie on the bed sheets, walls or clothes.

Again. A mess the moment after I cleaned up the room.

Again. The fighting of siblings.

Again. Not being a part of a conversation at a restaurant because I'm struggling with a two year old that doesn't want to sit still.

Again. A load of laundry.

Again. Removing myself from a party to feed or nap a child.

Again. Again. Again. I was a free spirit, and this job tied me down to a daily routine and struggles that I wasn't ready to embrace. I allowed motherhood to rob me of my joy. The kid at heart had left the building. In my mind was a picture of what it would look like to be a mom. My reality didn't look anything like the picture I had created. When I had a newborn, I would apologize to my husband that the dishes weren't done or the house wasn't clean. He would encouragingly respond, "As long as you are both alive at the end of the day, that's what matters." I think part of me took that phrase into the rest of parenting.

I'd get to the end of the day and encourage myself with the thought that the kids were at least alive. I was surviving. However, I wasn't thriving like I had always imagined. I needed a change.

Starting a blog was born out of my inclination and passion to do it better. I wanted to pursue all of the goals I had for being a mom. The struggles had overcome me, and **I was determined, with pure grit, to begin to thrive**.

The desire to pass along all that I was learning on this parenting journey was also a motivator. If I was struggling so much with the great role models, education and mentors, how are other women surviving this livelihood? The blog also became an outlet for my own creativity and a way to express myself.

Starting Meaningful Mama was a turning point for me. It held me accountable to live out all of my "I should..." moments, and I had a lot of them.

"I should really embrace the mess more and do more crafts with the kids."

"I should learn to jump in puddles and play in the rain."

"I should have tea parties and dance parties."

"I should be more consistent in my parenting."

"I should laugh more."

"I should focus on teaching my kids about how to have character and be intentional about teaching them about God."

The "I should..." list could go on and on. It was a great list and with the motivation of blogging, I set out to become the kind of mom I could be proud of—the kind of mom the kids would enjoy and respect.

My motivation was high, and I decided this blog would be my 365-day journey to doing it better. I made the goal to blog three times a day, with a focus on character development, a craft or activity, and a parenting tip. I knew nothing about blogging. I didn't even follow one blog. I just knew I needed this kind of accountability to do the job well.

I made it. 1095 posts later, I had completed my first year. Did the incentive of the blog turn me into the perfect mother I had always imagined? Not even close. There has been nothing more humbling than the parenting journey. Becoming a mom was a reflection of all my shortcomings. It made me acutely aware of my selfishness, impatience, and even anger issues I didn't know existed. Further, I developed a passion for blogging, and it has taken me a while to discover a good balance for my family. I never wanted to be a hypocritical blogger who said to her children, "Leave me alone so I can blog about how to love you better." Finding that balance took trial and error.

However, the motivation was there. I worked hard to do the parenting gig right so I could help other moms. I was suddenly more inclined to come up with creative ideas to do with my kids, become engaged in activities with them and embrace the mess that can come with making things fun.

What if the blog was taken away from me now? Would I still be working to fulfill the "I should..." moments? I would. For me, I needed the blog to get going, but what I want for my kids and for our lives together is the driving factor. What do I want my kids to look like 5, 10, 15, 20 years from now? If that's the goal, how do I get them there?

I also discovered that the joy that I had lost at the beginning of parenting could only be reclaimed if I had an internal transformation. The metamorphosis took place when I changed my internal dialog. I had to learn to assume the best and look for the good. Approaching life with gratitude was key. Claiming Scripture to embrace truth was also a part of the journey. I learned to lean on other moms' wise advice, take an honest look at my own emotions and motivations, and allow imperfections in both my children and myself.

I need to trust God and embrace the thought that we should "rejoice in our sufferings because we know that suffering produces perseverance; perseverance, character; and character, hope." (Romans 5:3) I also love the Carl Perkins quote that says, "If it weren't for the rocks in the bed, the stream would have no song."

Storms are going to come in life. We often cannot change our circumstance. However, we can change how we choose to respond, and that response is a testimony to who we are at the core.

We have been given the most important job. We are raising the next generation. What a privilege! You were made for this position. Reclaim your job. Keep heart, and find the motivation to live out more of your "I should..." moments.

It Will Be Okay

Jessica Smith

longestdays.com

I was a terrible babysitter. One summer, I watched three boys while the parents worked. It was only a few hours, but the boys knew that as soon as they asked for a movie I would conk out. The movie would end, and I would wake up to an empty room, and sometimes an empty house. I felt so guilty that I was a terrible babysitter that, when the mother asked if the job was working out for me, I said no. We went our separate ways, and I never babysat again in my teenage and college years.

When the nurses handed me my daughter eleven years ago, I was scared. So scared, in fact, that I threw up. I could blame it on the epidural they gave me, but I knew I was terrified. How could I be a mom when I couldn't even take care of kids I babysat?

The first few weeks at home, I asked my husband if I could pick up our daughter, every time. I didn't feel like a responsible adult. I was still surprised they let us walk out of the hospital with so little understanding of how to take care of a newborn. I wanted to argue with them that a one hour class on zero sleep was not enough to prepare me for the next eighteen years of caregiving. I received more training on how to buckle a seatbelt in an airplane.

My husband went back to work, though, and I realized I needed to up my game. In the past, when I didn't know about something I went to the library and read. It was how I learned to play basketball, how I learned gymnastics, and how I learned to play tennis. The reading didn't help me excel at these sports, but I could fill up a conversation with the mechanics of each of them. With the advent of the internet, I could Google with one hand, hold my daughter in my lap, all while flipping through *What to Expect in the First Year* on the table in front of me.

The books didn't tell me how much guilt I would feel as a mother. Mother guilt came the first time I cut my daughter's fingernails and I clipped a bit of her skin. She started bleeding like crazy and I called my husband in a near breakdown. He thought something terrible happened. I learned that day that fingers bleed a lot even if the cut isn't that big. Her finger healed, but my guilt stayed.

Guilt sat on my shoulders when I thought back through the week and realized my daughter hadn't pooped. No book told me that sometimes babies can go a week or more without pooping. Thankfully, the doctor explained in a patient and kind voice that there wasn't anything to worry about because newborn digestive systems are still developing. If was still an issue in a few days, I could give him a call. New moms take note: find a doctor who listens, but doesn't entertain the crazy that builds up like a steam valve in your head.

As the days passed, I grew more confident. They went by faster, and 911 was no longer typed in my phone ready to hit call. I learned to relax and roll with what life threw at me. Every day was different, though anytime I thought I had it down, I still just knew something new loomed on the horizon. It's a thought that can send a parent into a cone of shame, but every week I kept my daughter alive I gained more confidence.

And then we made it a month, then three months, six months and one year. That is truly why parents throw such a big party on a child's first birthday. It is because they need to memorialize their ability to keep a baby fed, clothed and healthy through the first year of life! At her first birthday, I thought to myself that maybe, just maybe, I wasn't as terrible a parent as I thought I was.

Motherhood is just as hard as I thought it would be. Toddlers, preschoolers, school-age, and teens are all as challenging as those first few weeks with a newborn. It never gets easier; each new plane of development presents new challenges. What did change was the guilt, as it lessened over time. As my daughter grew, I learned, that, although it is hard, no matter what happened, she would be okay and so would I. Motherhood isn't about having all the answers or being the perfect mom. It involves a lot of trial and error, with healthy doses of "I'm sorry," and "Will you forgive me?" Now that I am a parent of three kids, I know that no mother ever has it all together, but we have one thing in common. We all love our kids and want the best for them. **All of us moms do the best we can with the tools we have.**

In my late twenties, I was diagnosed with cancer. After surgery and radiation, I have been cancer-free for nine years. It has changed my life, my day to day physical health, and most of all how I parent. In order to treat the cancer, they removed my thyroid, and I now regulate my thyroid hormone with medication. But a pill doesn't always do what the body does naturally. I have a lot of ups and downs. There are weeks my medicine is off and I have no energy. It is all I can do to get through a day, then sleep, and wake up exhausted to do it all over again.

There are months when my body stores too much of the synthetic hormone and I can't sleep. My temper is short, my anxiety is high and my kids are there to witness it all. I wish there was a book I could read to help me manage a chronic condition while parenting, but like the rest of my mom life, I learn as I continue my habit of saying sorry, asking for forgiveness, and explaining to the kids that it isn't their fault. I have found this pattern to be the most powerful parenting tool of all.

All parents have challenges. For some it is money, for others it is single parenthood, children with special needs, and like me, a lot of moms struggle with health, whether it is cancer, a chronic illness like diabetes, depression, anxiety, or the myriad of other ways our bodies betray us. All of it adds to the challenges and guilt we face as mothers.

No matter what our challenge is, we will be okay. Our kids will be okay. Some days, we wake up and make a mistake before our feet hit the floor. Other days will breeze by and we'll appreciate the grace of a present moment. Regardless of what kind of day I have, I remember that I am not called to be a perfect mom, but I am called to be an example for my kids. Every single one of us makes mistakes. Every single one of us can be forgiven—by our children, by our spouses, and especially by ourselves.

If I were ever to write a book on parenting, it could be summed up by one simple line, *"Guilt doesn't raise children—forgiveness does."*

When we forgive ourselves first, we set aside guilt, every mom's nemesis. We tell guilt that it has no place in our lives. This allows us to accept our mistakes for what they are: mistakes. And it helps us change course and improve our lives and the lives of our families. At its core, the only true mistake I believe we mothers make too often is dwelling in the land of guilt.

Whether it is guilt over not doing the right thing, not giving our kids the right opportunities, a bad day, not enough time with them, a wrong decision, or not being the mom we think we should—guilt is a constant passenger in the minivan of motherhood. It is something we joke about with other moms and accept as a part of our lives, even though it has no place.

We have the power to take our lives back from guilt, change our family trees, and never let a bad feeling change how we parent and how we love our kids. Guilt doesn't affect our lives only; it affects how our kids live, how they will parent, and how their kids will live and parent.

It is what I needed to hear when the nurses handed me my daughter for the first time. If only they had said, *"It's okay. You will mess up more times than you can even fathom, but she will be okay. You will be okay. Forgiveness and I'm sorry go a long way in this world."*

Today, remember you will mess up, your kids will mess up, and your spouse will mess up. The school your kids attend will mess up. The coach who leads your child's team will mess up. Your friends will mess up. We are all so very human, but that isn't the end of the story. Because after you do what you wished you hadn't, gather your child in your arms, look them in the eye and say "I'm sorry. I shouldn't have yelled," or "I'm sorry I couldn't follow through on a promise I made. I know you are disappointed. Will you forgive me?"

Watch the way your child's face lights up. How their tears slow and their anger releases. How astonishment will fill the space where guilt was. Your child will realize that even mom messes up, and when she does, she says sorry and asks for forgiveness. It will change their life.

Put away that badge of honor we wear as mothers. The button that says, "Mommy guilt." Forgive yourself for being human. Confess your shortcomings, change your actions and move forward. It is what our kids need; it is what our families need. And most of all, it is what we all need as we navigate the treacherous waters of motherhood.

I am no longer afraid of acknowledging that I am the responsible adult, because I am leading my children the best way I know how—through forgiveness and grace, not guilt.

Fighting Siblings

Elaine Mingus

superradchristianwriterchick.com

"Fine. Just stay away from me!" she yelled. My daughter's door slammed and I heard her crying. "Why do you always do that!? Why are you always so mean?" my other daughter yelled back as she stomped into their shared bedroom. The door slammed again.

Lots of arguing followed.

It was one of those mornings. The two oldest siblings had spent most of it at each others' throats for various reasons, and I had enough of their bickering. I determined to find a solution to the morning's chaos once and for all. I walked firmly across the hall and opened their bedroom door, "Both of you have chores. Together. Go. Downstairs. Now!"

They groaned and went downstairs scowling at each other. "See what you've done," one of them said to the other. "Me? This is all your fault," the other replied.

"If you keep fighting I will give you more chores," I threatened, but the message didn't seem to sink in. because for the next thirty minutes the two girls griped about how each other did the specified chores.

"You're supposed to wipe the counter this way!" "Stop telling me what to do! Mom, tell her to stop telling me what to do!" Instead of entering into the fray, I continued to add more and more chores until they got the message that they wouldn't be free from working until they stopped fighting. Despite themselves, they finally stopped. After their reluctant cease-fire, I decided to add one last "chore."

"Get your shoes and take the baby for a walk. Together," I said.

Then, a funny thing happened. They smiled. "Okay, mommy." They quickly got their shoes and the baby stroller. They even offered to take the toddler. Call it mommy wisdom or divine inspiration, but I finally got what I set out to achieve: peace and sisterly friendship.

There is a famous photo on social media of two small children with tears in their eyes huddled together under a oversized t-shirt that reads: "This is our get-along t-shirt." Though I'm not sure I'd take that route, I think the sentiment has merit. So many times, we moms think that when our children are fighting we should separate them. We assume that the further they are apart, the less they will fight.

Not true! In fact, two people who are struggling in any relationship need to figure out the correct way to communicate with each other by practicing. This requires the investment of time together, even if it means occasional (or sometimes constant) squabbling.

I'm a firm believer that siblings will eventually be some of our best assets in life. They know where we came from and how we got to where we are. They intimately know how we were raised. They can identify with us in ways that no one else in the world will ever be able to. For most of us, the sibling relationship is the longest relationship we will ever have. It will last longer than the relationship with our parents, who will leave this earth long before us, or our spouses, who enter our lives long after our siblings usually do.

I remember one time, my sister and I were driving down the road when I saw a landmark where we had experienced something as a family. "Do you remember when..." I started, but before I even said what happened, she answered, "Yes." I didn't have to finish the thought. That was the end of the conversation. My sister knows me because we've spent so much time together. We don't even need words sometimes.

Maybe you didn't have a great sibling relationship; maybe your interactions with your sibling were even painful. Maybe they still are. You don't have to let history repeat itself! Today, you can choose to be an active participant in making sure that your children experience the joy of a sibling friendship.

In order to do so, pay attention to what causes your children to fight. Do they fight more after a certain friend comes to play? Try limiting their interactions with that specific friend. Are they watching television shows where the siblings are constantly at odds? Consider finding some sibling-friendly shows. Are they bored, hungry or tired? Have they just experienced a major transition such as a move, the birth of a new baby, or a divorce? These things can make anyone a little cranky!

Your children will fight. That's nothing to be ashamed of. Some adversity is a necessary part of the growth process, it strengthens us as individuals, but constantly being at war with each other can etch away at a potentially beneficial relationship. Every good mom deals with their own variation of sibling rivalry, but it is how we handle their natural tendency to snap at each other that counts.

When my children returned from their walk, they were chatting happily. I don't know what happened in the 20 minutes they were gone, but they had forgotten their problems with each other and were reminded of the sweetness of sibling fellowship. It was a win/win. I got some chores done, and their got their attitudes straight!

The way you handle your children might look different than mine, but making serious steps to nourishing the connection that your children have with each other is essential. It is one that can be easily overlooked when you are dealing with the urgent call of putting out the fire of a disagreement. Many times, we have to think on our feet as we try to figure out a way to get them to connect despite their own emotions (not to mention our own!). Sometimes it might be best to wait until everyone has had a little time to calm down before reconnecting. Whatever your method, don't give up. Remember that most likely **another fight is inevitable, but that doesn't mean you've failed**. Navigating the waters between siblings is a marathon, not a sprint. Eventually all your groundwork will pay off as you see them into adulthood as friends instead of enemies!

Elusive Time

Meri Stratton Phelps

As the sun starts to seep in through the bedroom window, I realize that another night has faded away. How did the next day come so soon? My body is tired, and I wish that I could steal a few more hours or even minutes of sleep. But reality reminds me that I should get up and start my day. Extra sleep is a luxury I cannot afford anymore. The house is quiet, and maybe I can have a few moments to myself before my son's voice starts calling.

I try to shake the sleep from my head and wander to the kitchen to get my cup of coffee, now a necessity to help with the morning wake-up ritual. The early morning time that I have to myself is my own special treasure. I have always been a morning person, enjoying the quiet time of the day while most people sleep. The sunrises are always stunning, and the time alone lets me dream about the day ahead.

The day stretches out before me like an empty road. Uncharted territory. A new day, complete with 24 new hours. How will I choose to spend my time today?

I hear his voice softly calling "Mama, turn." His persistence reminds me that I need to go and reposition him. Because he always sleeps on his side, turning him takes a bit of work. I remove the blanket, and the pillows along his back and gently cradle his hips to turn him on his back. I straighten the tangle of his legs, then I move one arm, and then his head, which is tricky because I don't want to disturb the BiPap mask that covers his little face. Last night, he wore the mask that has a leopard print, so when he's awake I'll ask him if "The Kitty" slept well overnight. After turning his head, then his body, legs and arms are properly repositioned on the other side. I replace the pillows behind his back, between his legs, and between his arms to provide him with the support that he is unable to give on his own. Finally I place his beloved stuffed polar bear between his long fingers. He sleepily squeezes the bear as it is returned. After being tucked in under his blanket, he drifts off to sleep again, and I watch the monitor as his heart rate lowers into the restful sleep zone.

I still have some time. A few more precious minutes to plan out my day. How will I spend my time?

Time has always been an elusive treasure. Despite having exceptionally punctual parents, I was never quite able to follow their lead, and to their great disappointment I was continually five minutes late. For everything. I blame my obsessive tardiness on my almost 2 week late arrival into the world, as my mom had to carry me well beyond her due date during a very hot summer. I actually do have a great grasp of the concept of time and the amount of time it will take to do something, but I always want to try to fit in just a few more activities than the clock will allow. Time doesn't seem to compromise well, and the clock continues to count down the minutes of the day whether I can keep up or not.

When I learned I was pregnant, I dreamed of activities I would do with my child, first when they were a baby or a toddler, and then later when they were in school or when they finally grew up and moved out of the house. Our baby was even given the nickname of "Little Future" since we didn't know the sex of the child before they were born. I imagined Little Future and I going on long walks together, then I saw myself teaching them how to ride a bike. In my mind, we would explore nature in the back yard, plant gardens, look for earthworms in the dirt, and watch spiders spin their webs. We would go camping and enjoy summer picnics on the beach. I would take them horseback riding and would eventually teach them how to drive a car. So much time with my new little baby. So many years of activities to plan. If they stayed at home until college, that might give me 18 years. Then of course there would be the visits home from school during the holidays, and eventually visits with that special someone who they would choose to be by their side as they grew into adulthood. With luck, the grandchildren would come and visit, and we would travel to go visit them. So many years ahead of us. A lifetime to spend together.

When I first saw my son's face, I was in awe. Finally, it was my time to be a mother. My heart exploded with love and an immense feeling of responsibility to this little person. My baby. My Little Future had arrived, and I couldn't wait to start our life together.

But as a new mom, my days were flooded with responsibilities that at times, and after countless sleepless nights, seemed overwhelming. I had this new little person that was completely dependent on me. And now, the regular home projects accumulated even faster. Piles of unopened mail sat on the counter, and the dishes and baby bottles seemed to pile up faster than ever. Unfolded laundry, which now included baby clothes and blankets and diapers, sat untouched. Before my son was born, I considered myself an organized person, but now I felt overwhelmed, disorganized and frustrated. The 24-hour day was never long enough, and the wonderment of motherhood faded as my son's life became eclipsed by the chores and everything else that I thought was essential and important. My son did not get the very best of me during those times.

And then, when my beautiful little boy was just three months old, we sat in a neurologist's office and my hopes and my dreams of a life together with him were crushed. The doctor told me that my perfect baby, my Little Future, had a degenerative neuromuscular disease. It was genetic, and it had a name. Spinal Muscular Atrophy, or SMA, had suddenly shattered my future. My son had the most severe form of the disease, and his muscles and nerves were already dying. He would never be able to hold up his head, or sit up, or crawl, or walk. There would be no bike rides. No walks to the park. No baseball games. No graduation ceremonies. My son would not be able to hold my hand, or give me a hug or a kiss. He would eventually lose the ability to swallow, to smile, and to breathe. He would die before the age of two. There was no hope, and the host of doctors who examined him told us to take him home, and love him for whatever time we had left.

Time. So expansive. So elusive. Before my son was born, time seemed so plentiful. Limitless. I had imagined a lifetime with him. Now, my son's days were numbered. And mine as a mom were numbered, too.

When faced with a terminal diagnosis, I have heard people talk about how they finally started living after they realized that they were mortal. That without fail, their time in the hourglass of life would soon trickle away. After my son's diagnosis, I knew that same reality. I had believed that, as a mother, time would be my friend rather than my nemesis. But now, time became a measured entity. Clocks now would count down the days in my son's life and our time together. What I discovered in that first week after my son was diagnosed with SMA is that time is not promised. Not for me. Not for my son. Not for anyone. Instead, **time is a gift, and every moment is to be treasured**.

How would you spend your last day with your child, if you knew that 24 more hours would be all that you had? Would you let those dishes pile up in the sink? Could the laundry go unfolded for a little bit longer? Would you turn off the radio, the TV, the computer, your phone? What would you do if you just had one more day?

As the time began to pass from the diagnosis day, birthdays became monthly events for my son, with big celebrations, balloons and singing because we never knew if the next month would arrive. We took trips and went on adventures, trying to fit a lifetime into a few years. I discovered that the chores and home projects that once seemed so essential could wait. I started to use my time to notice and cherish the small wonders of my son, like smiles and coos. I spent time running my fingers through his thick brown hair and staring into his big brown eyes. Even tasks like changing his diaper and feeding him and giving him a bath became a joy as I imagined a time in the future where I would no longer be able to touch and hold and care for my son. Snuggles and quiet moments with my son filled my days and refreshed my soul. Home chores and work projects were relegated only to times when my son was asleep and didn't need my attention. I made sure that, during the time he was awake, he would get the very best I could give him each and every day. He would get my time, and he would get my love.

As mothers, we weave a tapestry of memories for our children. We fashion a quilt of love for them that they will carry throughout their life, whether they are close to us or far away. It will become the strength they need, and the answers they seek in a world that can be hard and, at times, cruel. It will remind them of their own precious soul, and how very much they are loved with the type of love that only a mother can provide. Just as our mothers did for us, the quilt will be there. It is there when we need consoling, when the tears flow, and when we don't have any answers about how to make them stop. It is there when we enjoy the greatest celebrations and victories in our life. It is there when we need answers about how to manage our own children. It is there when we are alone, and when only the love from our mother is enough to comfort us during a crisis. Some of the memories shine in bright golden tones, while others are a bit ragged on the edges. Because that is life. It is the good with the bad.

The amazing with the mundane. The joys with the sorrows. Mothers give the most precious gifts to their children. They give their love, and they give their time.

The sun is higher in the sky now. My son is awake and now calling for my attention. As I walk into his room, he greets me with a soft "Good morning Mama. I love you," and my soul is refreshed. My son will celebrate his 7 ½ year old birthday next week. I have been blessed with more time with him than I ever imagined, and I am beyond grateful.

Today, the chores can wait. Today, there is still time left in the hourglass. Today, I have time to fit in a few more memories to enlarge the quilt. I realize now that the quilt is as much for me as it is for my son. It is filled with precious memories that I will always carry in my heart. Today, I promise myself that together we will add another brilliant square to the tapestry.

If Our Rocker Could Talk

Kelly Bingham

kellyrbingham.wordpress.com

The gliding rocker in my son's nursery has seen a lot, although I haven't gotten to use it as much as I would have liked. I pictured spending countless hours gliding and nursing my son, but I only got to nurse him for two weeks. As is often the case, the plan or vision we have for our lives goes awry, and all we can do is adjust as we go along.

Ten days after my son was born, I got a sudden fever, which led to a diagnosis of mastitis in both breasts. The pain made breastfeeding a torturous chore that I dreaded every two to three hours instead of a joyous time to bond with my son.

Then, just two days after the diagnosis, extremely high blood pressure sent me back to the emergency room, where a diagnosis of postpartum preeclampsia kept me in the hospital for two more days.

It took all that time to get my blood pressure to an acceptable level, and fluid around my lungs meant the traditional treatment—magnesium—wasn't a good option because it could cause respiratory distress. I was basically in the early stages of congestive heart failure. For a day or so, all I wanted was to ensure I lived to see my son again.

The medications I was prescribed to keep my blood pressure and swelling down also prohibited me from breastfeeding. At that point, I gave up on breastfeeding and pumping completely.

I have to admit, though, that moving from breast milk to formula was a giant weight off my shoulders. Feeding was no longer something I dreaded; now I could enjoy providing nourishment for my son without the anxiety and pain that I'd come to associate with breastfeeding.

While I was incredibly disappointed, one of my doctors pointed out that feeding my child should be a time of bonding and joy, and for some women, breastfeeding just isn't an option. She assured me I did the best I could, and that any amount of breast milk my son received was good.

I began taking my son downstairs to one of the couches to feed him, especially at night, so as not to wake my husband who was already back to work. Since we already had to go down to the kitchen to make a bottle, naturally we just made our way on into the family room.

So, for months, instead of using the rocker to nurse and hold my son, it became an extension of the closet, where clean laundry began to pile up when I didn't have the time or energy to put it away. As my son got older

—and grew much bigger—it became a place of limbo for clothes he outgrew.

At some point, I discovered that my baby ate better in the rocker, because it was quiet and free of distractions in his room—no dog barking or wanting to play, no television noise. I finally donated or put into storage all the too-small baby clothes and began rocking him and feeding him his bottles in the glider.

That chair became a place of peace and quiet, where my thoughts could ruminate, or I could just sit in silence with my baby.

In the morning, often before it was light outside, I would relish being able to hold and feed my little boy in darkness and quiet, before he'd even fully woken up. He would be still and calm, and I could enjoy some quiet time to think about the day ahead. My favorite part of those minutes would be leaning down and smelling his hair, fresh, soft and clean from his bath the night before.

Sadly, that rocker was also the place I cried many tears. When my son was three months old, I was diagnosed with postpartum depression and anxiety—yet another twist in life I had not anticipated.

I'd always been a bit moody, and I noticed I was having difficulty getting everything done I needed to since my son was born, particularly since I'd gone back to work. I also noticed I was much more emotional, but I attributed all these things to having given birth, the stress of being a new mother, and my hormones.

My husband was concerned and suggested numerous times that maybe I should see my doctor or talk to a counselor. I've rarely benefited from counseling, though, and I was sick of seeing doctors after a full-term pregnancy and postpartum preeclampsia, so I did not heed his requests at that time.

More and more, I'd find that I could barely get a shower each day, but I'd justify it in my mind: "I have an infant to care for, and I'm exhausted. Who cares if I don't feel like getting a shower?"

But depression increased until even taking care of my son was a major task, and the crying became a daily occurrence. Often, I would cry multiple times a day, and I couldn't seem to stop. I would have panic attacks that would paralyze me and make it impossible to even decide what to do next. The smallest thing would seem like a giant mountain to me.

I began to feel more and more like a failure, as if I weren't a good enough mother, a good enough wife, or a good enough employee. And the negative thoughts just compounded until they became like walls around me. No one could really get in to help, and I surely couldn't break out myself.

It was on New Year's Day 2015 that my depression seemed to culminate. I started crying before I'd even gotten out of bed and couldn't stop until almost two in the afternoon. I didn't have an interest in eating. Taking a shower was a major accomplishment that day, as if I'd successfully completed a marathon. Blow-drying my hair was not even an option; I hadn't touched my makeup for weeks.

All I wanted to do was run away. It was then that I accepted the fact that I needed help. Running away would not solve my problems, and I could never leave my child and husband alone anyway.

But even after I sought treatment, the depression and anxiety didn't go away for several months. The nights I spent feeding my son in that rocking chair came with tears, with prayers, with silent thoughts of whether I should even be a mother at all; I wondered how I could ever be a good enough mother to my son and if he deserved better.

I mourned my life pre-pregnancy, which only led to feelings of guilt and shame and ungratefulness. So many of my friends would love to be mothers and can't, or they fought through many obstacles to finally hold children of their own. How could I be so ungrateful and unappreciative of the healthy, beautiful baby boy I had?

Then, one day at 4 a.m. in that rocking chair in my son's nursery, I reached a point where I felt all the sleeplessness and fatigue and chaos and anxiety and depression were worth it.

Despite having been fed and changed, my son seemed to just want to be in my arms. He was eight and a half months old and just getting over a cold. No matter how many times I laid him down in his crib, he would wake back up until I held him again.

He didn't cry or wiggle around like was so often the case; usually my son wants to be active and moving. But on this early morning, he would just lay in my arms with a pacifier in his mouth. Only the dim ocean friends dancing across the ceiling from his nightlight projector gave me enough light to see his eyes falling closed as I rocked him.

Despite my alarm being set for 6:30 a.m. and a long day of work ahead, at 4 a.m. my son just wanted to be held by me, his mommy, and for once, I was content even at that early hour. And it was at that moment that I thought, "How did I get so lucky that such a beautiful and perfect little human loves me so much that he just wants my touch? I'm certainly not deserving of this."

Since that night, I would love to tell you that things were wonderfully perfect, but I can't. My whole family was sick for months: my husband with pneumonia, my son with double ear infections and sinus infections, myself with ear infections and tonsillitis.

I'm still battling the postpartum depression and anxiety, but having gotten the medical assistance I needed, and I'm making progress. I still take blood pressure medication since my postpartum preeclampsia diagnosis and have a long way to go to regain my physical health fully.

Most days, I'm fairly certain my body and mind are forever changed. I still grieve what I lost from time to time.

But if my rocking chair could talk about all those moments since my son's birth, it would say that every mom walks a different journey. It would say there will be days where all you can do is pray. Some days there will be tears; some days fear; some days even anger. Some days you may feel as though nothing will ever go right again. But it will. Then other days will bring unimaginable joy, boundless love and unbreakable faith. And it's all normal.

What I learned through these hours in my rocker with my baby boy is that motherhood is truly the hardest calling on earth. It is a journey, and no matter how well planned, life always tends to throw curves.

Some women, like me, may face a rockier road. Others may see nothing but smooth sailing. And that's okay. The important part of motherhood— and of life—is to keep going. All of those moments in the rocker in my son's room are memories that make up my life, the good, the bad and the downright ugly.

There are some moments I am not particularly fond of—or proud of—but they composed my life, and no matter what, I can say that my son is most definitely worth it all.

In Her Honor

Kellie Van Atta

familyserviceclub.org

Slightly blind without my glasses, I slipped into my daughter's room when I heard her crying around 6:00 a.m. I picked her up and brought her into bed with me. She quickly fell back to sleep. Gazing over at her chubby cheek, I smiled, so thankful to be a mom.

Motherhood hasn't always been easy for me, in fact, it usually isn't. My oldest, Paxton, is now four, and when he was born, I was a total mess. One night, when he was six months old, while he slept soundly in his crib, I cried desperately in my closet. I felt so lost, so alone. I love my husband, and I love my step-mom, but I wanted to talk to my *mom*.

As a good student and successful teacher, I was used to feeling competent in my daily life, but I didn't feel this way when I was at home with my infant son. I faltered through my first few months of motherhood feeling completely inadequate. *How could I get my son to sleep for more than three hours at time? Was it detrimental that he was taking every nap in the sling? Would I ever feel normal again? Would breastfeeding get easier?* While many women would consult their mothers about these questions, I cried in the closet. My dad travelled a lot when I was growing up, and although he is an amazing person, he doesn't remember anything about my early childhood. Did I sleep in a crib or in bed with my parents? Was I fussy or content? These questions remain unanswered, and for this and many reasons, I felt (and sometimes still feel) really clueless as a mom.

You see, I lost my mother when I was 17.

I will never forget a conversation I had with her just weeks before she passed away. After a long night out with friends, I called her into my room to talk.

I lived in San Luis Obispo, California, with my sister, my mom, and my step-dad. We had moved there, driving away from my dad and childhood friends, halfway through my sophomore year. Trying to placate me during a tough transition, my mom told me that if I ever felt like California wasn't the best place for me, she would consider letting me move back to Utah to live with my dad. That night, I had made my choice. It had been over a year, and I was ready to move back. My mom sat down on my floral comforter to hear me out. Outlining many reasons, I explained that, although I would miss her terribly, I thought I should move back to Utah for my Senior Year. I had prayed about it a lot, and I felt it was the right choice. My mom was a really kind woman, but her first response was no. "I would miss you too much," she explained.

Always a people-pleasing momma's-girl, I told her I understood. Sadly, I settled down to sleep as she left my room.

Much later that night, she knocked on my door, woke me up, and changed my life. After thinking about it, she told me that she didn't want me to move out, that she had been dreading my departure to college and that she would be sad for me to leave earlier than she expected, but she told me that I could go. Tears forming in her eyes, she told me that she wouldn't have to worry about me because she was confident that the Holy Spirit was leading me. She explained, "I don't always have to be with you: I know that God is leading you."

I've been a Christian as long as I can remember, but **I had never seen such an inspiring illustration of faith.**

About a month later, my mom passed away unexpectedly. My sister and I were with my dad on a trip to Palm Springs for Easter Break. On Thursday, April 1st, 1996, I talked to her on the phone, and while I don't remember much about the conversation, I remember that we exchanged "I love yous" right before bed. On Good Friday, my dad woke me up in tears. My mom suffered an asthma attack, and her lungs had collapsed during the night. Characteristically unselfish, she was in my sister's bed as not to awaken my stepfather with her coughing.

Of course, dealing with my mom's death as a 17-year-old wasn't easy. While I experienced great peace two days later on Easter, and I truly felt assured that my mother was in Heaven, I still suffered. I couldn't understand how my friends could buy prom dresses and go on with normal life while my life was altered forever. Bouncing between denial and sadness, I made my way through High School and college. I missed my mom every day, but I felt my heart was healing.

And then I became a mom.

I had gone through some therapy at one point, and my therapist warned me that having kids would revive my grief in new ways. She was right. From the minute we brought my son home, I mourned her loss in a totally different way. I was constantly filled with questions, and every book I read seemed to contradict the one I read before it. And though I remembered her faith that the Holy Spirit would lead me, I was having trouble feeling lead by anything other than my desire for sleep.

Long days turned into short years, and even though my husband and I really struggled in the early days of parenthood, one night, on a very rare family trip, we sat on the porch of our hotel room, watching the sunset and discussing the possibility of having another child. We had previously decided that we were done having kids as it was hard for both of us, especially me, but as time passed and the fog of sleep deprivation lifted, I began to feel more confident. I felt the Holy Spirit leading me, and I often defaulted to helpful parenting strategies that my mom had used many years ago (I didn't really even remembered them, I just found myself using certain phrases that she taught me). So even though things had been challenging, we had learned to love parenting, most of the time, and we decided we would try to have another baby.

During my second pregnancy, as my son got a little older, I started to mourn the loss of my mom as a grandmother for my kids. Don't get me wrong, they have wonderful grandparents, but I have often cried, imagining what an amazing grandmother she would have been. How much she would have helped with Paxton while I was pregnant, the types of food she would have made for us, the games she would have played with him. I joked to my husband that my mom would have loved being a grandmother so much that she may have bought a house next door to us so she could help out with the kids. During our nightmarish potty training experience, I imagined her knocking on my door, offering me a break and some more baby wipes. I fantasized about calling her to catch up, to ask questions, to talk about things we loved, like Jesus and cooking. Praying for God's peace in this area, I realize that my kids will never know what they are missing. But I do, and it is a lot.

Nineteen weeks into my second pregnancy, I received shocking news. My sweet baby was a girl. My sister has three boys; I already had a boy, and for some reason, this news was incredibly unexpected. Throughout my pregnancy, I didn't really think that having a girl would be much different, but as soon as my daughter was born, I realized that I was wrong. I love my son more than my life, but as my daughter grows, I feel like I'm rekindling a mother/daughter relationship from the other side. I still miss my mom daily, and I would give almost anything to have one more hug from her in her silk robe. But when I hug my daughter and envision a future that I never had with my mom, my heart swells. Projecting onto an unknown and uncertain future, I can at least hope that, Lord-willing, while I will never have long weekly talks with my mom, my daughter might call for some girl talk when she is older. We named my daughter Everly, and one reason I like this name is because it feels like a combination of "happily" and "ever." My husband, my son, and my daughter are part of my happily ever after.

Part of me is still a broken teenager, and another part of me is still a clueless mom, but when I hold my sleeping baby and rub her forehead and cheeks, God's blessings and love are tangible. When I remember my mother's words in a tough parenting moment, and when I feel the Holy Spirit guiding and comforting me, I know that my mom was right so many years ago. She doesn't always need to be with me because, with the Holy Spirit's leading, I will be okay.

I Was Going to be the Perfect Mom
Drea DeyArmin

I was a perfect mom. I had well behaved kids. I was well rested. I was fit. I had a wonderful social life. My house was clean. My world was a role model to all. This was exactly what my life would be like in my head before I was even pregnant with my first child. I was ever so amazingly wise before there was ever an actual little human in my life as my own child. As a teenager, I was the recommended babysitter in the mommy circles. I spent a few summers being a nanny to two little girls. I had nephews I spent many hours with. And so, since I had been paid money to only watch a few kids for a set number of hours without the responsibility of having to clean the house, worry about the child's future, or the family budget, I figured I should have this whole mothering thing figured out when it was my turn. If only the mother whose baby is wailing would ask my opinion. If only the mom whose kid is throwing a temper tantrum in the store would seek my advice. With all that wisdom, maybe I should have written a parenting book.

Truth be told, I should have written that parenting book right then. At that moment when I had all the answers. Well, the moment that I thought I had all the answers.

At age 25, I gave birth to my first son armed with all these answers. I should have realized the moment I gave birth to him in a two-door Honda Civic on the side of the road that my mothering journey had already begun veering away from how I had planned for it to go. I thought I was still in early labor feeling intense contractions. We lived on the fourth floor of an apartment building and had to take the elevator down to the car. While I was walking down the apartment hall, I had to stop and work through a contraction. In the elevator, with several other people inside, I had to get down on the ground and work through a contraction. Right outside the elevator door, with others surrounding me with curious glances and hesitant faces, I dropped to the ground to work through another contraction. My husband finally got me to the car. Not even a mile down the road, I reached my hand down, touched something, and shockingly said, "Honey something is coming out!" My husband chose denial and said, "It can't be. We aren't there yet." At that moment, absolute instinct kicked in and I put my feet up on the dashboard and pulled my pants down.

My husband looked over and could see the top of the head. He pulled the car over, called 911, got over to my side of the car, and held onto the baby as moments later his whole body appeared into this world. Neither of us said a word to each other until I uttered the most precious phrase a mother who has just delivered her child has ever said:

"Do you think we should turn the hazards on?" My husband with equally precious words responded, "Oh, right."

What a wonderfully smooth arrival of our first little child into this world. And the next year of his life was just as equally smooth.

The hazards on a car, like the ones flashing on our mobile labor and delivery unit, are there to warn others driving by that we didn't really intend to be there on the side of the road, so please be careful around us. We likely should have had hazards flashing around us our entire first year of parenthood.

"New mom attempting to breastfeed!" Please be careful around me.

"Exhausted mom unable to speak of anything but diapers." Please be careful around me.

"A mom with a body flooding with hormones she has never experienced before." Please be careful around me.

Our newest member of the family was not happy to be out in the world. He screamed. He nursed for five minutes. Then he screamed. He would have his diaper changed. He would scream. He would go into the car. He would scream. He would fall asleep for 15 minutes. He would wake and scream. He was checked out by a pediatrician, and we were told that all was fine. He still screamed.

With all that screaming, I started screaming myself. Only mine came in the form of tears. Lots of them. And there was no hour of the day that was safe from the screaming or the crying. I was trying desperately to nurse. I absolutely could not believe all that was happening. This is very hard for me to admit, but I did not love my child. Oh, I wanted to. I did think he was adorable. But I didn't love him like I wanted to love him. I struggled hard with my emotions. I spent many days crying while he screamed. Then he spent the days screaming while I cried.

I spent a while trying to pretend that we were okay. Babies just cry. I am overreacting. I am not strong enough. After all, don't people have babies all the time? Even the animals seem to have this all down! I just must be doing something wrong if I can't figure this out.

After a while, though, my exhaustion and emotions prevented me from hiding the struggle. When people would ask, "How are you doing?" I got to where I would blurt out "Awful! Please pray for me. He doesn't ever sleep." I would say that to whoever asked. My usual screen of social politeness dropped. I remember telling friends, but then eventually anyone naive enough to ask—even the drug store cashier. **I was just too tired to try to pretend.**

One particular Sunday, an older lady in my life who was a grandma to me came to church and was parked a few rows from the front in her wheelchair. I had my son in a front pack and walked up to her and knelt down so she could see him. She was one naïve enough to ask how I was doing. And she heard the struggle. She began to just stroke my hand that was resting on her chair and say, "It will all be worth it. It will all be worth it. He will be worth it." Our conversation didn't last too long as he began to scream again and I couldn't see through the tears that began to flow in response to her encouragement.

When my son was around six months old, I believe I began to like him. Nursing was not smooth sailing at that point, but at least he latched for longer than five minutes. His sleeping stretches were slightly longer. I had spent a lot of time those first six months walking outside.

I've been asked if I walked because he would fall sleep on walks. No, as a baby, he didn't fall asleep on walks, but his crying sure seemed a lot quieter outside in the air than it did inside those four apartment walls. At first, I would put him in the sling, let him scream, and just walk. By six months, though, he would finally start to sleep on those walks. By the grace of God, we were making it, one day at a time.

At some point, we moved out to a new state and started living with some family until our new place was ready. We were starting to figure things out together. He would smile, laugh, and figure out a few words of his own. I guess you could say the fog was starting to clear. I don't know exactly when it started, but it eventually cleared.

On one particular night, everyone was gone for one reason or another, and it was just my almost one-year-old son and me in my family's house. We were listening to some lighthearted music and rolling a ball back and forth. Then, at some point, we hugged and he just kept his little arms around me and we started to dance to the music—me on my knees and he in my arms. And as I smelled his skin and swayed, I told him "I love you." And I started to cry, almost all of the tears that flowed those first awful months.

I realized that I did love him. I had said that I loved my little man during that first year many times. I had said it to him. But with all the struggles, I don't think I really felt it. And in that moment, I realized that I hadn't really loved him at the beginning. But, now, I loved him so much and was incredibly grateful that he was in my life. I thanked God for my son. I thanked God that we made it through that first year. I thanked God that I loved my son fully. Earlier, the fog started to clear, but now the sun was out! This was not the beginning of a perfect life with my son, but it was a defining moment indeed.

In the movie Cheaper by the Dozen, the mom says at the end, *"I guess you could say...we had a mess of theories about how to raise children.*

We still have a mess of children, but no theories." I believe my mothering a newborn started out with a whole bunch of theories and rules of how I was going to be a perfect mom surrounded by perfection in every area. That first year did not go as I had planned at all. But then, I was left with a dependence on God to get through it all, few theories, and a beautiful love for my baby.

I will take that trade.

The book I would write now on parenting would sure read a lot differently than the one I would have written before I had kids. If any of you heard any of those early thoughts that would have gone in my book, please discard them. The new book reads a lot differently. And I'm so glad it does.

Even Gestational Diabetes Has a Silver Lining

Tiffany Spire
sparkandpook.com

I've always been a fan of thinking positive and finding the silver lining. For example, when I had to leave all my friends and family and move to the other side of the country for the sake of my husband's career, I saw it as an opportunity to explore a part of the country that I might never have seen otherwise. I learned in the very beginning of my journey into motherhood that no matter what, even an illness such as my gestational diabetes, everything can have a silver lining. I didn't always think so.

I was 35 years old when I found out I was pregnant. My family physician recommended the midwife team at our local hospital to manage my care since I was in such good health. I wasn't overweight, and I had no known family history of major health problems. My initial meeting with the midwife went well, and I remember her telling me that I could eat as much as I wanted. As an afterthought, she added, "Just watch the carbs." At the time, this struck me as an odd comment, but in hindsight it was full of premonition. I dismissed the suggestion immediately since I didn't plan on pigging out on donuts and the like, though I didn't stop to think about the Coca-Cola I drank on a daily basis.

As my journey toward motherhood began, I was elated at the prospect of finally becoming a mom. Of course, I experienced all of the typical inconveniences of being pregnant, such as nausea, indigestion, back pain, and exhaustion. But the way I saw it, all of those things were simply reminders of the life that was forming inside me. For several months, I was filled with joy because of this long anticipated baby-to-be, and I was truly enjoying my pregnancy.

A few weeks into my third trimester, however, things changed. It was time for the glucose screening. This is a blood test performed on mothers-to-be to determine if their hormones have started to affect them in such a way that they have become glucose intolerant, or worse, have developed gestational diabetes. The process for this screening involves taking a baseline blood sample. Then the patient is given a large quantity of a very sugary substance to drink rapidly. After an hour, another sample of blood is drawn. The glucose levels of the blood samples are checked to see if they are within normal range (meaning, the insulin in your body is able to do its job).

I felt a little queasy after the glucose screening, but I didn't think much of it until I received a call a few days later to inform me that my glucose levels were higher than normal. This meant I would need to go back to the medical center for the more involved glucose tolerance test. I would have to perform all the same steps as the screening, but with two additional blood draws making it a three hour test. I remember they were only able to get two of the blood samples drawn before my body suddenly decided it could no longer tolerate the sickly sweet concoction, and up it came!

The next couple of weeks were a blur of follow-up tests and consultations that resulted in my diagnosis of gestational diabetes.

I was shocked and angry. *Why me? How could this happen to me? I'm healthy!* I was furious that someone else was now going to dictate how I should eat, and I'm the kind of person who doesn't take well to being told what to do. And then the pity party began. *Look at me, I have to count every single carbohydrate I eat. No more rosy pregnancy for me. No more eating what I want. Instead, I get to prick my finger four times a day to check my blood sugar level, and then feel like a failure when it turns out to be too high.*

At some point, a few weeks into the diagnosis, my anger and resentment simmered down into frustration and resignation.

Also around that time, the husband of a dear friend of mine was diagnosed with Parkinson's disease, a life-altering illness. This sad news put things into perspective for me. While my gestational diabetes altered my life significantly, it was a temporary condition that was treatable and had a high chance of being eliminated once the baby was born if managed carefully.

I gave up feeling sorry for myself—and also gave up my daily soda. I followed all of the nutritionist's advice and even consulted her regularly for additional help. But I still couldn't manage to get my blood sugar to stay low enough.

At this point, I was transferred to the care of the high risk doctor on the OB team in the hospital. I had initially been resistant to the idea of taking meds for my condition, but upon learning about all of the possible risks to the baby when mothers have gestational diabetes (including hypoglycemia, increased need for c-section, possible preterm delivery, and still birth), I knew I needed to do whatever it took to keep my baby healthy. What mother wouldn't? My attitude had completely changed from "woe is me" to "I got this!"

As it turns out, I only needed a low dose medication for my body's blood sugar to finally get back in balance. I was also required to go in to the medical center twice a week for a non-stress test. This required me to be hooked up to a fetal heart monitor for an hour each time in order for the medical team to monitor the baby's heart rate and level of movement.

I finished out the remaining weeks of my pregnancy under this regimen of finger sticks, strict diet, medication, and continual monitoring, all the while hoping and praying that it would be enough for the safe delivery of a healthy baby.

The proof would be in the pudding, so to speak. The doctors would need to know immediately upon delivery if the baby's blood sugar had been affected. *Was she hypoglycemic? Is she in respiratory distress? etc...*

After 30 hours of labor, I did end up needing a c-section because the baby was in a bad position. As soon as my daughter was born, blood tests were done on the both of us. The results were immediate; we were both declared healthy, with normal glucose levels.

What relief washed over me! I was filled with such happiness and a sense of triumph that I had been able to get things under control (including my attitude) and keep my daughter from harm.

I also felt a sudden sense of freedom. Now that the placenta was no longer shooting my hormones out of whack, I could, once again, eat what I wanted. While still in the hospital, I ordered the first Coke I'd had in weeks. In fact, I got so caught up in this newfound "freedom" that I went on a carb binge, just because I could.

So how does all this mean that gestational diabetes has a silver lining? Well, once I calmed down and stopped binging on carbohydrates, I began to eat a more balanced diet. Thanks to everything I had learned from the nutritionist who had worked with me through my treatment and all the research I did on my own about carbohydrates and glucose and blood sugar, I now understand a great deal more about what eating healthy really means. Before my diagnosis, I would not have thought twice about putting mashed potatoes or rice or pasta on my dinner plate. Now, I know better.

I lost a lot of weight after my daughter was born. In fact, I'm smaller now than I was before I got pregnant. When people ask how I did it, the only thing I can attribute it to is eating a lower-carb diet—and Coke is a rare luxury these days.

If I hadn't developed gestational diabetes, I don't think I'd be aware of just how harmful carbohydrates can be, especially considering how prevalent they are in the typical Western diet. I would probably just be steadily gaining weight as I had been before my pregnancy, and possibly working my way toward diabetes and a host of other problems.

Gestational diabetes was a big dark cloud for me during my pregnancy, and at the time I couldn't see the silver lining. If I'd had a better attitude about my situation, I could have handled it better, sooner. Luckily, I eventually came to grips with my condition and faced it head on. Because of my illness, I am now in a much healthier place, and my family is benefitting from that, too.

There are many kinds of dark clouds in the realm of motherhood. I've come under a few more of my own, but now I know to stop and look for the silver lining, because you only see it if you're looking for it. If you're currently stuck in a dark cloud of your own, I encourage you to look for your own silver lining.

A Legacy of Love

Leona La Perriere

My mother was at the kitchen sink rinsing some vegetables when I came into the kitchen. "Miss Yvonne called this morning and she would like some help with her Christmas cards this afternoon." Then she turned around to face me with that radiant smile of hers and added, "After thinking about your schedule for today and checking on it, it looked like you would be available to help her, so I told her that you would be there around 1:30 pm." I was a little disappointed about that, not that I really had any great plans for the afternoon, but going to Miss Yvonne's was not what I'd prefer to be doing. Yet there was no way I would want to say that to my mother. You see, Miss Yvonne was an older blind lady that lived alone, and our family had chosen to be her friends, her helpers, her guardians. So that's how I spent the afternoon, and it turned out to be a rather nice day after all.

As I walked in the door after my visit, my mother mentioned that Miss Yvonne had called her and said how she had felt my smile all afternoon and that it had really lifted her spirits. Another dazzling smile and a kiss and hug from my mother as she thanked me for being so thoughtful and cheerful and for making our family proud. Yes, I did get a lump in my throat and a little more pep in my step knowing that I not only did the right thing, but I did it the right way.

Mom and Dad strongly believed in caring for others, being there for others, developing responsibility in their children and helping them learn how to do things in as cheerful a way as possible. I can still hear my mother singing as we cooked a meal together for a neighborhood family who needed an extra hand since their mother had just come home from the hospital with a new little baby girl. We did this several times that month, and my mother got a meal train going with other families in the neighborhood to deliver meals, too! It was only later that I realized that with four other children in the family (all under ten years old), no other family members that lived close by to help her. Having had a very hard time with the delivery of the baby at the hospital, that Mrs. Hebert needed us and appreciated the help so very much.

Then, there was Mr. Lund, a very nice older widowed gentleman who lived by himself, who commented several times to my mom and dad how he loved watching our family go to church together on Sunday mornings. I heard my mother mention to my dad that she thought he sounded a little wistful and lonely and they asked him if he would like to join us. The biggest smile crossed his face and... Yep, you guessed it! Mr. Lund started joining us for Mass each Sunday and a light breakfast after that. It was a nice start to our week.

As you can imagine, growing up in a family of six children—four girls and two boys—was not always a bed of roses. We did have our moments, and mom and dad were as diligent in showing us the same care and respect that we were being taught to show to others. They felt that it was even more important to do this for family and not just for others.

I now appreciate the way they delegated our family jobs. As we grew older and if the jobs required some learning curve, our parents taught us how they wanted them done. When we had mastered them, those jobs became our responsibility. It was all part of being a family. We discovered that team work worked to our advantage. When some jobs were taking longer to do, we would all pitch in to help the others and get the jobs done more quickly. As my parents used to say, "The faster the work gets done and gets done right, the more time we have for fun things!" And we did have a lot of fun together.

School and learning were sacred in our family. I think we got perfect attendance nearly every year. I still remember how our parents instilled the love of learning in us by "studying" with us every night. They took this role of a parent very seriously and often reminded us of the rewards of a good education.

I learned about mediation in the way that my parents did not take sides when a situation arose between some of the brothers and sisters. They made us talk it out together, discussing what happened and what was to be done about it. We always needed to be respectful to each other, even though we would probably rather have duked it out! If a punishment was in order, my parents made sure that the punishment fit the crime. We were not always in agreement with this, but looking back, they did a pretty good job!

These are just some examples of life in the Dupont family. Positive attitudes, respect, doing the right things the right way, taking responsibility for your actions, putting your best foot forward, and knowing and remembering that what you say and do will always reflect on our family are some of the tenets we were raised on. Little did I know when I was growing up that being encouraged to move through these "challenges" on a daily basis would instill in me the leadership qualities that helped me be successful in so many parts of my life.

Lucky for me, my husband's family had many of these same guidelines. I am proud to say that my husband and I have chosen to make these same tenets a part of our family life. Our children grew up hearing the stories about our childhoods—the good, the bad, and the ugly—and how our parents were the best parents they knew how to be. They grew up realizing that our parents were great role models and that we wanted to honor them by being the best parents we could be. Together, we participated in walk-a-thons, bike-a-thons, helping out at soup kitchens, sorting out Thanksgiving baskets for needy families, ringing the Salvation

Army Christmas bell, delivering homemade meals to help families in time of need, and so many other activities where we learned just how important it was to care for others.

When our daughter, Michelle, was at Children's Hospital in Philadelphia recuperating from an emergency brain surgery, the outpouring of support from so many people was overwhelming and totally unexpected! They wisely reminded me that, "one good turn deserves another," and now it was their turn to help me! I learned how to be gracious in accepting their help.

When our son, Dan, was in medical school, he also volunteered at a local hospital in their indigent/homeless out-patient clinic in what little spare time he had. The United Way funds for this program had been cut drastically, and he wanted to do something to help get the medicines these people needed. He called me about what needed to be done to organize a 5K run to raise funds for this program. Of course, I objected that he was in medical school, and how will he ever find time to do something like this? His response: *"Mom, this is what our family does. This is how we were brought up. Please help me with this since you have experience with chairing some St. Jude's Bike-a-thons."* Guess he told me! He and several other medical students put together a very successful 5K, and after all the bills were paid, they were able to present a check to the hospital for over $2,000.00!

Our daughter, Monique, was born with hip dysplasia, not life threatening, but serious enough. She had her first hip surgery at eleven months, then another surgery when she was in first grade, then another surgery when she was a freshman in high school. The toughest one was the high school surgery. She was very involved in many activities and the surgery set her back quite a bit. Yet every afternoon after school she had quite a few friends and even teachers stop by the house to visit and/or do homework with her. Her positive attitude and smile kept them coming.

Another family activity was to work with Habitat for Humanity. It was quite rewarding to be working alongside the family whose house we were helping to build. When our children were too young to actually participate in building the houses, they were busy making sandwiches or running the errands that needed to be taken care of. When they turned sixteen, we officially presented them with their own tool belts and tools so that they could now build with us. It was a proud moment for all of us that lasted through the years. When Monique and her husband were living in Philadelphia a couple of years ago, she proudly wore her tool belt as she worked Habitat in Philly.

School and learning were a high priority for us, too. By participating in school activities and being active participants in the learning process, we wanted to instill in our children the love of learning and the pride that comes from a job well done.

They learned the rewards and consequences of their actions, studying, and team sports—such as earning scholarships or having to sit out of a game.

Our children are always watching us and learning from us. We are the examples for their future. Parenting is the ultimate form of love. It takes a lot of hugs and kisses, help from others, tears, laughter, understanding, courage, integrity, laughter, inspiration, prayers, strength, and did I mention laughter?

There is certainly a ripple effect that I see here in motion... From when my husband and I grew up to our own family and now our children's families. We will keep those ripples going—who knows where they will take us!

In That Moment

Claire Ditowski

It began with one sentence: "I'm so sorry, but the situation is very grave." It was that one moment, the moment that began a new chapter in my life. It was then that I knew my life would now be divided by the time before this loss and after. It's a line we create when experiencing a great loss—a loss of any kind, really—one that cuts down to your soul and creates an ache that doesn't go away. Oh, it may ease with time, but the scar remains. And it almost becomes welcome, one that we are loathe to miss. In feeling the ache, we remember. And in the remembering, comes the validation of the precious thing that was lost.

We all experience various losses throughout our lives, as I had before losing my little boy. The year before, I had an early miscarriage. Brimming with excitement, I had barely begun sharing my happy news, and then it was over. When I finally became pregnant again, it was with a mixture of such hope and anxiety. The joy was complete as I passed that "magic" number week 12, only to be dashed as I ended up in the emergency room. Put on bedrest, I was determined to make it through to the end. My family and friends rallied around us. My parents, who lived close by, along with a friend who came to stay with us for days on end at a time, took care of my two little boys and our home. Friends came with meals, bearing gifts of books and magazines to pass the time as I lay in bed or on the couch.

Then one day I went in for a checkup. I had been very lightheaded for a few days, actually passing out at times. I asked for an ultrasound to make sure things were ok. The doctor didn't think I needed another one and recommended that I start to move around a little more. It is still with regret that I remember that day, wishing I had had the courage to stand up to him and demand an ultrasound. But, we chose to trust his knowledge and we went home. I tried to do what he said, even having short bursts where I felt better. One morning as I woke up, I knew that something was wrong. My belly was so large, far bigger than it should have been at the time. And every time that I tried to do anything, I felt as if I would faint. As I was sitting in the doctor's office, waiting to be seen, another expectant mother came to sit next to me. Eager to share and connect over swollen bellies and ankles, we compared due dates. "You're so big, you must be having twins," she said. With that comment came the confirmation that something was indeed wrong. As soon as the doctor saw me, she measured me and immediately sent us to the hospital. It was there that I received the ultrasound I had requested days before. The screen showed a belly full of blood, a placenta almost fully abrupted, and a sweet, baby boy not long for this life. The doctor's next words as he sat on the side of my bed were, "I'm so sorry. I missed it." And that is how the next week in the hospital became my new timeline division. The one I refer to as my before and after in my journey of motherhood.

People are so kind. They want to help, to comfort, to take away your hurt. The love that was poured out on us was amazing. But, there are some who said things like, *"it wasn't the right time,"* or *"try not to think about it,"* or *"just be thankful for the boys you have."* And I didn't get frustrated because I knew. I had been the one before who tried to find the right thing to say or do, even though I had not experienced that pain.

There were also the ones who seemed sent from heaven to comfort my heart. It was these few who stood beside us and a tiny hole in the ground. On a beautiful, warm May day, my husband and I were surrounded by those few. There was the dear friend who did truly know my pain, a pain that I had not understood as we buried her little boy on a cold, wintry day just a few years before. The family members who stood by my hospital bed and prayed for a miracle for our two lives, helping me keep my faith when only one of our lives was saved. And my two little dark haired boys, who only knew that now, instead of just one, two of our babies were in heaven. They stood there next to us as I looked down at them with very different eyes. I had loved being their mother, devoting my whole life to them to do it. But, in that moment putting that tiny box into the ground, I had a new perspective; one that I had never wanted.

A few weeks ago, I ran into someone I went to college with over twenty years ago. Full of hope and anticipation, we had stepped out into our futures. In that time, our only contact had been peering into each other's lives through social media. As we stood there, trying to fit twenty years into a few minutes, I was amazed at how quickly the subject of losing a child came up. We both were fortunate enough to have four children, but with quite large age gaps between a couple of them, explained by the losses of our babies. How quickly the invisible bond that draws two hearts together is woven. **Because in that moment, you are understood.** Another mother who knows the heartache of knowing one or more of her children are missing. A child that she loved from the moment she saw the line on the test, a child that she dreamt of holding and loving, a child whose future is not in her arms, she understands.

I looked at her beautiful face, more lined, her hair laced with gray, and saw not the young woman twenty something years old, but a mama who has experienced that joy of expectancy and the pain of loss. We spoke of this bond. We spoke of how sad it is to have it, and yet so comforting to just be known. We spoke of how perspective changed from the moment that line is drawn. It's in the after that we begin to see how precious life is. We see how fragile it is and how quickly it can change. The loved ones we have begin to be seen through different eyes. We don't always remember to appreciate the moment, but when we are reminded of what we have lost, we remember that difference.

In the end, there are some mamas who don't show the heartache, suffering silently, wondering if people will understand. Any woman who has lost a baby to miscarriage, a stillbirth, and even an abortion, has lost their child. I learned so much during that time from those around me who showed me that they understood, that shared their stories with me. And those who may have not had the same loss that I did, but still reached out, willing to hurt with us, bringing comfort in our loss.

I learned it's ok to grieve, and it's important to have something tangible to remember the one who was lost to us by. Every year, we go visit that grave, to remember, to feel, to not forget, and to look at the boys we have with us as the miracles they are. We watch them grow, some looking down at me now, with their arms wrapped around me, and we know that as full and as wonderful, and as miraculous it is to have them, there are ones missing. Not with us now, but never forgotten. And when I am privileged enough to have a precious woman share her story with me, I get it. I understand.

And somehow, whenever that happens, a tiny piece of my heart heals.

Children Gave Me Confidence

Crystal McClean

castleviewacademy.com

Everyone has their own story, their own struggles and challenges. However, we all change forever with the birth of our children, and it was no different for me. One lesson that has been difficult for me to learn is how to believe in myself. Over the past seven years, I have been trying.

Tristan was born premature. I trusted the doctor who told me everything was fine and to head home and continue on with my day... Only to return back to the hospital in later in full labor. I didn't trust my body and what it was telling me—I believed the doctor. It wasn't until they tried to stop the labor 14 hours later that I knew for certain what was happening, but by then I knew it was too late. Rushed by ambulance between hospitals in different cities, I almost gave birth at 100mph. At 28 weeks and 5 days, Tristan was born at 3 pounds and 7 ounces.

The next five and a half weeks were very stressful, trying desperately to express milk and deliver it each day to the hospital, which was 35 miles away, and dependent on a ride from my sister-in-law on the days my husband worked. The hospital-grade pump was my constant companion. We'd meet up every two hours around the clock. It went everywhere with me. Even so, I was barely keeping up with Tristan. There were many occasions when I would call the hospital to check in with Tristan and the nurse would tell me that if I didn't get milk there in the next hour he would be getting formula. My body was still letting me down.

Overall, things went pretty smooth while Tristan was in the neonatal ward and special care baby unit, with just a couple of frights along the way. A heart murmur and worries about his retinas cleared themselves by the time of his due-date.

Tristan came home five weeks before his due date (not receiving a drop of formula!)—a wonderful surprise, as we were told he wouldn't be released until at least his due date. It was a bit of a rush to get Phil and the car seat to the hospital before the cut-off time. Otherwise, it would be too cold outdoors and he wouldn't be released.

Phil and I had talked about getting an angel mat that would alert us if Tristan's breathing stopped, as he was still occasionally having periods of apnea in the hospital. He'd only been disconnected from all of the wires and tubes 48 hours before, and the nurses said this was a stressful time for them. But we decided to trust in Tristan, and in ourselves.

We need not have worried, as the only time Tristan slept was in my arms or while in the stroller while out walking! To tell the truth, I could be assured of one hour each night that I could sleep as well as Tristan. This was at 3 a.m. when ER was on TV. The sounds of all the beeps and blurps on the show must have made Tristan feel comfortable as he'd sleep right through the only show I had any interest in. Until just last month, he still wouldn't go to sleep without at least a night light, and he still needs background music to doze off.

At times I actually thought I was going crazy due to having only about 3-4 hours of sleep over the course of 24 hours, and not all at once. But I knew this wouldn't last forever. **Babies are only babies for a short period of time, even if at the time it feels it will never end.**

I breastfed Tristan, as I knew for so many reasons that it was the best thing for him. And for me. I felt it was the one thing I was doing right. It helped so much with bonding when I was in the depths of depression and didn't even have the energy to speak out loud. It was not always easy with a premature and very colicky baby, in the country with the lowest rate of breastfeeding in Europe. Even many health professionals from midwives to psychologists told me to stop from the first day out of hospital. But I had faith in myself in this one area, if none other, and I didn't stop until after our second child was nearly a year old.

Just when I thought I was getting the hang of this parenting thing, we were thrown a curveball. Tristan had a bit of a cough, and the health visitor sent us to see a doctor as he was also pale. We were then sent to the hospital, where Tristan was given a blood transfusion because his iron levels were almost undetectable. They said if his cold moved to his lungs that it could very well kill him. Tristan was a happy, healthy little babe, and I didn't even know he was so ill. It really shook me to my core that I hadn't realized this. So exactly six months after his due date, I sat holding Tristan while he received the blood of a generous donor into a vein in his head.

Twenty-seven months after Tristan came into our world, Kallista was born 24 days early. This time, I was more prepared, and we were home the same day. After a later weekend stay in the hospital for some light-therapy due to jaundice, things were much easier than they had been with Tristan. Kallista has been a very healthy little girl and always brings a smile to my face. Kallista's birth definitely had a healing effect for my mind.

I continued breastfeeding, going tandem for almost a year. In fact, things went so much easier this time, that I was able to donate over 24 liters to the milk bank. Doing this made me so happy, and it helped me to have more faith in my own body after its betrayal of early births and lack of milk in Tristan's early months.

After overcoming these early obstacles, our next hurdle was to begin our homeschooling journey. Once again, I was not taking the same path as the majority of the population here in Northern Ireland. My husband was totally supportive, and that's all that has mattered. I just couldn't send Tristan to school as were finally beginning to properly bond. Compulsory school age here is four, the youngest in the world, and I didn't want my children to have the stress of homework at four and for them not to get to know each other in childhood and bond with each other. I had never considered homeschooling before having children, but it something that I do trust myself with. It isn't always easy, and there will be tough times, but that's just family life in general. It was meant for us. Our children can learn at their own pace and learn what they are interested in. We spend all of our time together, and we enjoy it.

To help me overcome my self-doubts, I have tried to ignore the people who are critical of the way we raise our children. When needed, I have found people with similar interests and who are supportive. When I was breastfeeding, it was a nearby La Leche League group. When I'm feeling isolated now, I turn to connecting with friends back home in Canada and around the world through Facebook. I have also joined many Facebook groups that are focused on premature babies, breastfeeding, and homeschooling. I am very much an introvert, and although I tend not to speak up much in these groups, I know they are there when I need them, and I gain a lot just by reading through and feeling part of a community.

Even so, I still go through many periods of self-doubt about everything (sometimes on a weekly basis), and I know I always will. But I try to remember that everyone does. It's normal and it's okay. There are and will be many others who are also dealing with similar thoughts and emotions.

I try to take my worries and turn them into something positive when I can. This year, I will be more involved with Tiny Life, a charity that helped me when I had to leave Tristan behind at the hospital. I'm looking forward to helping to make their services and information more accessible. By doing this, I will be helping other parents get more information (and thus power) to believe in themselves and their relationship with their premature child. Having trust in myself helps with the bonding process, which is very important.

Another way that I try to give back and lift myself up is through blogging. I can share what we do at home with others. I always hope that someone will enjoy our activities and give them a try. Spending time with my children and seeing the way that they totally trust me makes me want others to enjoy the same pleasures.

From time to time, I also blog in support of charities, and I always feel better for it. It helps me to put things in perspective, remembering how far we have come and how fortunate we are.

Looking back with some perspective, I can see that a lot of my doubts weren't actually my own, but rather the voices of others who didn't understand what I was doing because it wasn't the "normal" thing to do. I couldn't control the premature birth of my children, but I have been healing emotionally by believing in own body, mind, and soul once more.

If you had told me when I was twenty that twenty years later I'd be a breastfeeding, baby wearing, homeschooling mom in a foreign country where I don't agree with the politicians, the fighting, or the riots over religion, I'd have looked at you like you had three heads. There's no way I'd be anywhere but my hometown with kids in the public school system. It's taken a lot of courage to accomplish what I have. And an undeniable trust in myself to achieve it. It doesn't always feel this way, but looking back and thinking about conversations I've had with Phil, it was the birth of my children that gave me confidence.

This Wasn't My Plan

Renee Kemper
thatsjustlife.com

There is an age old saying, "Everything happens for a reason," or maybe you have heard it as, "God meant for it to be." However you look at it, I have said it probably a million times myself. Usually it is said to someone to make them feel better when they are going through a difficult time. Throughout my life, lots of people have said those words to me. I would reflect on them, but never really stopped to think about how true it might have been. There are lots of small, seemingly unimportant events, which lead to me being a mom of two pretty incredible teenagers.

Being a mom has lots of different meanings to people. I think there is an image out there of the perfect mom, but I am here to tell you, that image does not exist. At least not for me. At 18 years old, I was married and pregnant with my son, Dakota. Of course I had dreamed of all the magical things about being married and being a mom. You know the fairy tale stuff that most girls dream of. That was me. I thought I had life under control—I had dreams. I had my plans all mapped out.

After moving out of state, my son just over a year old, I found myself filing for divorce and officially becoming a single mom. I don't even think *scared to death* could begin to describe how I felt. I was 500 miles away from my friends, family, and most of all, my mom.

How was I supposed to deal with all of this alone? How had I let myself get into a situation like this? My head was full of fear and anxiety. Somehow, I woke up every single day and pushed through it. People told me, "It will all be okay, everything happens for a reason." But what reason could there be for this? Then, things started to happen, although I wouldn't know until years later just how important all those small events would be. That should have been my first clue that I had no control, but I didn't see it yet.

Through the days, weeks and months that followed that 500 mile move and divorce, I made up my mind that I could be a single mom. I could be strong and I could raise my son no matter what the circumstances. I went back to college, I got an amazing job, and before I knew it, I was living my life again and happy! It was not easy, and I do not mean to make it sound like it was. But the trials I went through to get to that point would take a full book to get through. My point is that anyone can do it. You just have to make up your mind and then take the steps. Don't be afraid to lean on people. Sometimes, the people you might think are least likely to help wind up being the people who help the most.

I made some lifelong friends along the way, but probably the most important friendship that came from all of this was my friendship with Aaron, who is now my husband. Again, with the "everything happens for a reason"—I didn't know at the time just how important he would be in shaping me into the mom that I am today. I had become stronger than I ever thought I could be, and I was sure I could be everything my son needed. But after seeing the relationship that he and my son had built, I knew I was wrong. That was a big turning point for me. Even though I always felt like I had a handle on things, someone or something would creep up on me to test my faith, my strength and my knowledge. I realized at that point, I would never fully have it all under control; I just had to live on faith. As I am sure many of you know, it is *hard* to give up that control!

I hope as you read this, you can relate to where I am at this point. In a very short amount of time, I went from being married, having a son, and moving 500 miles from my hometown, to being divorced and a single mom, to finding my soul mate. What an insane two years of my life as a mom! It felt like I went from being a teenager to a real life adult overnight.

Fast forward six years, we had moved back to my hometown and were trying to get pregnant. I love being a mommy and I wanted another little life to fill our hearts. Just like any couple, we made plans. We knew what we wanted, and we did everything we could to make it happen. But no matter what we did, we just were not having any luck. So, once again, we decided to just let go and trust that there was a reason and a plan that we just didn't know about yet. I found myself as a mom and a wife, yet again struggling to give up that control, to **give into the truth that I really had no control to start with**. And if I didn't truly believe it then, over the next three years it would be undeniable.

We lived in a nice house, in a nice neighborhood with great neighbors. Sounds like everything a mom would want for her kids, right? I talked my husband into moving back to my home town because of the lakes and rivers. He loves to fish, and that bonding time with him and my son was invaluable. So when our neighbor told us about a house for rent out by the huge lake in our town, I knew we had to check it out. The yard was huge, and it was close to the lake, but the house was so small. It was less than half the size of what we were living in at the time. While my mind was telling me *no way you are moving into that house*, my heart was telling me *it had to happen*. So, we called the guy and told him we would take it. Much to my mind's relief, he said it had already been rented. I felt bad for my husband, but was secretly thankful, because that house was definitely not a part of my plan.

Days and weeks went by, and in spite of all of my plans and rationale, I could not shake the feeling that we needed that tiny house by the lake. I didn't know why, but I just could not get it out of my head. About three weeks after we were told that the house had been rented, the guy called us back to tell us that the original renter had backed out and that the keys were ours if we wanted them. How weird that I could not stop thinking about that house, even though there were parts of me that didn't want it, and then there it was. It was ours. So without knowing why on earth I agreed to it, we started packing and moved into that tiny house.

No sooner did we get moved in, it was time for school to start. I couldn't believe that my son was about to start 1st grade! And I was really excited to see that there was a little girl that lived across the street from us. It was always very important to me for him to have close friends, especially since he was an only child at the time. Dakota and Dom hit it off from the start. They were together at the bus stop every morning since that first day of school, and played together every day after school. She was at our house pretty much all of the time. But the more she was with us, the more we realized something was not right.

As a mom, you know when something is off with a child, even when it isn't your own. Everyone has a different parenting style, but that isn't what I am talking about. I could not put my finger on it. I was still a new mom, in my eyes. I don't care how old your kids are, you are always a new mom, because every day brings a new experience as a parent. But even know moms have that gut instinct.

Then it happened. One small moment in time, that would change our lives forever. She came to me one day before heading out to swim, along with a friend's daughter, to show me the bruises. Bruises that spanned her entire body, front and back, from head to toe. My heart sank, my stomach in knots, I had no idea what to do. As I was on the phone with my friend, the dad stormed through my door, cussing and freaking out— telling her to get home (I'm not going to repeat his words to her). At that moment, I knew what I had to do. I told her to stay put, told him to get out of my house, and I called the police. I was shaking uncontrollably, alone in a house with three kids, standing up to this giant man. Where in the world did that strength come from? Then, I realized I was not only shaking, but crying, and on the phone with 911. At this point, anything I had gone through in my life as a mom was trivial in comparison.

The police came, DHS came, CASA came. All these people in my house, so much happening so quickly. They took pictures, they talked to her, and then it hit me; I had just changed her life forever. She had to pack a bag, and they were taking her to a foster care facility. Within an hour, I was watching her ride away in a car and was told that we could have no communication with her. Even though I knew I was doing the right thing, I felt like my heart had been ripped out, as if she were my own daughter and I was never going to see her again. My husband reminded me, once again, that I am not in control and to just keep the faith. So I did just that. I called and emailed relentlessly to check up on her and get as much information as I could, though it was not much.

I had to be in court the next week and there was not enough notice for anyone to get off work to go with me. I felt my strength being tested once again, walking in there alone. I keep saying I had to let go and live on faith, but that is kind of the point of my story. It seems like the instant I let go, that is when things happen.

Remember back when we talked about getting pregnant? Well, it turns out that we were to have another child, but there were other plans in the works.

Her attorney came to me that day in court and told me that Dom wanted to stay with us! Without a second thought, I told her *yes!* Make it happen. We could not be foster parents, because that would have meant her staying in foster care for another three months while we did classes. We wanted her back into semi-normal life, so we opted for guardianship instead.

And, in that instant, we had two kids.

We moved out of that house, back into town. It gives me chills to think back to when I didn't want to live in that tiny little house. And it is even clearer to me now, than ever, why we were there in the first place. She went through some really tough times. My son stood by her side and fought for her, too, which at the time seemed normal. I think about how courageous he really was, to be eight years old and dealing with all of this. Nothing of course, could compare to her courage. Courage she had because, for once in her life, someone was standing up for her.

I would love to put on a happy face and say that we just got through it, but that would be lying. I spent many nights crying big, real tears. Sometimes I think my uncontrollable emotions came because, once again, I had no control. All I could do was give her unconditional love, help her learn and grow, and teach her to have strength, because that is what moms do.

In March of 2010, we adopted Dom. She was officially our baby girl. My son had a sister. From that day on, I have been a mom living simply on faith. I make small plans, but not big ones. Because I know that no matter what my plans might be, I ultimately have no control. What I do hold for certain and have learned after all of this, is that I am a mom. I am not perfect, and I never will be. But I have strength, I have love, and I have faith. Because of that, I have two incredible teenagers who fill my life to the brim with stress, happiness, and unconditional love. I would not have it any other way, even though this wasn't my plan all along.

More Incredible Than My Dreams

Christina Mathis

thetransparencychronicles.blogspot.com

I always knew I wanted to be a mom. What I didn't know, though, was just how much this was going to require. When my husband and I first married, we talked about having as many children as God would give us, and just a couple of months after we were married, we found out we were expecting our first child. Sadly, this pregnancy ended in a miscarriage. One year later, though, we did have a beautiful baby girl. A couple of years after that, we had another beautiful girl. She was followed just 15 months later by our chubby, full-of-life, baby boy. I was ecstatic! My heart was full caring for my children.

My husband, however, was not at all happy. After some rather difficult years, he left our family. It was now up to me to be both mother and father—sole provider, comforter, and spiritual guide. The burden of caring and providing for three children was great. Thankfully, I had the love and support of my family, friends, and church. God made Himself evident in more ways than I can count. As trying as this time was, these are the times my children and I look back on fondly. One of them will say, "Remember when we used to make a fortress in the living room every Friday night and watch movies?" Another will respond, "Oh! That was so fun! We'd try to sneak out of Austin's fortress because he kicked us in his sleep."

Austin... The love of my life, my heart, my forever four-year-old. He seemed to be a healthy baby, but in reality he wasn't. He was born with a tumor in the core of his brain. It grew and grew until it couldn't grow anymore; then when he was just four years old, it took his life. There were no outward symptoms until right before he died. Even then, his doctor didn't suspect a tumor. It wasn't until after Austin had passed away that the tumor was discovered. Looking back, I can see this was God's grace. It was an inoperable tumor. But instead of watching him suffer through his final days, we have only good memories. Easter of 2004 was the last time we would all be together. I remember laughing at his silliness as the kids hunted Easter eggs at my parents' house, watching him sit on my dad's lap and help him open birthday presents, taking what would be our last family picture.

After Austin's death, keeping my little family together became even more of a priority. It was now just me and my girls, and over time we became inseparable. The next few years brought many tears as we worked through our grief, much laughter as we told stories about Austin's antics, and plenty of reflection and thanksgiving on God's faithfulness through it all.

And He was faithful, even through the dark days that lay ahead. As we each worked through the grief in our own way, I noticed that one of my daughters was having more trouble than the rest of us. She was depressed and opened up to me that she had been cutting and had tried more than once to take her own life. She had been losing weight and was refusing to eat, so I knew also that she was struggling with an eating disorder. Years earlier, a friend had directed us to some wonderful Christian counselors who helped us deal with our grief following my son's death; now, they would help save my daughter's life. Because of client confidentiality, the counselor could not tell me what was said in their time together, but she did tell me the best thing I could do for my daughter was to let her know she is loved—no matter what. No judgment, no lectures, no speeches on what was right and what was wrong. She already knew that. What she desperately needed to get through this time was unconditional, unwavering love.

Unfortunately, not everyone in our lives was saying the same thing. Family and friends were telling me she was too far gone. Because of her dad's issues, there was no hope for her. She was doomed for a life of hurt and shame. I should stop fighting it and just let her go. Because their father wasn't involved in their lives, my girls were destined to live their lives searching for love and acceptance through giving themselves to men.

I refused to accept this, however, and devoted myself to relentlessly praying for my children. Just as Deuteronomy commands, I claimed God's promises over them. I prayed Scripture over them. I spoke God's love into them. **I reminded them that God has bigger plans for their lives than they could ever imagine.** That the struggles they had faced weren't pointless—God had a reason and He was going to use them in great ways. I used every opportunity, every situation, every circumstance to point them to Christ, His love for them, and what He was doing in their lives.

I knew that in order for my daughter to heal completely, she needed a fresh start. Life had been grueling the past few years. We all needed to start over—just the three of us. Where we were was becoming toxic to my children's emotional and spiritual well-being, so I began earnestly praying that God would open doors to move us somewhere that we could all heal. Somewhere that showed grace rather than judgment, love rather than condemnation. Just a few weeks later, I was presented with a job opportunity in a town about 100 miles north from where we were. It was exactly what we needed. In the two years that we have been here, I have seen my daughters grow emotionally and spiritually like never before.

They have become the strong Christian women that I knew they could be. They have had the chance to tell their stories and help others who have faced the same struggles.

It's not unusual for our home to be full of young people. And, to my heart's delight, most of them have "adopted" me as their mom. They talk to me about their problems. They come to me for advice. One even moved in with me during the (very brief) time my children were visiting their out-of-state grandparents. She couldn't stand the thought of me being alone!

These kids might not be my biological children, but I sure do love them like they are mine.

As I am quickly approaching my empty nest days, I am so thankful for the experiences that motherhood has brought. I wouldn't trade the past 20 years for anything in the world! Every sleepless night, every tear, every joy, every heartache... It has all been worth it to see my daughters thrive and live their best possible lives. Motherhood has ended up being even more incredible than I dreamed it would be!

Acceptance
Monica Brietenstein
mommee-truths.blogspot.com

Late one afternoon in the summer of 2013, my husband and I sat anxiously awaiting the results of a series of psychological tests that our six-year-old daughter, Bronwyn, had taken during the previous weeks. Until that point in time, our experience with the medical community had been less than ideal.

No one, thus far, had been able to provide us with a satisfactory explanation for our daughter's cognitive, developmental, and social delays. We simply wanted an answer; a definitive reason why. Neither one of us, however, was prepared for when the psychologist said simply, "Bronwyn has Autism Spectrum Disorder (ASD)."

All I remember about the rest of that meeting is that I held my husband's hand a little too tightly and tried a little too fiercely not to blink, lest the tears spill over. During the drive home, I struggled to accept that a professional had just formally diagnosed my child as having special needs. In so little time. so much had changed—Bronwyn had ASD. And yet nothing had changed. Bronwyn would only ever know what she and all children are deserving of—acceptance.

It has always been my belief that "knowledge is power," so I took to the internet in search of help. I was determined to learn all that I could about ASD to ensure that my child could be given every opportunity to live her best possible life. I was fortunate enough to find a group of phenomenal women—all of whom were mothers of children with ASD. Although I was scared and apprehensive, I willed myself to attend one of their weekly meetings. And the truth of the matter is that I cried throughout that entire first meeting. Yes, I felt sad, and yes, I felt extremely overwhelmed. I realized, however, that I was not alone.

In each and every one of those extraordinary women, I found encouragement and support, compassion and understanding. I felt reassured, knowing that I would never again have to walk the journey alone. That group of women showed Bronwyn and I what I had promised myself she would only ever know in this lifetime—acceptance. Acceptance for the amazing girl that she was.

What I learned about ASD is that it affects all whom it touches differently. That is why people with ASD are referred to as being *on the spectrum*. Each person's symptoms and severity differ. Sometimes the difference is mild—other times, vast. Although people with ASD are regarded as "different" from what is defined as neurotypical, they are not less-than and should only ever know acceptance.

Bronwyn understands that ASD causes her brain and body to sometimes think and act differently than other people's brains and bodies. As she matures she may come to understand that, in more technical terms, ASD impairs her neurological development, her social interactions, and her verbal and non-verbal communication. That time is not now. Now is the time for Bronwyn to know, as should all children, acceptance for who she is. My daughter is absolutely beautiful in the way that matters most—on the inside. Her smile is infectious, and she is kind and compassionate.

Although Bronwyn has all of these remarkable qualities, ASD interferes in her social interactions with others. Interpreting social cues and non-verbal communication are daily challenges for her, and expressing her thoughts clearly and understandably can be difficult. As her mother, I have cried many tears on Bronwyn's behalf. I have stood at a distance and watched proudly as she has tried so hard to put into practice the many skills that she has been taught at her therapy groups. I have watched her attempt to make friends, to engage peers in conversation, and to sustain play with them. And I have also watched heartbrokenly as those same peers have ignored her, run away from her, and laughed at her. In spite of how those children have treated her, though, Bronwyn's beautiful spirit soars. Even more incredible is that she harbors no ill-will towards those children. Bronwyn has only ever shown them what they, like her, are deserving of—acceptance.

This past winter, my daughter played Novice Girls hockey. Her position was right-wing, and throughout the season that never changed. The coaching staff understood that in order for Bronwyn to thrive within that environment, familiarity, consistency and routine were essential for her. Before each practice and game, my family would ask Bronwyn what it was she was supposed to do once she got on the ice. By the season's end she had learned that she needed to "skate hard" and "chase the puck"—two simple concepts. During her time as a Wilmot Wolverine, Bronwyn's teammates showed her patience, kindness and respect. They only ever showed Bronwyn what she and all children are deserving of—acceptance.

The concept of acceptance (not to be confused with approval) has been at the forefront of most of my life. In my late teens, I made a decision that my family would not accept. Having been on the other side of scathing rejection myself, I vowed that should I ever become a mother there were very few choices my child could make that I would not accept. I naively believed that the question of acceptance would arise when my children were older. I had thought that it would concern issues such as who they would love, what political party they would support, or what religious faith they would join.

I never imagined that the question of "acceptance" would present itself to me in the form of a beautiful little girl with special needs.

Not once have I questioned whether to accept my daughter for who she is. As mothers, I do not even believe that that is a choice that we are even given. You just do. I desperately wanted a child, and I loved Bronwyn from the moment I realized that she was growing inside of me. The fact that she was born with Autism Spectrum Disorder did not change that. I am her mother. She is my child. And until the day that I draw my final breath, I will strive to ensure that in Bronwyn's lifetime she only ever know what it is that she and all children are deserving of—acceptance.

It Matters
Amy Bottorff

It is fleeting. I see it leaving him. Ten and a half short years, and it is leaving. How does time do that? I'm not ready yet. Sometimes it is in full-force stick-turned-weapon overhead, running without caution to conquer yon pirate ship. He is in command of his world, lost deep in make believe. Things can be as he wants. Worlds are within his reach.

Then it comes—the thief of wild-eyed abandonment: "I'm too old for this." It might just be the last year he dons a costume in excitement and runs house to house. Oh, he might wear one again, but not in the same way. Conformed to its likeness, really being what disguise he had chosen. Not at all worried what others might think. I'm not ready for you yet. I'm not ready, Time. You are producing tears as you take my little boy into adulthood. Tears of joy that I am able to witness his growing and changing as it should be. And tears of loss that I will never hold that infant again. Or never hold that two-year-old's hand, soft and chubby. He is growing and I am beyond blessed in watching. I am trying to fight back; I try hard to let every moment infuse into my being.

As I stop my mind from pondering these things, I rise from the park bench I had been sitting on and walk toward my boys who are ten and a half and seven. I think of how my heart wasn't always bent to be grateful in the present moment. I grieve for that time lost. But someone changed my heart forever. Someone in bright colored workout clothes with a sense of humor and joy for the mundane moments of motherhood that I am positive will forever be unmatched.

We met like most young mommas do, at the park for a play date through a mutual friend. Right from the start, Mary was full of smiles and laughs. I appreciated the way in which she interacted with her boys. She was always willing to help and to open her house to other children. The thought of having eight boys together for a play date unnerved me straight to my core. Not Mary! "Drop your boys off, go relax, we are going to have a blast!" And they always did. Early in our friendship, on a summer day, I was unfortunate enough to get strep throat. I was horribly sick. She demanded that she pick up my boys. Not only did she care for them all day, but she took them on an epic play date to an indoor trampoline jump zone.

She showed kindness in the most mundane and experienced joy in the process. I wasn't that mom. Coming into motherhood, I was a terrified mess. I was bitter at the loss of control for my plans. I wanted a clean house, perfectly timed naps, and even more perfectly timed bedtimes. In the preschool years, I wanted the perfectly behaved child. I didn't want the one that was disruptive and hitting. But God has a way of releasing your grip on what it is you think you need.

She adored my youngest, who wasn't quite fitting into the box that his preschool wanted him to fit into. I worried about him. She would always find herself laughing at him so hard she would be in tears. She would say, "I just love him! He is going to be ok. He has a spunk and a joy for life that is going to take him far." And she was right. It took her to soften my heart toward him and his sometimes out of control behavior. I worried less about my youngest, who does live every moment to its fullest. The way he embraces life, I have found, has many positives.

Yes, precision and order and control aren't really what this mothering thing is all about. What is it about control that we all desire so much? I thought that if I had control and order I would win at the big moments of life. Really, as Mary demonstrated, it is the tiny, simple everyday moments that define a life.

Everyday moments matter. The moments that we pause to extend kindness and place others in front of us. They matter. Kindness matters. It matters—maybe even most to those we share our home with. The moment we encourage another mom who is sick or who doesn't have the perfect preschooler. It matters. Kindness counts. It counts in our parenting; **it transforms lives and leaves a legacy that continues**.

How can I be so certain that kindness leaves a legacy? Because we lost Mary less than seven months ago. She was taken from her mothering here on earth suddenly by a heart condition she did not know she had. The hole that is left is large. The questions are endless, and the grief gripping. Her memorial service was full of accounts of the love, joy and kindness that she always extended.

I can say without a doubt that my approach to mothering has been forever transformed. Those things that I used to see as a chore I view much more clearly as a privilege. Dealing with another bad choice on the playground? Privilege. Pausing for a moment to break up yet another brother dispute? Privilege. Why? Because I get to be here—I get to show up. I am fighting hard to not take the everyday for granted. Is motherhood magically easy or without strife? Of course not. It is still filled with everyday struggles. But I have been changed by a gift of perspective that will forever be tucked into a pocket in my heart. A gift given to me by a woman in neon workout clothes who extended smiles, joy, and kindness in the simplest moments of motherhood, and for that, many lives will be transformed for years to come.

In honor of Mary Ann Mitchell Feb 28, 1975 - Oct 25, 2014

Provision & Faithfulness

Kim Dorman

It started in 2012—a few months before I lost my job. I've always wanted to be a stay-at-home mom, but after both of my wonderful maternity leaves in 2010 and again in 2012, I reluctantly rejoined the workforce as an emotional, postpartum mess. I kissed my babies goodbye at the daycare each morning and drove to the job I was lucky to have. The job that had evolved into monotonous days of impossible demands from my manager and confusing assignments for which I didn't have the training or aptitude to complete well. I knew the only reason I wasn't let go with the rest of my team after the restructuring was the fact that I was pregnant at the time.

Now, about four months post-maternity leave, my manager had me in her sights. I sat in the parking lot one weekday morning, soul-weary, beaten down and dreading going into my office building. Strategizing how to avoid my manager, wondering how she would belittle me or my work that day—like all the other days—and questioning if the fat paycheck, nice bonus, and health benefits were really worth it. But my family. We have debt. I earn the most. I have the benefits. I need to do this... Or do I?

What about God? What if I give it to him? That morning, as with so many others, I wondered what it meant that, "God has not given us a spirit of fear, but of power and of love and of..." something else I can never remember (II Timothy 1:7). But I know whatever it is, it's not a spirit of fear. That morning, I had had enough of my fear. With my husband's support, I walked into my boss's office and asked if we could meet. I told her, "This isn't working. We need to figure out an exit strategy for me—whether it's to another opening within the company or an exit from the company altogether. I have an internal lead. Will you work with me?" And the burden slipped away before she even said yes. It was a freeing moment I will never forget.

The next several months were hard. I continued in my role while working on that lead, praying hard and purposefully disengaging from work in the evenings so I could focus fully on my family. I finally interviewed for the position and got rave reviews. The hiring manager assured me it was in the bag. Then a month of silence followed by the posting being "temporarily" suspended and a meeting with HR thanking me for my years of service, and here's a bit of severance. And freedom. Blessed freedom. A Year of Jubilee smack in between our 6th and 7th wedding anniversaries at home with my children to recover and live and scrimp like never before. To create, to realize the power of regular dates with my husband (free since I swapped services with another mom), to be there for all the firsts, and to begin to know God. To rely on God. My husband looks back at that year and says there's no human way we could have afforded to have me home, but I was home. With my kids. My dream that we could never have achieved on our own? God planned it Himself and it was far more than I could have asked or imagined.

As I began to feel whole again, I started to really see the world. To love the oppressed. My introduction was through a weekday Bible study, where I learned about Amy Carmichael, the 19th century missionary to India who rescued girls in the temples from unspeakable evil. A spark ignited as I read her biography, then on to George Muller, my personal hero and the rescuer of orphans from the streets; and modern-day abolitionists and Christ-followers like Hillary Allen and family, who went from Raleigh to Southeast Asia to spread the gospel and aid the oppressed; Christine Caine, founder of A21, the organization that rescues and restores victims of human trafficking; Kristen Welch, founder of Mercy House in Kenya that takes in teen mothers-to-be who are victims of rape and abuse. I devoured books, blogs and articles on saints and warriors who chose to take on the heartbreak. In my mid-30s, I started to see a clearer purpose for my life for the glory of God. He has given me a passion for the orphan and the oppressed. I don't fully know where it's leading yet, but the journey has begun. **It started when I gave up my fear and let God take over.**

I still try to take it back. I'm still working at consistent prayer and time in his word. But I'm being made new. My husband sees it. My kids see it. They see how far I still have to go, but also how far I have come. God has expertly layered my life, and I think the best is yet to come. Big changes are soon happening for our family, some of which we know already—like our pending adoption, which after six long years, will take place this summer. Others of which we are unsure. Inevitably, change is coming. I'm excited and trying hard to live well today, because sometimes I just want to get to what's next. But what is now is important and I need to learn what God has for me to learn and do what he has for me to do today.

Just over a year after I lost my job, renewed and still in the process of being remade, I started my new job. The one I'd applied for over a year earlier. God saved my spot and brought me to the role when I was ready to enter into it. The money in our emergency fund lasted until the month I started back to work. My kids love their day care. I am a contractor now, so I leave on time every day and see more of my family than I did last time around. My husband and I are stronger together. When we bring home our new daughter soon, I will once again have the privilege of being a stay-at-home mom. But before we did some creative number crunching to make staying home a possibility for me, I came to be at peace with the idea of getting off the plane from our two-week, unpaid-time-off trip to China and going back to work the next day after giving my newly adopted daughter to the ladies at the daycare. Not because I thought that was best, but because I trust God to do what brings glory to himself. And once I fully gave control of my daughter to God like Abraham did with Isaac (though in a much less dramatic fashion!), he showed us a way for me to be home with her and our other kids from the beginning.

Daily and in every way, my Father proves himself faithful, and I can't wait to see what else the days ahead hold. The peace that has replaced my fear and the joy that has replaced my worries are transforming my family. To God be the glory!

There is Always Hope
Natasha Westerhoud
natashawesterhoud.blogspot.ca

I am sure some of us can remember a time when we were just little girls pretending to be mommies. They all say it's a dream come true to get married and have children. And I was no different. I had, at one time in my life, wanted to have eight children. I love kids. Always have. Especially teenagers. It was a few years after I got married that we had realized that having a child may be difficult for us. Both of us had medical concerns that were complicating the issue. It took us a few years to come to a place of closing that chapter in our life—a few years of grieving over the loss of dream and the idea of a family of our own. At that time, we had not considered adoption and were not in a position to go there. In those years, we may have been silently grieving, but we also decided we needed to continue to live. We worked and played and lived life to the fullest. We invested in other people's children, and it blessed us greatly.

Then one day it was a like a light bulb turned on and we both decided that we would like to take a look at what it would take to adopt a child. We investigated the different options and decided that we would try to adopt a baby girl from China.

The process of adoption was very foreign to us. We had to take many classes and fill in what seemed like hundreds of pages of information. We had to get complete medical checkups and police checkups and be interviewed by different social workers. Interviewed about whether we were worthy or not of parenting is what all this felt for us. It was a hard and humbling process, but we kept moving forward and trusting that this was God's will for our life, and we are indeed doing the right thing.

As one can imagine, this all takes time. Nothing happens overnight. Originally, they had said it would be a 9- to 12-month wait, and we were fortunate that the kids were moving out of China quickly. We had been waiting for about eight months when, out of the blue, we received news that we were no longer acceptable candidates for adopting out of China.

The Chinese government had changed their qualification on who could adopt, and we did not fit their idea of an ideal parent. We were devastated. We had already been accepted—now what? We had already invested not only financially but whole heartedly. Our hearts were set to bring a child home to call our own.

After some investigating and persistence, we were allowed to be pushed through as accepted, but now they told us the wait time could be up to 5 to 8 years. More devastating news. We were already older when we originally started the adoption process—now we will be much older if this our little girl ever gets home to us. We decided to keep our names in and wait. Trusting and obeying that this indeed was the plan for us. In the meantime, we lived our life. I started working with students and my husband started his own company. We worked, we organized mission trips, and we travelled to many countries, helping and serving. We set up our home and continued to trust. But then the waiting got to be too much for us. We went ahead with private adoption attempts, and they all turned out very sadly for us. The birth mother changed her mind, leaving us with much grief and pain and suffering. All the while, wondering why this is happening to us. At that point we decided we were no longer going to try.

We just pushed forward and left behind the idea of having a family. We were fine, the two of us, and we would be ok.

We worked and lived life, trusting that this was the course we were supposed to be on. Then, what seemed a life time later, the phone call came. We were matched with a little 10 month old girl. Eight years of waiting, and the waiting was done. In a matter of weeks, we were flying to China to meet our girl. We spent two weeks in China, getting our paper work done and getting to know each other. I was overwhelmed and scared. I had no idea what I was doing. I was a mom. Just like that. One minute I was just sitting in a chair, then a few seconds later we had opened the hotel door and they had dropped this little angel in our arms and left.

We were too busy trying to figure out what it looked like to feed her, change her and bond to her, nevermind giving any thoughts to what the change might do to me.

Then we flew home. I thought I was ok, but I was not. I was severely jet lagged, more than I had ever been in my life. I am sure it had to do with not only traveling but having a baby with me as well. I was so tired. I don't actually know when I started to get depressed. It might have been a few months after I got home. My life changed. I felt alone. I felt trapped. I felt tired. I felt angry. I felt *alone.*

I think that was the hardest part. As social as I was, I had to stop. I had to bond and attach. I had to spend all my time with my princess. I had to make sure she knew I loved her and cared for her and was her mom. That was my call—she had to know that I loved her and that I am her mom and not just another caregiver. She had to know that I will never abandon her. But that meant I could not go out as I used to with my friends. I had to say no to things. And had to watch as others went on with their lives. I watched on social media as everyone's world was just so full and amazing, and mine was so different that I had no idea how to cope. My whole world changed, and I was spiraling into a deep depression.

No one told me about this. I had no idea.

Working for over 20 years and being married for 17 years without children, we were use to a way of life. And as much as I wanted this new life, I had no idea how hard it would be to adjust. I felt it wasn't fair that some made it seem so easy. Why was I having such a hard time? It was hard to talk to any of my family members or friends. I would get things like *this is your life now or this is what you wanted—you need to make new friends with kids same age as yours*. So, I stopped sharing with them and pulled myself away from everyone. I wanted my old life and old friends with my new daughter. But that was not going to happen.

I had no idea how to cope.

It wasn't until my husband had mentioned to me about postpartum depression that I started to think that this is what I may have been dealing with. I didn't think it applied to me since we had adopted. After some investigating, I realized it was possible and was likely what was happening to me.

I was obsessed with my child, attaching and bonding with her. I had developed this huge fear of not attaching. We had gone through so many classes and warnings of "what could happen,"—it was just too much for me. I had developed an extreme anxiety of how I was parenting and the things I was doing, sure that everything I was doing was wrong. I was on my own, or felt on my own, trying to figure out being a mom, yet still being me. Frankly, I had not changed. Much of me was still the same.

I wanted to have a support group but did not know where to look or begin; I still believed I needed the same friends group that I had before. I was living in the same community that I loved, yet I felt so alone. I did not know how to be the same me, but with a daughter. I had this high expectation that everything was going to stay the same with friendships, family, work and life. I wanted things to stay the same. Instead, everything changed except me. I had the same ideas and passions and dreams and likes, yet I did not know how to live them out now.

Slowly, I started to realize that I needed to do something. I was tired of crying and being depressed. I had this amazing little girl in my life and needed help. I finally came to a place where I needed to let go of what was and look for opportunities to share with someone who would understand and help me through this process. The first two years were the hardest. I look back and wonder how I did it. The anxiety, the pain and the loneliness were too much to bear at times. As I look back, though, I can see how God placed specific people in my life to help me along the journey. I am glad I was open enough not to resist. Open enough to say yes to the help of new friends and yes to the professional help I eventually sought. All of it helped me to move on and into the new life that was waiting for me.

I had to let myself be vulnerable and stop isolating myself. For some reason, we tend to be so hard on ourselves as moms, thinking we need to have it all together. I am here to say, you don't. That kind of thinking will hurt you. It hurt me. It is ok to grieve what was, but then look up, look around you, and see what is.

The change in my life was a huge shock, and I did not give myself permission to understand that. We waited so long for our girl that I just expected that everything would be perfect, that I would be only happy and excited. I had no idea about postpartum adoption depression, and depression wasn't even on my radar. I thought my surroundings would not change, that my environment would stay the same. But it did not. And I was not prepared. I felt so guilty about feeling the way I did. I thought because it was every girl's dream to have babies and the fact that I waited so long, I should be happy. I should be content. I should just be like everyone else said I should be.

We need to be kind to ourselves. We all have different needs and deal with things according to those needs.

Today, three years later, I am working full time and doing what I love to do. I spend an amazing amount of time with my precious daughter, and we have a close and wonderful relationship so far! I have friends that I feel safe with. I see a therapist when I need to and have a life coach and a few other mentors in my life. I have found joy once again, and I am happy. I have found a way to be me again, alongside my daughter.

Seek out the help that you need, and allow yourself to be vulnerable with them. Accept the changes that are happing in your life. Find friends and professionals that will help you through the journey. There is always hope. Be kind to yourself.

Do not give up, and do not feel that you are the only one who is feeling this way. I thought I was. Everyone looked so happy and perfect. And then realized that many are not. Live into the life that you were created to live. Be bold, and try to find your joy again.

You will find it.

You will be ok.

You will feel like yourself again.

Be encouraged, my friend.

Walking Through the Pain
Mackenzie Rollins
livinghiscall.com
cheeriosandlattes.com

"Mackenzie, it's the baby, she's not breathing!" She cried into the phone.

"Call 911! Jeff's nearby, I'll call him, he'll be there soon!" I quickly replied. That was the extent of my conversation with our sweet babysitter. My heart sank and began pounding. I ran out of my office at school and called Jeff as I ran down the hall. "Jeff, you have to get to the babysitter's, Zoe's not breathing, 911's on their way. Hurry!"

I ran into the Upper School office and told the secretary that Zoe wasn't breathing and I needed her to drive me; I knew I couldn't drive. I texted our small group to pray as soon as I got into the car; one sweet friend texted back, *Jesus breathe into Zoe.* I clung to that as I began praying aloud, "Jesus breathe into her, Jesus breathe into her." I couldn't stop, I couldn't cry, I could barely breathe. I continued praying, and pointed directions to our secretary as she drove me.

Traffic seemed worse than usual for that time of day. I just wanted to hold my baby girl. I scanned the roadway looking for the flashing lights of an ambulance. Nothing. I strained my ears to listen for a siren. Silence. I finally got up enough courage to text Jeff again, I asked him if I should go to the babysitter's house or to the hospital. My heart raced as I feared the reply. *Here.* he responded.

As we grew closer, my prayers got louder, I didn't know what else to do. A part of me couldn't get there fast enough, but another part of me didn't want to arrive; I didn't know what I was going to find. I peered down the street as we turned onto the road where the babysitter's house was, just a few streets away from our home. I saw an ambulance, I saw cars, I saw people standing outside, I saw Jeff in the driveway.

I ran up and hugged Jeff, he held me. "She's gone." he whispered.

"No! Tell them to help her, tell them to go help her!" I cried. He held me tighter. I knew there was nothing we could do, we were helpless. We were powerless. Night had enclosed around us on the beautiful afternoon of May 7th.

After talking with the emergency personnel and reassuring the babysitter that it was not her fault, that we still trusted her, and we were so sorry that she had to experience this, we went home. The house seemed empty, yet there were reminders of Zoe everywhere—bottles drying on the drying rack, her swing in the living room, burp rags on the edge on the couch; everything was waiting for her to come home with us. Our two older boys were at Jeff's parents house just around the corner. His mom had picked them up before I arrived at the babysitter's house, and they still weren't quite sure what had happened during their nap time. We sat with two of our pastors and asked for advice on what and how we should tell them; we knew they were going to be heartbroken. They reassured us that there weren't words for something like this, but that God would give us the words to say. Finally, we called Jeff's parents and nervously waited for them to come home.

"I want to play with Zoe!" were Jayden's first words as he walked through the door; his words pierced our hearts. We sat them down with us on the couch and slowly explained to them that she wasn't coming home. Jesus had taken her up to be with him in Heaven during her nap today; her room was ready and her "special job" that God had for her life here was finished (or in many ways just beginning). All we could do was cry together.

The next day, was filled with hard things—waking up to realize her cries would no longer wake us up, continuing to pump milk (as I had still been nursing), going into Zoe's room for the first time, looking at the pictures that I had taken of her just hours before she passed away, the list could go on and on. However, as I made the choice to walk into the pain, each time, I was able to come out stronger and healthier than before.

Typically, we try to avoid pain; it's natural. Perhaps that is why most people say the first stage of grief is denial. We don't want to feel pain because it's unpleasant and miserable at times. I didn't want to feel the pain of losing Zoe. None of us did. I had such a hard time as family and friends wanted to "help us" by putting her things away—I kept thinking someone would bring her home to us and she would need all those things again. It was just a nightmare. We had to move forward with our new reality. That we would now carry the pain of loss with us the rest of our lives. We couldn't avoid it; instead, we had to walk into the pain.

Pain is an indicator. It communicates to us that something is wrong. This is true of both emotional pain and physical pain. It is a message that causes us to react. When we touch a hot stove and feel the pain, our first reaction is to jerk away. Emotional pain has the same effect on us; however, we must to respond differently to this type of pain. We must sometimes keep our hand on the metaphorical burner and allow ourselves to experience emotional pain in order to become healthier.

Rather than backing away from the emotional pain that we were feeling as a result of Zoe's loss, we needed to process it and move forward with it as a new reality in our lives. We had to choose to walk into the pain, because in doing so, we could walk through the pain and continue living our lives. We had to reject the guilt of moving on and accept the truth, that she was even happier in her new home, and in the arms of the Father who gave her to us in the first place. She was in the best place she could be!

"I need to shower, shave, and get dressed." Jeff shared with me that next morning. "I'm afraid what will happen if I don't." It was his way of saying that we can't allow ourselves to get stuck. Just as I used to teach my students as a swim instructor, when you go under the water, the best thing to do is push off the bottom. We were at the bottom. We could either sit there and emotionally die ourselves, or we could push off the bottom and trust that God would take us back up, for our sake, and for the sake of our grieving boys.

It was evident that, as we walked forward into the pain, we knew that we weren't walking alone. We knew we were being carried forward each day by someone who had walked through this pain before. He knew well the pain of losing a child. Without Him to walk with us into the pain and even carry us some days, we would never have been able to walk at all.

Today, walking into the pain looks different than it did one year ago, but **even though the pain still lingers, the peace and joy are both very real**. Today walking into the pain looks like:

• Not turning the radio off when a song that stirs my emotions comes on but allowing myself to cry through it,

• Sitting and watching videos or looking at pictures of Zoe that bring tears of joy,

• Allowing myself to picture her with our family today and what she might be doing,

• Allowing myself to stare at another baby I see and remember Zoe's tiny little fingers or sweet little nose,

• Sitting down and writing out my feelings and what I'm learning.

One of the many things that I have learned through losing Zoe is that true hope is so much stronger than even our worst circumstances. As a mom, one of the biggest fears I had was losing one of my children. I now live that reality, but I live it with hope.

Because I do have the hope of knowing I will see and hold my precious girl again in heaven one day, I have been able to commit to walking into the pain, then existing on the other side, healthier than before. I will walk into the pain, and I will walk *through* the pain, but I will not live in the pain.

Making More of My Dreams
Laura Wilkinson
laurawilkinson.com

God uses motherhood to stretch, grow, change and kick us right up and out of our comfort zone. Being a mom is sanctifying, purifying, and gratifying. There is truly nothing else on earth that compares to having the honor of wearing the badge of "mom."

I was an athlete for most of my childhood, and even most of my grown up life. I finally retired at the ripe old age of 30 and couldn't wait for my next adventure—starting a family.

Unlike most things I had set my mind to do, getting pregnant didn't come easy. But honestly, as much as I wanted to be pregnant, I wanted kids more. Having an adopted brother, the adoption route made sense to me and was a normal path to take next. However, my husband had reservations. Big ones.

The following summer was one of the hardest of my life. Most of it was spent grieving the fact that maybe having kids was not something God wanted for me. And I wasn't okay with it. It took several months of soul searching honesty to finally get to a point where I knew Jesus would be enough in my life, even without kids.

As I was coming out of this mourning period, still feeling a little dazed and confused, God up and changed my husband's heart. Unbeknownst to me, walking into church one morning, my husband was praying that, if adoption was what God really wanted us to do, He would make it really obvious.

For some reason, as the worship music was ending, the choir director stayed up on stage and out of nowhere started sharing the story of how he was adopted. As we walked to the car after the service, my husband's expression was serious and his face was drained of all color. He didn't say a word until we sat down in the car. The first thing out of his mouth was, "I think we should adopt."

My heart leapt with joy! On our seventh wedding anniversary, we signed with an adoption agency. I was going to be a mom. I could have jumped to the moon.

Then came the waiting. Waiting. Is. Hard.

I thought once I knew I was going to be a mom, it would be easier. But the excruciating longing you experience is just gut wrenching. Praying is all you can really do, and pray I did. But how do you pray for a child you don't know, and for biological parents you know are going to give up their baby? It's difficult to navigate. My heart longed to pray for reunification, for healing and restoration. And while I did pray for that, I knew those prayers were not for my child and her parents, because for me to have a child, she would indeed be abandoned.

This was my first glimpse into the painful side of adoption.

A year into our wait, on our eighth anniversary, we had another surprise. I was pregnant. We were in shock and beyond excited. We were actually going to have two kids! God was not only answering my prayers, He was exceeding them.

After our daughter, Arella, was close to a year old, the wait for a baby in China had slowed down dramatically. When we first started the process, we were told it would be around three years; now it was estimated at six, and it was still slowing down.

My heart sank. When you know you have a daughter out there, you just want to go get her right then and there, bring her home where you can love her, keep her safe and make sure she's taken care of. But God used this dreaded wait to push us further.

We began to look at the waiting child program, for children with special needs. Now, it's one thing when your biological child is born with a special need. You can assume that God gave this child to you with this need, so He's going to equip you to handle it. But when you're asking for a special need, you begin to worry that you're checking too many boxes and maybe not the ones God had in mind.

Fortunately, God is sovereign, He knows us and He will, in fact, equip us for what comes when we trust Him. We nervously checked a lot of boxes for different types of special needs with the guidance of our pediatrician who is also an adoptive parent of a child from China.

The very first month after submitting all of those checked boxes, we were matched. And we fell immediately and madly in love with this little peanut across the world in a small orphanage. And her special need was simply that she was born without a left ear, but could hear fine out of her right. The coolest part about this was that my dad had lost his hearing when he was young, so suddenly he got excited and felt attached to her, too.

Beautiful.

I had read all the books and every blog I could find about people adopting from China. I knew all the possible scenarios and even that we would probably face an entirely new scenario. Basically, I knew to go in with an open mind, flexible and ready to just roll with it.

As an athlete, I had travelled to China on numerous occasions. Just that part can be very stressful for families, but it was easy for us. The hardest part was having to leave my 18-month-old Arella, whom I'd never spent more than a night away from. We would be gone for a little more than two weeks on the other side of the planet.

Most of the videos and stories I had read about seeing your son or daughter for the first time in the Chinese adoption process involved a packed room of anywhere between 20 and 75 families waiting for their names to be called to go see their child. It was loud and crazy with lots of crying.

So when we walked into the Civil Affairs office and it was eerily silent, I assumed we were going to be waiting a while for everyone to show up. But as we walked through the door to the waiting room, I saw two people inside—a young, petite Chinese woman holding a tiny little girl in a big, puffy red jacket.

I didn't have time to prepare myself, my heart, my camera—anything. There she was, just staring with wide little eyes at us, curious.

In all my research I heard it was common, even good if they were scared of you, cried or tried to get away. It meant they were capable of forming attachments to caretakers. Many kids that grow up in orphanages or foster care have attachment disorders. My husband and I were as prepared as we could be for that. But it didn't make it easy.

The Orphanage director put Zoe down on the floor where she promptly took the director by the hand and tried to march her out of the room and away from us. I finally had to pick her up while she tried hard to get away. She would calm down for a minute, then rally again. My husband took a turn with the same result. Eventually, I had to hold her as she began to cry and wail her little heart out, kicking and wiggling with all her might.

But I held on. I talked gently to her. I showed her things. I rocked her back and forth. I sang to her. After a long fight, she gave up the battle and fell asleep in my arms. Then I finally let my pent up tears fall.

I cannot even fathom what she had to go through. I imagine one of my biological kids being ripped away from us without warning, having to go with a stranger who looks different and speaks a language they've never heard. Heartbreaking. While adoption itself has much beauty in it, it is born out of great tragedy. I can't ignore that or pretend it didn't happen, because it's part of Zoe's story. It's a part of who she is.

But God turns messes into masterpieces.

Zoe was terrified because she had no idea what was going on, who we were or what was about to happen to her. But we knew. We had a plan. We had a room prepared for her and a sister excitedly waiting for her to come home. She had a family that was in love with her and would do anything for her. But she didn't know us or the plan.

God has really shown me a deeper look at my relationship with Him through this adoption journey. I'm a lot like Zoe. **I don't know what the future holds or what the path to get there looks like, so I scare easy.** Sometimes I just want to run away and avoid it.

But God continually asks me to trust Him. He has a plan. He's preparing a place. He's not going to leave me.

Zoe has now been part of our family almost three years, and she has blessed us beyond measure. I cannot fathom life without her or the joy we would have missed out on if we hadn't adopted her.

That also teaches me that if I don't trust God's plan, it's not just me that misses out. Who else will miss out on blessings and joy because I run away instead of follow the path He's laid out?

I love how He teaches us and grows us through our children.

We had such a hard but amazing experience adopting Zoe that, six months later, we started another adoption, this time from Ethiopia. Three weeks later, I discovered I was pregnant again.

Today I can laugh with exhaustion, joy and a very full heart. I'm now just sitting back and enjoying the ride as God takes my dreams and changes them into realities that are much, much greater than I ever desired.

I Never Wanted to be a Mother

Roxanne Foster

thefosterparenthood.com

Really. Never. I can't remember having a single longing thought or desire in my entire 25 years of life before becoming a mother. I always assumed there was something wrong with me that I never wanted children.

When I was a little girl, other girls were playing with dolls and playing "house" and I was proudly declaring that I wanted to be the first woman president. Having children and being mommy to little life sucking humans were just not in the cards for my ambitious, road to presidency heart. When I met my always-wanted-to-be-a-daddy husband, I made it very clear I never-wanted-to-be-a-mother. He will tell you now he never believed me, but we entered marriage understanding it may just be us and that would be enough. People would regularly tell me I had no idea what I was talking about, and I would smugly think, *you clearly don't know me very well.*

I'll be extremely honest: even after several years of marriage, I never did experience baby fever. My husband, however, was meant to be a father. I could see it in his soul that he longed for the day someone would call him daddy, and I started to wonder if I was just being selfish. After a lot of prayer, we decided to just "give it a shot" and see what happened. I want to be clear. Though I still never felt longing for a child, I understood the decision I was making. I was prepared to lay down my selfish desires for my child. I was also certain God knew what was best for my family, and I was confidently stepping out in faith that He would guide our path.

One try, and my sweet Scarlette Grace was conceived. I know, I know, fertile myrtle over here. I know how blessed we are to not have struggled to become pregnant. I wish I could share with you the first few words out of my mouth after reading the positive test, but that may cause me to lose my credibility in trusting and following God. I couldn't believe it happened so quickly, and my heart was nowhere near prepared.

Pregnancy was a horrible experience for me. I hated almost everything about it, save feeling her move around. I was extremely ill, laid out on the floor of my office's bathroom for at least an hour every morning. I not so lovingly referred to my growing baby as a parasite (textbook definition if you haven't researched a parasite lately), which my OB got a real kick out of. Charlie-horses would leave me crying in pain for hours. But more than the pain, swelling and snissing (for the LOVE—the things no one tells you!), my heart was full of fear. The kind of fear that cripples you and steals your joy.

I spent nine months agonizing over becoming a mother. But I played the part so well. Her nursery was the prettiest Pinterest-worthy thing you ever laid eyes on. We found the best daycare Oklahoma City had to offer after touring all the top facilities. Four baby showers, maternity pictures, custom clothes and all the top of the line baby items you can imagine, helped me keep my mind off the thoughts that sent me into panic and left me feeling empty. From the outside looking in, I was ready for motherhood and was going to be damn good at it. I had a plan, and nothing was going to interfere. But on the inside? On the inside, I was falling apart.

I'm not going to love this child. This was a mistake. Why did I agree to this? I am not motherly. I don't even like kids. What was I thinking? My body will never be the same. Speaking of my body, oh my WORD how is this baby going to get out? Haven't they figured out a way to do this thing painlessly by now? This is all my husband's fault. What's so wrong about being selfish anyway? How will I pretend to love this child? People are going to know I'm a terrible mother. Why don't I feel connected to this thing in my body?

I know it will sound cliché, but the second my arms held that sweet baby girl, love filled every pore of my soul that was once burdened with fear. I knew immediately my life was different, and nothing would ever be the same. Old desires were laid to rest that day and replaced with new dreams for this perfect little creature who resembled her daddy. Those first few hours with my girl awakened parts of me I didn't know existed. I became a completely different person. A person who was capable of feeling emotions deeper than before, whose love was overwhelming and whose plans were foiled.

Within minutes of Scarlette's birth, I looked at my husband and said, "I'm not going back to work, I can't leave her." And just like that, my career-driven road to presidency was blown up indefinitely. Designer clothes, lavish vacations and a picture perfect house were al happily replaced with snot-stained clothes, a trip to Disney World and a house that regularly embarrasses my mom. I was ill prepared for the whirlwind that would come over the next few weeks of adjusting to life postpartum. But my heart was anchored in this newfound love for my baby.

Love is powerful. One look at that precious, perfect, tiny face and I knew immediately I would do anything for her. As in, all of a sudden I contained enough raw emotion that I would kill anyone that hurt her. If you would have asked me before she was born if I could kill anyone, I would have said no. But now? **Love cultivates deep, giant feelings and can make anything possible.** I had no idea I was capable of such strong emotions.

That sweet little girl will be blowing out three candles this year, with her 11 month old baby brother by her side. Our family is in the beginning stages of becoming a foster family, and we hope to grow our family through adoption one day. While I feel confident saying I would have enjoyed my life without children (hello, Italy!), I would have had no idea the true beauty I would miss without them. I wouldn't trade the joys of motherhood for any of the luxuries this world can offer. You can't replicate the feeling of joy the first time your child says "I love you, momma" of their own accord. No amount of money is worth missing out on that.

I did quit my job to take care of my daughter and, now, son. I don't regret that decision for a minute. Some days, I can't believe I am the same person who used to proudly declare she was never having children. What an idiot I was. Sure, there are times I wish I could go back to pre-children, life-of-leisure Roxanne—who doesn't? We mothers had no idea what we had going for ourselves before kids came into the picture, am I right? I mean, reading for fun? Sleeping in? Uninterrupted sleep? I don't even know what those things are anymore.

I know not everyone's story plays out exactly like mine. Postpartum depression, lack of immediate bonding and traumatic births are barriers to growing the mother-child bond, I understand that. However, I firmly believe that love is powerful enough to heal all wounds. Greater than that, a mother's love is potent enough to rewrite anyone's personal history or pain. It may take time, but a mother's love is pure and powerful. Don't give up hope. Reach out to people who are safe and love you. But believe that the love you have for your children can heal.

A mother's love can do extraordinary things. It has the capacity to change lives in ways we could have never imagined. It can heal all pain, all sadness, and all regret. A mother's love is what bonds us all together in this chaos of raising children in an increasingly scary world. We pour out our souls for these tiny humans, day in and day out, doing our part to better the world by raising up the next generation to love more deeply than we do.

Love is our common thread. I am so grateful to have experienced this deep pool of love which I did not even know existed before meeting my child. Without it, we wouldn't be on a journey to grow our family through fostering and adoption and give new life to children who are hopeless. So while I never wanted to be a mother, I'm eternally indebted to a God whose plans are higher than mine. I would have never had the chance to feel a mother's love. Without it, I wouldn't have ever learned who I truly am.

Going Home
Janet Faubert

The summer of 1983 would change my life. I was at my parents' place to spend most of my holidays at the beach. My mom called to tell me that my favorite Nanny had passed away.

I didn't live with my parents when I was a child. My mom was busy with work at the hospital, and my dad was gone often being a truck driver on the road most days. I stayed with my Nanny for ten wonderful years. She was the best. Life was to be very different after that phone call.

I stayed with my parents for a couple of months to regroup my life. *Now what was I to do,* I wondered. So, I was in a new school with new friends and a new place to live. I got engaged too young. I thought I was ready and that, at seventeen, I knew it all. That was a growing time and a wonderful experience that gave me my first son. For this amazing gift, I am so grateful. My ex-hubby and I grew apart, but we are still friends today.

A few years later. I was blessed with another son. Well, that son grew, and one year when he was 14 he wanted a dog for his birthday. I did not want a dog. I wanted a cat, but we got him his puppy. The first day our Odie came home, it was love at first sight for all of us. We got a new family member that day. My mom said not to let him sleep in the beds and not on the couch. That rule didn't even last one day. That sweet dog is seven now, and we can't imagine not having him in our bed each night.

My mom was funny at times. I didn't really know she had a sense of humor until I was an adult. I got to know her much better when I had my own children. We would talk and laugh over our lunch plans each week. We talked about everything. She had fun with her grandsons. She enjoyed being their Nanny.

Life was good, and the pictures in our family albums show the joys of captured moments with the boys.

My mom got older. She was quiet now. I brought her to the hospital to get checked. I thought something was not right, but I didn't know what was wrong. I thought it might be part of the *getting older* stage of life. I noticed small changes at first. I was in denial that she was different, but she was.

She had moderate dementia. When I first heard that word I didn't even know what it was. So I learned. My sister and I were on a new journey with our mom. She wanted to go home. She was in the hospital for three months. She had also had a stroke, then a second stroke and some other health problems. I had to make sure she was safe, so going home was not going to happen for her. It was time for a retirement home. It was not an easy time for my mom. She loved her own place.

We did pick out a place together, but she was not happy some days about having to move and I understood that. She had her own room, and it was sunny and bright with her own sink area. I brought her things to her, but she still wanted most of her belongings to stay with me at her place.

I would help her have a shower. She didn't like shower days, but I was patient and kind. I didn't rush her. I would tidy up her room and bring her laundry home to do for her. These things would have been done for her by the staff at the retirement home, but she wanted me to do that, so I did. I didn't mind at all. When she was content and comfortable, I was happy. She wanted her treats every visit, too, and that was ours to share. We liked our movies. The movies would make me laugh or make me cry. Some days, I would just watch my mom as she watched a movie. I did know that one day I would miss that beautiful face.

I stayed at her place to clean and take care of her mail, bills, and things. Her place was homey, so I was good. I could get on a bus and be with her often. We didn't have any long conversations, and that was fine. We were together, and that is all that mattered to us. I would stay for a couple of hours every couple of days. My sister and I would take turns, so she was not alone often.

I like her room here at home, where my parents lived since the early '80s. Her color was purple. The curtains match, and the breeze from her window makes me smile when I think of her every day. **I miss her so much.** There are fewer tears now and more happy memories. I decided not to move yet. I am not ready.

I have time now to do some scrapbooking in this house of hers. A new hobby that will take me back in time, walking down memory lane. I won't run. I will walk slowly and enjoy each photograph.

As I grow older, I have to stop and notice that I do have some of my mom in me after all. It's funny at times. I think *oh there she is in me,* and I laugh and talk out loud to her.

She was loved.

Our plan is to stay here for now and move when I am ready to leave my past behind me and start a new chapter in my life. We will buy our cottage near the water. I will garden, and my hubby will fish all day long. Life does change.

They say when you are born, you come into this world crying—crying because you miss Heaven, but all your family and friends are so happy to welcome you with smiles and laughter.

When you die, you are so happy to be back home with God, with no tears. But all your family and friends are crying and sad because they will miss you.

Mom is so happy to be back home.

Never a Mistake
Meghan Boyce
themontessorimoms.com

Some would call my journey to motherhood a mistake. Some well-meaning people even at times refer to my beautiful, perfect, daughter as "a mistake." Or, an "oops baby," or my favorite: "a lapse in judgment." But like all good things in life, I know my journey to motherhood was all part of God's perfect plan.

At eighteen years old, I was a good girl. I listened to my mama, got good grades in college, and was a tried and true friend. I was modest with my looks and with my body, and I made levelheaded decisions almost all of the time. The summer I was eighteen was a tough one for me. My high school sweetheart and I parted ways, and I left my freshman year in college feeling very alone and unsure of myself. My parents tried to force me out of my shell, and when I took an interest in a young man four years my senior, they encouraged me to pursue him. It didn't take much. His rugged good looks and New England fisherman charm won me over almost immediately. I thought he'd never ask me out, so when he called me at work and invited me to dinner on his boat at the end of August, I nearly swooned. I remember driving up to the docks where his boat was, watching the thunderstorms roll in over the sound while he prepared our dinner, and I remember him fixing me a glass of pink lemonade.

And then I remember waking in a fog, praying for it to end. In that moment, that one moment, my innocence was gone. It was exactly five weeks later when my journey to motherhood began, when I miscarried the child created in that unspeakable violence.

I remember feeling God had failed me, that I had failed myself, and that my body was no longer my own. I cried for the way I first experienced pregnancy, the way I first experienced motherhood, for the way I first experienced the loss of a child. At eighteen, I had decided that I never wanted to feel that way again. As with all things, life keeps moving. I met a man who showed me what it was like to feel respected, appreciated, honored, and once again I felt the pangs of motherhood. I imagined myself holding a newborn clutched to my chest while my future husband wrapped his arms lovingly around me, keeping us safe and protecting us from all of the negativity in the world. **For where there is tragedy, there is also great joy.** My late teens and early twenties were filled with great love stories, a newfound sense of self, and an incredible self-confidence that only continued to grow. I was twenty-four when I felt the pain of motherhood again. At six weeks. I miscarried my second child, one whose existence I did not know of until that point. My body had betrayed me again. It seemed my womb was only a place violence and tragedy, and it was worse this time because the child I lost was made of love. I couldn't bring myself to tell many people. Even my most trusted confidants could not understand how this "mistake" happened. *How I could be so careless? How I could be sad about losing a child born out-- of-wedlock, whom I could not provide for, who would interfere with all I've worked so hard for?* The words stung so harshly; I remained ashamed. I didn't see how motherhood could ever complete me as it seemed to for the women in the parenting magazines.

Three years passed. I embarked on a grand adventure with the love of my life and moved 10 hours away from the closest person we knew. I had just accepted a spot in a local nursing program, and I felt like God had opened a door. My life was full of big changes, and I finally felt confident in the path I was on. My partner and I were on cloud nine, working so hard, but our goals were plainly in sight. It was about two months after our move that I knew something was different. I hadn't been feeling well lately, and being pretty well versed in medical knowledge at that point, knew that many of my symptoms were akin with early pregnancy symptoms. I didn't know how to tell my partner.

We were actively trying to stay a party of two, and this would change everything we had worked so hard for. Once again, I felt as though God was testing me, giving me more than I could handle. When I finally took the pregnancy test and saw the two pink lines, I nearly screamed. The thought of growing and birthing a child seemed like another act of violence on my body. It seemed like once again someone else controlled me, and I had never been so afraid.

That fear stayed with me throughout my pregnancy. What should have been a joyous time was intermingled with bouts of severe depression, anxiety, and a sense of failure.

My daughter's birth was traumatic. See, what most people don't know is that birth can subconsciously reawaken the trauma of sexual assault. Recent studies have found that as many as 80% of women who were sexually assaulted needed birthing interventions during the birth of their first child. This includes the use of vacuum extraction, which is how my daughter made her eventful appearance into this world. Pitocin or not, assault survivors have been shown to stop having strong contractions at the end of the delivery process. That is when God showed me one of the greatest gifts of motherhood: finding the strength and beauty in your partner. My, now husband, supported me, comforted me, and showed me a gentleness my life had never known. He was so assured that this was God's plan, and calmed my fears with his confidence and unwavering faith. When people would ask "How did this happen?" he would simply reply "We are so blessed." And so it came to be, that the first time I set eyes on my beautiful daughter, I knew no truer words. None of it had been a mistake. She will never be a mistake. We are so blessed.

Sharing the Journey
Elizabeth Lovelace

I've never felt as alone as I did in the midst of grief and loss. Everyone's experience with grief and loss is different. While others try to reach out, my grief isolated me. I felt very vulnerable, and in an attempt to protect my heart, I tried to stay away from people as long as possible.

I dreaded going back to church, seeing neighbors for the first time, answering the questions of why I wasn't pregnant anymore. But I felt safer on social media, so that's where I went to share my thoughts and feelings. For the most part, people were kind and supportive. In my head, I knew I wasn't alone in my experience. Women miscarry all the time. But I wasn't hearing people talk about it. I knew babies died; I wasn't naïve, but I only knew of one couple personally who had experienced it.

I discovered something extraordinary, though. As I spoke about my loss and the challenges of daily grief, I started hearing from others who had also experienced loss. Some women were older than me, and they told me of the babies they miscarried or lost in infancy. Some were my age, and shared that they, too, had miscarried. I soon discovered I wasn't as alone in my grief as I thought I was.

Let me share my story. I am a mother of four. You wouldn't be able to tell by looking at my family, because I am raising just two of my children. My daughter recently turned six, and my son is a roly-poly eight-month-old. In between my two on earth, I conceived two more who are now in heaven.

In February, 2012, I was about five months pregnant with our son Maximilian when I started feeling contractions. I was put on bed rest and assured that I just needed to take it easy and all would be well. Something told me it wasn't going to be. The contractions came and went, and a few days passed. Almost a week after the contractions started, I was a centimeter dilated. The pit in my stomach only grew; the fears began to consume me. In bed that night, I confessed to my husband, as I sobbed into his shoulder, that I was afraid we were losing our son. He tried to reassure me that Max would be fine.

Max would have been fine if he had been able to stay safe inside, but he was born at 24 weeks. At the time, we didn't know what happened, we had no answers. An emergency c-section was performed in order to give him a better chance at survival. I had been planning a home birth for him. I wanted a calm, beautiful birth. It was the opposite. I wasn't in control of my birth experience; I was at the mercy of the doctors operating on me.

Max was a fighter, but his underdeveloped lungs couldn't handle the rigors of breathing. He lived for two days. My husband and I were able to hold him while he lived, and Max passed in his daddy's arms. We buried him the following week. We were living in Argentina at the time, so only a few family members were there to pay their respects. My worst fear, losing a child, became a reality.

The following year, I was able to conceive another child, whose face I never saw. The pregnancy test was positive one Thursday, and on the next Thursday I slipped down the stairs landing hard on my hip. I miscarried the next day. I had one week with that baby.

My husband wasn't even in the country at the time, so I had to e-mail him to tell him I was pregnant. When he landed back in the country, my brother-in-law picked him up at the airport and told him I had lost the baby. There was no ultrasound, not even an e-mail to immediate family to let them know of the pregnancy. All I had was a positive pregnancy test and feelings of confusion and anger. In my heart, I was once again at a cemetery burying another child. The miscarriage sent me to a darker and lonelier place than when I had lost Max.

Because I had given birth to a child who then died, my heart and mind knew only to associate the new loss to the old one. I spoke of my first loss freely. In my efforts that people should not forget Max, I had become quite outspoken about infant loss and grief. In a way, I was trying to do what I could to mother my son in the only way I felt I could. It felt hypocritical not to also talk about my miscarriage. If this was also a child I had lost, what kind of mother would I be to speak of one child lost and not the other? So I told family and friends, and my Facebook world, that I had suffered a miscarriage.

While miscarriage and infant loss are a lot more common than we would like to think, they're, understandably, not talked about much. According to current statistics, about a quarter of pregnancies end in miscarriage. Yet, the majority of adults don't think it's that common.

Why? Because we don't talk about it. Perhaps it's because I'm an introvert (we tend to spill all on social media), or perhaps because I had an urge to speak of my children—all of my children—but either way, I did just that. I shared my own thoughts, I shared online articles that spoke to these topics, I joined groups on social media that pertained to miscarriage and infant loss, and I read a lot.

Something happened along the way that I wasn't expecting. Women started sharing with me.

I knew my mom had miscarried when I was a child, but I didn't know she had miscarried twice and named those babies.

One college friend wrote me to tell me she had had a miscarriage. She said, "Every time I read one of your posts sharing about your own journey, I think, 'I should tell Liz, she would understand.' So I am. Thank you for being so transparent." And, "Just struggling a lot this week, and sometimes you are the first person I think of to share with."

A childhood friend felt compelled to tell me about her miscarriage. She told me, "I know you (understand). Something about loss makes us reach out to others who 'get it'. Thanks."

Sometime after Max died, I was praying with an elderly woman in our church. We talked about Max for a bit, and she shared some details of the passing of her adult son. On the outside, she and I had nothing in common. And even though the ways our sons died were very different, we found common ground in the grief we both shared. She opened up to me in a way that I did not expect.

After my miscarriage, I put a question out on Facebook in search of ideas. I wanted to honor my child yet didn't know how. Several women responded. One had planted a tree, another had purchased Willow Tree keepsakes for each child lost, and another confessed that she had not done anything outwardly to honor her children. But seeing others speak of the ways they found to remember their children gave her some ideas to do the same.

Another friend told me, "I have to thank you so much for being so open about what you have gone through. It really helps to know that you're not alone. Hardly anyone talks about this, so people don't realize how common it is."

Looking back now, I realize that my reasons for being outspoken were selfish, really. No, not wrong, but I wasn't motivated by others' needs. What motivated me was a mothering instinct—as a photographer, I love to share pictures of my living children, and since I couldn't do that for my dead children, I did what I could. I spoke out of a determination that my dead children be remembered. I spoke out of the need to mother still.

I wasn't expecting the responses I got, and the ways other women reached out to me. I had given them a safe place to share their loss, to speak about their grief. I wasn't trying to be that safe place, I didn't invite anybody to share their stories with me, but **revealing my brokenness showed others it was safe to do the same.**

I learned that there is power in sharing our stories—I was strengthened by giving my grief a voice, and others were empowered to give their own grief a voice as well. Perhaps you have a story to tell, and others will tell you, "Thank you so, so much. I really appreciate being able to talk with you about this," as my friend said to me.

And you'll both find that you were not alone after all.

They Just Know

Paula Rollo

beautythroughimperfection.com

"MAMA!" she calls.

It's 3 a.m., but I go running to her room, just as she knows I will.

The next morning, she crawls into bed next to me as we both wake up, without a worry in the world.

As we go through our day, I can't count the number of times she calls and I answer.

I sit and read a book in our favorite comfy chair. A stolen moment of peace to myself as they run and giggle through our home. Before I know it, they are both on top of me, my book has gone unnoticed as they know they are the only true center of my attention.

We talk and we laugh, they climb on me, never once thinking I may not welcome it. Never considering that I could find their presence on my lap for the hundredth time today, anything less than wonderful.

And it's true, I love them and I cherish our times together. There are times that I lose my patience. There are moments that I yearn for a break, or just a moment where I'm free from all the touching. Even so, I love that they never doubt their place. Their place is with me.

They do not doubt my love. They don't wonder if they will be welcome in my arms, because they know they always are, and always will be.

Because this is motherhood. It's kissing one more scrape, changing another diaper and enduring ten more tantrums than you thought possible. And all in the space of an hour.

It's finding that your patience is much shorter than you ever imagined, and your love much deeper.

It's knowing love more than you ever thought possible. Because even in the times that the little ones are met with a "hold on" or a "just a minute," they are not deterred by this. It doesn't make them doubt the love that we share or the fun that we will have as soon as that minute is over. They know our love, and it's enough for them.

They know we belong together. They understand family more fully than many adults, because they know love, acceptance and where they belong.

And I hope they never forget it.

Not What I Expected

Kristin Smith

therichesofhislove.com

Motherhood didn't come in the way I originally expected it. Like many young girls, I had dreams of my prince charming, the white picket fence, and the proverbial 2.5 kids and a dog. It seemed easy and perfect.

And then at the age of 21, while a junior in college, I got pregnant. I was shocked. I was a "good girl," and things like that don't happen to girls like me. Or so I thought. I was terrified. Sure, I was in love with the guy I had been dating. Yes I wanted to marry him. But like this? It wasn't at all the way it was supposed to work out. There wasn't a fancy dinner and a proposal story. Rather, a commitment to one another and to God to raise this child in a family, together. So a few months later while my belly started to swell with the baby I carried, we vowed to one another to stay together, in sickness and in health, till death do us part.

I was selfish and unprepared for what being a mama would be. I stayed in college the fall of my senior year, before he arrived. Hugely pregnant, donning my only piece of comfortable clothing, denim overalls and a plaid shirt. I cringe at the sight I must have been. I felt a bit like an outcast. As I would walk across campus, I felt so very out of place. Everyone was happy and seemed so carefree. I was carrying a life inside of me. It was monumental at times. Excited but scared, I was full of fear and desperately didn't want my water to break on campus. *Anything but that, Lord.*

The morning before his arrival, it happened at home. I woke up to my water breaking and knew it was time. We rushed to the hospital and then spent the next 18+ hours waiting. Well, let me rephrase that: my husband waited, and I cried. The pain of labor was more intense than I had imagined it could be.

Having back labor throughout was excruciating, and I was certain that I couldn't handle it any more. And then came a flurry of women dressed in blue who told me to push. I did, and he was here. Our Isaac. Our firstborn. Dark black hair and 8lbs 15oz. He'd prove to be our largest baby overall. My doctor had prepped me for a 7lb baby based on my measurements—boy were we all surprised when he was weighed after birth!

He was perfect, and we couldn't have been more proud. He was ours and we would do anything for him. We left the hospital changed. The roads seemed more daunting now that there was precious cargo in the back. And then, as so many mothers experience, the sleepless nights and colic came. The crying seemed nonstop, and I can remember so many times sitting in the rocker in his room with nothing left in me but my own tears.

And the guilt, can we talk a minute about the guilt?!

Incredible guilt for getting mad about his cries, for not being able to fix his colicky behavior. I was certain that I was failing as a mother. Breastfeeding wasn't easy, he didn't sleep through the night and couldn't self-soothe at all. All of the things I knew were so important didn't happen the textbook way I understood they should. There weren't really books out there with moms sharing their real life experiences, only how-to's that I clearly could not master.

I felt alone and isolated.

Have you ever found yourself there, mamas? Today, with the internet and blogs, it is easier to find someone who has had similar experiences, but it is also easier than ever to find women who seemingly have it all together. Their kids are perfect, they sleep through the night at three weeks, they never cry or fuss or have attachment issues. And full on diaper blowouts—oh no, doesn't ever happen to "perfect mom." If there is any doubt up to now, I have not and will not ever fit into that category!

No, my journey as a mother has always been filled with messes. Sometimes those messes are funny. Like the time my daughter was able to open a full jar of diaper ointment and wipe it ALL OVER herself and the carpet and her changing table. Oh yeah, and she climbed up the changing table to get it while she was unsupervised in her room for a short time.

Can we say *Mother of the Year Award?*

That is my reality, friends! Sometimes it is messes that I create by my own doing. I am short-tempered and harsh to one of my little people. I hold unrealistic expectations of others and not myself. If there is a parenting mistake that could be made, I have likely dabbled in every one of them.

Other times, it was the mess of the journey, one filled with sadness. You see, my journey towards being a mom a second time wasn't easy. I was naive in thinking that because we got surprised by pregnancy the first time, when we were actually trying it would surely be easy.

Six years and scores of negative pregnancy tests later, my hopes had dwindled to nothing. My doctor said there was a less than 3% chance that we would get pregnant on our own. We couldn't afford other treatment options and weren't sure how we even felt about them, so we resigned ourselves to the idea that we might have an only child. And then one day I got heartburn.

For many, heartburn isn't significant, but for me it is the one true sign that I am pregnant. I was over the moon excited, and we anxiously prepared ourselves and our then six and a half year old for the new brother or sister that would join our family.

Gabriel came much more quickly than his brother, as in we almost didn't make it the 30 minute drive to the hospital. At one point, I may have screamed that my husband needed to "Speed it up because this baby is coming." We had about an hour to spare, so it wasn't an emergency, but it was cutting it close!

When he was nine months old, he came down with RSV and nearly died. As an unaware parent, I didn't know the warning signs of respiratory distress. He had seen a doctor the day before and was diagnosed with "just a virus." The following day, he was fussy and lethargic but I thought it was his body fighting the illness.

My parents happened to visit that night and took one look at him and calmly told us to pack a bag, that we needed to head for the emergency room. That 35 minute drive was the longest of my life. My dad sat in the backseat with a flashlight shining on him making sure he was still breathing. Our doctor later told us his little heart likely had 30 minutes left before it would have given out. We spent nine long days in the hospital before he was just well enough to go home.

I would have done anything to save him. And yet I was never more helpless. I will always be grateful for the doctors and nurses that cared for him in the hospital, and the perfect timing of my parent's visit.

We later decided that we weren't finished with our family and started trying for a third. Months turned into more years, and once again tests revealed that natural pregnancy was highly unlikely. But one day, the heartburn returned. I could hardly contain my excitement. My husband and I walked around with silly grins, trying to protect our "secret" for a little longer from the kids. Dreaming of all the what-will-be's.

But then, the bleeding came. I sat on the floor of my bathroom and begged God to spare this baby. A few hours later, it was over, and the darkness that I felt was overwhelming. I was bitter and angry. Everywhere I went, I saw women with round bellies. *Why them and not me, God?!*

After six grief-filled months, I saw a therapist. I wanted to be happy again, wanted to trust that God had something good planned for me, and

I was unable to see the blessings on my own. The therapist recommended I write a letter to my child, a goodbye of sorts. This simple letter brought me back to my love of writing. As a result, I started a blog and began to share my difficult walk through faith, family and motherhood.

In the fall of 2008, I had a procedure to "clean out my tubes." On the day of the surgery, I took a pregnancy test, and it was negative. A few weeks after the procedure, I had heartburn. I took a pregnancy test as a second thought, and it was positive. I was stunned. We went in for an ultrasound, and there on the screen was our 6 week, 6 day old son.

Somehow, the egg must have implanted on the very day of the surgery, thus the negative test at the time. It hung on during a procedure that could have wiped it out, and 8 months later Elijah joined our family.

He remains a strong fighter to this day.

Because we had so much trouble getting pregnant, I didn't even consider birth control after Elijah was born. He stopped nursing after nine months, and in four weeks I was unexpectedly pregnant again.

In August of 2010. we saw 4 letters on the ultrasound screen I never expected to see—GIRL. Named after my best friend who went to be with Jesus at the young age of 35, our girl Karlena is a constant reminder that we must hold strong to our faith. **God has been with us every moment of parenthood.** The trials that we have faced have been many and the journey has not always been easy. But God has been there with us every step of the way.

None of it happened like I had originally hoped or expected, but each moment has been a gift. A reminder that this life is precious. Unexpected at times, yes. But oh, so beautiful.

Seeking Joy

Danielle Olson

wellyouwellness.wordpress.com

Motherhood rarely turns out how you planned it. You know, the huge, ranch-style house surrounded by the perfect white picket fence, with the knight in shining armor, and three, beautiful, healthy and intelligent little kids frolicking in the yard.

I don't know about you, but that's not exactly how it turned out for me. Before I even had my first child, the knight in shining armor rode away, and I had to figure out how to pay for that house by myself, unemployed. I remember crying out to God, with a big, round belly, *How can this be in your plan?*

Sometimes, no matter the situation, whether our partners leave, our children fall ill, our dream job is taken away—we cannot see how God can work in this situation, or how it could be a blessing from Him.

We normally agree that God can make a bad situation better, but not that this "bad" situation is God's best, God's plan. I challenge that.

Have you read the Bible? How about some of the stories of women in there? They zip my lip about my problems faster than you can say "Ruth." I'm convinced God can not only take your tough situations and make them better, but it is in these exact situations where you will find Him, at work, planning, caring. Each and every one of us has battled, or is possibly currently in such a battle in our lives. No two situations are the same, but most are along the same lines: tough circumstances we can't change. If we could blink and change the circumstances, we would; but alas, we can't. We have to suffer through the current problem to reach the day where we wake up without it. But, have you noticed that the problem has one other element to it? Your attitude about it. Often, whether the problem goes away or not, when we change our attitude towards it, we change the entire outlook, and thus the final direction of our so called problems.

Somewhere between the full time job, the toddler's tantrums, the cleaning, laundry, bills, personal hygiene (anyone?), and the basic challenge that is my everyday life—I knew I was missing something. No, not another sock that had to be washed in the few hours I was actually at my home a day.

It was joy.

Being content with my situation, no matter the ups and downs, and no matter what my version of motherhood looked like. And thus, I began the grandest search of my life: seeking joy.

I began at the beginning of my Bible and wrote down every Bible verse that mentioned joy. After looking them up, I did not find my answer. That pesky joy was going to be harder to find than a quick Bible page flip. Drat.

I have learned what joy is by earnestly seeking it. As Paul said, the secret is being content no matter what circumstance comes your way:

> *"I am not saying this because I am in need, for I have learned to be content whatever the circumstances. I know what it is to be in need, and I know what it is to have plenty. I have learned the secret of being content in any and every situation, whether well fed or hungry, whether living in plenty or in want. I can do all this through him who gives me strength." – Philippians 4:11-13*

Being content when there's more month than paycheck? Yes. Having true joy when your little one splashed 99.7% of the water out of the bath again? Yes. Even at 9:30 p.m., when you're cleaning 257 Cheerio's off the floor? Yes. But how?

Being content and having joy because you are grateful for what you do have. Truly, being grateful and having a hopeful disposition is the same concept. When I became a single mom, my "have" list was a heck of a lot shorter than my "don't have" list. Husband, income, family nearby, a plan? Nope. What was on my "have" list was a God greater than those problems, and a blue--eyed little blessing He still gave me, even though He knew what would happen. Through Him who gives me strength.

No matter how much you want to fight it, being grateful for what you do have in your "don't have much" situations is the key to joy, the key to a full life in Christ. I know the last thing you want to do is think of how grateful you are to have a hard wood floor to put your feet on when you're cleaning off those 257 Cheerio's, but truly mama, you should be. You need to be.

"Give thanks in all* circumstances; for this is God's will for you in Christ Jesus." 1 Thessalonians 5:18

*I am still searching the footnotes for what exactly "all" includes, but unfortunately, to date, I have not found an exclusion for laundry (or anything else). I will keep you posted. About ten months after my divorce was complete, I moved back to where I grew up to be closer to family. One of the first Bible verses I wrote on my new chalkboard-covered décor was Psalm 37:4: "Take delight in the Lord, and He will give you the desires of your heart." This sounded pretty, and it sounded like the answer I needed, because there was not a whole lot of delight going on in my circumstances.

After a few weeks, I wiped it away in search of the next uplifting verse. We are always looking for happy circumstances. "Oh, God, change him/ fix this/give me that/help me with this." Instead, what we need to be praying for is a better view of our attitude. Show me how you can turn this into Your goodness. And refuse to see it {insert your situation here} as anything but God's goodness.

This is a lesson that I am still learning. Not long ago, in the throes of a torrential rain storm, my basement flooded. After working nine hours, I rounded out the day sweeping a never-ending stream of water into a tiny drain at one end of the basement floor. At 7:30 p.m., I finally got a re-heated leftover onto the table for my son's dinner. I sat down next to him in tears. To be honest, all I was thinking was how we didn't have anyone to help, how no one really cared, and how hard it was to handle motherhood, working full time, taking care of a house, and my own guilt of what seemed like not getting my son fed on time.

He came over to me with a magazine page we ripped out of a child sponsor program to which we subscribe. The photo was not of our sponsored child, but of two little boys carrying a five-gallon pail of water from a stream miles from their home. My son came over to my lap with this photo. "Mommy read this." I could hardly handle myself when I read about the boys' situation, and thought about the small amount of water I was wishing away, which was likely cleaner than what those young boys were carrying, was all they had to cook, bathe, clean and drink. That one hurt. Again, it wasn't my situation, it was my attitude and my negative thinking that ruined my night.

You may be looking at my situation and thinking that yours is worse; you may be thinking you've never gone through something so miserable. Both of these things are likely true, and I will tell you regardless of which side you fall on—it doesn't matter. **It doesn't matter if your current struggle is a bad hair day or you can't pay your rent this month —the truth is the same.** You can have joy in both of these situations, and every possible one in between. But with a negative outlook, you will never find joy in your situation, even if—and maybe especially when— your situation is great. I will even take that a step further. Even if your situation does get better, you will not truly find joy or appreciate it with a negative attitude. A negative outlook can find a problem with an all-inclusive Hawaiian vacation. No, you must be able to find the good in a hopeless situation.

One of the easiest ways to spoil your joy, even when you've learned to be grateful, is your words. You simply cannot have a positive life without positive words. You must delete phrases like "I can't handle..." "I never can..." and "I never will..." from your vocabulary. If you have to, speak life and possibility into the simplest of situations; even if that means you have to repeat, "I can eat whole grain toast," 500 times in a row. Sooner or later, you will start to believe it. If you're wondering if your words really matter, check out the verse below.

"The tongue has the power of life and death, and those who love it will eat its fruit." – Proverbs 18:21

Need I say more?

Fast forward to today... I not only understand, but am thankful for the path God placed me on. It helped me—no, forced me—to learn some valuable lessons about God and how to live life that I never would have in my "perfect" plan. To quote a popular meme, "What screws us up most is the idea in our head of what it should look like."

Unfortunately, that's true. When I feel the lowest is when I focus on all that I don't have that maybe those around me do have: a partner to help mow the lawn, money for pedicures (or time to give yourself one), a new dress for an event—it could be anything. Instead of even rationalizing that thinking, just stop. Think about what you do have that you are taking for granted. It's likely that a mama next door to you is praying for what you're forgetting about. Better yet, do something for her. Even if you think she has more time/money/health/whatever than you. The law of giving is backwards—the more you give, the more you get.

So did I find joy? Yes, I think I did. It's in putting my trust in a Savior who only has my well-being in mind. It's living in the hopeful expectation that He can plan a life out of my struggles better than I ever could have. I still have to drag myself— sometimes kicking and screaming—into being thankful in my everyday life.

I hope this encourages you to look past your circumstances into what I believe is God's true place for you, His loving arms. From there, you can see your circumstances from His point of view and rest in the security that He's got it —you don't need to manage everything, and better yet, you shouldn't. Cast your cares onto God, and seek Him and His joy today.

I'm Messy

Crystal Williamson

I got married when I was still in college. I was 20 years old, type B personality, and had never had to take care of an entire house before. I had two friends who got married the same summer as I did, and we each had little rent houses with our husbands near our college campus. I thought I was grown.

Even at that early point, I began to realize that I was not a natural housekeeper. Both of my sweet married friends had beautifully decorated houses that always seemed neat and tidy if we stopped by for any reason. When we came over for a visit, they somehow had the dishes all washed and put away before we left. I often didn't even see when they did it. People described my house as "homey." I tried to take that as a compliment. Sometimes, I tried really hard to get and keep my house clean, but when finals or other busy points in the semester came around, it would fall apart. We were clutter people.

That seemed to be a force we could never quite control.

My sweet 21 year old husband had never even done laundry except for the "man-proof" dorm machines that had actual buttons that said "Darks" and "Lights." Many of our early fights involved me feeling like he wasn't helping around the house enough. That first summer, I worked days at an office and he worked evenings at a restaurant. I would come home for lunch, and he would be just getting out of bed with plans to play with friends all afternoon and no thoughts of the dishes, the clutter in the living room, or anything else. It was really good for my mood and our marriage when he picked up a second job in the mornings.

By the time we finished college, got real jobs, and bought our first house, we had a bit more balance in the housework duties and sort of had a handle on things. Even during that time before kids, I often marveled at women who had seemingly effortless spotless houses. I was mad at sitcoms because they completely ignored this part of adulthood. Even Monica on *Friends*, who was a known neat freak, didn't seem to have to spend very much of her time actually cleaning. They were all off at the coffee shop or going on dates all the time, all while their beautiful apartments stayed sparkly clean.

As hard as I tried not to, I still compared myself to my friends who had the nice, perfect houses. On some level, I felt like less of a woman if I couldn't get my house to feel that clean.

And then, the babies came along. My first pregnancy was absolutely miserable. I threw up multiple times a day and felt nauseous pretty much constantly, well into my second trimester. I managed to keep my full time job, but I sometimes marvel at how I did that. That is about all I had the energy and motivation to do. By the time I got home at night, I pretty much laid on the couch, trying not to throw up until it was time for an early bedtime. Thank God for my husband stepping up during that time. For the most part, he took over with dishes and anything else that he could see needed to happen through most of my pregnancy. But, the detail work and deeper cleaning, the floors and even the bathrooms really weren't happening regularly anymore.

After my firstborn, Zane, was born, I went back to work full time after 12 weeks of maternity leave. Working full time with a baby was more exhausting and emotionally draining than I ever imagined. I know some women who love working full time with kids. They seem to thrive in the structure and busyness of it all. I was not one of those women. Every moment of my day was filled with work, caring for my son, or preparing everything for the next day when we would do it all again. Once again, we were barely maintaining the basics of the house—dishes and laundry. I would try to do other cleaning on Saturdays, but that was also our only real time for social interaction and quality time as a family. My house got out of control and overwhelming very quickly.

My bedroom is usually the worst room in my house. It is the room that no one outside the family has to enter, so it becomes the last priority. The floor would end up piling up with toys, clothes, and who knows what else. My room is where all the baskets of clean laundry go to never be folded and bags of Christmas presents we received sit for months before I actually have time to go through them. Luggage from our most recent trip will sit out for weeks before everything gets unpacked and put away. Being in my own room would sometimes put me on the brink of a panic attack.

I felt like a failure as a woman. "Women are supposed to be able to handle all of this," I would hear in my head. Our culture has an expectation of women to not only "have it all" but actually do it all. We are told that we can have the career and the kids, everything we want, but no one seems to mention how much work that is, and that it is so easy to lose ourselves in the process of it all. I had no more time to just be me and enjoy the things I liked anymore.

Because of the strain I felt from all of this, the loss I felt from having to spend so much time away from my son, and multiple other reasons, I began to pray seriously for some relief, for God's promise of an easy yoke and a light burden in my life. Over a period of about two years, we watched God do just this in our lives. Just before my second child was born, I was able to accept a half time job in my very same department at work that I would be able to start when I returned from maternity leave. The whole process was nothing short of a miracle for us.

I thought that my new schedule was going to solve a lot of my housework problems. I was going to actually be home more than I would be at work for the first time in years. The purpose of my new lifestyle was to be with my children more, but I figured that the house being a bit more manageable was a nice side goal.

Of course, two kids is a total game changer. My entire day could be devoured by potty training, nursing, "snack, please," temper tantrums, play dates (that I'm late to), "Will you play with me?" etc. Although the part time work schedule was very freeing and fantastic compared to what I had done before, I did not live up to my own expectations for my house... Again.

I felt like I could never rest or do anything I enjoyed at home. If I wasn't playing with or helping the kids, I felt compelled to do some kind of cleaning any moment that I was home and not sleeping. If I did sit down, I would find myself looking around and noticing the clutter on the floor, the leaves that needed to be swept up, the dust in the corner, and I would feel guilty for not working hard enough. "What kind of mom/wife am I?" I felt like a hamster on a wheel. Always running, but never seeming to get anywhere.

Eventually, I began to realize how unhealthy this mindset was. I noticed that, even in the Bible, God commands people to rest, to have boundaries from work in their lives. **God never said that keeping my house clean was a requirement to be a good mother or wife.** My husband never said that he would not love me as much if the house wasn't clean. My kids never actually cared what the house looked like.

Did I want my kids to remember that mom was always cleaning and never had time for other things? Wouldn't it be good for them to sometimes see that mommy is reading a book she likes, or writing, or just letting herself rest?

I had an epiphany that I had made my house cleaning an idol in my life. What I mean by that is that I had devoted so much of my time, energy, emotions, and feelings of self-worth into this one thing that I had allowed it to control me. I had become a slave to it.

To change my thought patterns and habits, I had to set some boundaries on my cleaning for a while. On my days at home, I would set a timer for usually an hour during nap time and only clean during that time. After the timer went off, I would allow myself to do something I wanted to do for the rest of nap time. After the kids went to bed at night, I would pick up some of the clutter that had gathered in the hallways. This was something small that helped me keep my sanity. When I allowed myself to enjoy some small bits of me time, I began to remember who I was again, more than just somebody's mom.

Through all of this, I realized that life is meant to be lived abundantly, not completely wasted away by attempts to live up to some kind of impossible imaginary standard. I learned to accept that this little flaw was part of who I am and no one loved me any less because of it. And also, no one cared even a fraction as much as I did about how clean my house was. My good friends love me and not my house, even if they stop by on a day that I didn't have time to tidy up first.

The funny thing is, while it would never pass a white glove test, we can still get the house "company-decent" when we get really motivated. And, I get to read books again, guilt-free. Win, win.

So, mama, go read that book, or paint, or sit on your back porch and breathe for a few minutes. It's okay to enjoy this life you have been given. Nobody really cares if your shower is clean today.

Loving Them Well

Cyndi Windy

I've heard it said you can never be a perfect mother but you can be good enough. Why is it we think that becoming a mother somehow equates with sainthood and super hero cape? Where in the process do we start to expect ourselves to be a deity, perfect and spotless? When do we determine we are capable of meeting our child's every need with patience and wisdom unknown to man, and how do we turn the ship when she starts sailing on the Sea of High Expectations?

My oldest is turning 30, my youngest 13. I've been at motherhood for a long time. That's a lot of years to get my act together, right? No. You see, I was growing up while they were growing up. I still am! Yes, at 52 I'm still learning how to parent. Experience in the name of "Hard Knocks" causes us to morph. As your babes grow, so will you. They will become awkward and clumsy, as will you. Who we ideally set out to be as mothers may not be who we see as we look in retrospect's mirror after we've gone about the business of living the nitty-gritty daily grind.

Not one of my babies came with an owner's manual. Not one. Just when I would give myself a congratulatory pat on the back for awesome parenting skills, I would turn around to completely mess up the next call to duty. There are times when you will instinctively know what to do and you will carry out your momma job with great skill and success. There will also be times when, because you and your children are imperfect human beings, you will take a shot in the dark hoping you hit the target—only to see by the light of dawn you missed the mark, by far.

You will stumble, fall, and scrape your momma knees, and because you are carrying little ones on your back, they might get hurt too. You will lie awake regretting the quick tongue, the words spoken in anger, and the scathing looks you sent your child's way. You will see their countenance fall, and you will know you were the reason. Guilt and uncertainty will be your bed partner many a night. **That's the messiness of motherhood. Just love them well.**

I am a military mother. My oldest son serves in the United States Army. He began as an enlisted man and took his oath as an 18-year-old senior in high school. He began his Army career as a medic for the National Guard and was then blessed with the opportunity to go active duty while in ROTC. For four years, I watched him from about four hours away as he married, earned his Ministerial Studies degree, and prepared for life as a leader in the Army. Every time we visited them, I would cry for the first two hours of that four hour trip. I was poignantly aware of what the future held, and I knew we would not live in close proximity for years and years, if ever. I knew a day would come when we would send him to a foreign country where he would live in harm's way. I longed to have him be that towheaded toddler again, in my lap, where I could engulf him in my protective arms and keep him from harm. Just one more time. Just one more time of being the shield from the ugly that is the world.

Instead, he held me. The last visit before his deployment, he held me. It was early am and the world was still sleeping. My husband and I needed to travel the 13 hours back to the kids still at home. We were all determined to make this as clean and clinical as possible because no momma wants to add to the burden of her son as he prepares to leave his wife and children for war. We had had a wonderful steak dinner and night out to celebrate their anniversary the evening prior, and we made "normalcy" happen. That's what military families do. It was a decided effort. But in bed... *How can I do this?* Repeated itself over and over like waves crashing on the beach, eroding away my resolve. *How can I do this? How can I say goodbye knowing it could be the last time? How do I do this?*

Early morning came, and we quickly shoved our last minute things in the car, filled the coffee mugs, and kissed our son and daughter--in--law before sneaking out the door. He got up and stood in the kitchen in his shorts and bare chest, and there, he held me. No, he wasn't little and needy. No, I was no longer his world. Now, he was big and strong and not so blonde anymore. And all the failures of all the years became insignificant in that moment. You see, I had been good enough. Not perfection, not even a glimmer of it—but loving him well and holding fast to beliefs and discipline was what had mattered. Yes, I loved him well.

My oldest daughter is a mother of four now. Oh, the complexity of the mother and daughter relationship! Your worst enemy, your best friend! Your harshest critic, your most ardent defender! It is often through your daughter that you will come full circle. You will pass the baton of messy motherhood to the next generation as you experience the intense and indescribable joy of grandmotherhood.

I was single-parenting her and her younger brother after a traumatic marriage and divorce from their dad. Failure was my best friend. I had lost it all—house, car, husband, pride, dignity. I had ruined our family's legacy of couples growing old and losing each other only to death. I moved the three of us back home to my mom and dad so I could afford the health insurance premiums and pay bills. Here I was, 28 years old and back home with two in tow.

My mom picked up all the shattered pieces of us. She cooked, cleaned, potty trained transported my kids to daycare while she continued to work as a teacher. She had my back in every area of life while all I could do was plow through the haze of despair over what my life had become. I was gone 11-12 hours a day for my job. Mom carried us. She loved us so well. As a matter of fact, I simply can't recall her being a messy mom even during my childhood. Something about that loving us well worked to erase things.

I hate to recall, let alone share, a night where my parents and children were privy to a fight between my ex-husband and me. It was ugly, but had sadly become our norm. My daughter went flying to the safety of my mom's arms upstairs and my dad eventually stepped in and stopped us to protect the others in the family. Failure at its finest. That's not just messy motherhood—that's a train wreck. Have you been there?

So, with that backdrop, know that my firstborn was a force of nature to be reckoned with even without the trauma of parents snared in selfishness. She didn't just push buttons, she jumped up and down on them while spewing out sass that could make Mother Theresa's head spin. My anger was always just under the skin if not sitting right on top of it. We were a horrible combination. I fought daily to keep her from self-destructive behaviors, and I didn't do it with grace. It was downright ugly at times. But, I loved her well.

As a new high school graduate, she left our home. She was done dealing with me. Done with living with me. Done with it all. She went off to college from another home, not ours, that fall. We would see her when her homesickness for her little sibs became great enough she was willing to see me as well. When the college curse of mono hit her, she came home for the care she needed. Know that as hard as the shell around their heart appears, there are momma-shaped holes that only you can fill. Just keep loving them well.

All the past pain and regrets visited me heavy that year. Turning off the video in my head became near impossible as I replayed the ugly over and over. Sure was I, that I had ruined this child. I deemed it a relationship that had suffered irreversible catastrophic events that would never be redeemed. Never give up on a prodigal. Just love them well.

Fast forward three years, she was marrying my favorite son-in-law (okay, he's the only so far) and they were finishing their last year of college. A few months after, a tentative phone call—she was expecting. She was afraid I wouldn't be happy since they were not yet settled with jobs. I assured her it was a life, a new life, and no I was not mad or disappointed. I hung up to return to the lunch room where the news started to settle and something deep within my heart just sprang to life. I wasn't even aware there was a place in my heart that could experience such deep emotion. My grandchildren still enthrall me. Each and every one of them.

We didn't know it, but that day started a very different kind of bonding that takes place when your daughter becomes a mother and you walk together, both in unchartered waters, both fiercely loving this child of hers, this child of yours. Together, you will both love this child well.

This daughter that left because she was done with me, returned home for the last portion of her pregnancy. Her husband, a Customs and Border Protection Officer had mandatory training out of state for three months. His training was ordered to take place at the end of her pregnancy in another state far from home. There was no negotiating.

I was with her. Just the two of us. She would have preferred to labor and deliver in a cave away from every member of society, but that's a little antiquated, so I emptied the basins as she vomited through hours of labor. I, in my messy mother way, did not sleep when she slept and ended up having a seizure as she was pushing. Yes, I had to leave her side and lay down while it passed. Awesome support, right?!

The doctor, who I knew, came in to get ready for the delivery, took a look at me, and said, "What's the matter, Cyndi? Is your baby having a baby?" in his deep Rwandan accent. At the time, I was angry and ashamed at my weakness at a moment when she needed me, but you know what? She didn't need me. I needed to be there for her. Those are two separate things that we must sort out as we parent—*what is my child's need versus what is my need?*

Momma, sometimes we are completely useless to our children. That's okay. SHE had to labor. SHE had to push. SHE had to do the hard and painful work to bear the fruit. Let that settle on your heart.

I took the pictures to send to her husband of this exquisite entity that had ruptured a floodgate in my heart. I thought my love for my children was overwhelming and unexpected. But this, this was beyond anything I had ever experienced in my messy motherhood.

The balance shifted. The weight of promise in the next generation was greater than the weight of my past momma messes and disappointments.

When I stood over my Grandma's casket and looked at her hands that had seen over 90 years, I saw my hands. The ridges in the nails. The shape of them. I saw the hands that played King on the Corner and put puzzles together. I saw the hands that made homemade, chunky, cinnamon applesauce. I saw the hands that held *Little House of the Prairie* books while she read aloud. I saw the hands that crocheted baby blankets for generations of grands. I could smell the Jergen's she used, always on the shelf by the sink. I knew nothing of her former messy motherhood. I only knew she loved us well.

So, make your mistakes. They are unavoidable. Drop your expectations, they serve no one. Don't strive for perfection, it's unobtainable. Do this: Love them well.

Full circle, dear momma. Full circle.

The Mom Quilt
Contributing Authors

Jodi Durr (Compiler) – *meaningfulmama.com*
Paula Rollo (Compiler) – *beautythroughimperfection.com*
Becky Mansfield (Compiler) – *yourmodernfamily.com*
Kristen Welch (Founder of Mercy House) – *wearethatfamily.com*
Brenda Sirratt (Editor) – *editallthethings.com*
Stephanie Jones (Designer/Editor) – *thestephaniejones.com*
Julie Brasington – *happyhomefairy.com*
Nicole Tolosa
Kelsey Wilkening
Mackenzie Rollins – *cheeriosandlattes.com*
Kara Carrero – *karacarrero.com*
Aleeca King
Meghan Boyce – *themontessorimoms.com*
Danielle Agnew – *inforlove.wordpress.com*
Crystal Williamson
Michelle Recicar
Caroline Vroustouris
Sara Reimers – *sunshinewhispers.com*
Annie Rim – *annierim.wordpress.com*
Stephanie Blake – *kingdommoms.org*
Kate Harden – *bellsthatring.blogspot.com*
Tabitha Dumas – *tabithadumas.com/blog*
Stefanie Davis – *simpleacresblog.com*
Kellie Van Atta – *familyserviceclub.org*
Kari Scott – *lanternno7.blogspot.com*
Drea DeyArmin
Tiffany Spire
Leona La Perriere – *hearapplause.blogspot.com*
Elizabeth Lovelace
Claire Ditowski – *5mamasandablog.wordpress.com*
Randomly Fascinated – *domesticrandomness.blogspot.com*
Charisse Segee
Kelli Pritchard – *axisministries.org/category/blog*
Kate Skero – *nourishinglittlesouls.com*
Lorie Huneycutt – *loriehuneycutt.wordpress.com*
Priscilla McConnell – *memoirsformemories.blogspot.com*
Janet Faubert
Crystal McClean – *castleviewacademy.com*
Kelly Bingham – *kellybinghamwrites.com*
Laura Falin – *peacebutnotquiet.com*
Meri Stratton-Phelps
Megan George – *jeansandbarefeet.wordpress.com*
Roxanne Foster – *thefosterparenthood.com*
Casey Snyder – *gracefaithcompassion.com*
Daphne Greer – *grievinggumdrops.com*

Laura Wilkinson – *laurawilkinson.com*
Kristin Smith – *therichesofhislove.com*
Cyndi Thelen – *soultracings.com*
Paty Pruet
Angelia Griffin – *mybestlaidplans.net*
Natasha Westerhoud – *natashawesterhoud.blogspot.ca*
Kim Dorman
Amy Bottorff
Monica Brietenstein – *mommee-truths.blogspot.com*
Danielle Olson – *wellyouwellness.wordpress.com*
Laura Brown
Becky Linn
Marilyn Biddinger – *glimpsedglory.com*
Christina Mathis – *thetransparencychronicles.blogspot.com*
Jessica Smith – *longestdays.com*
Elaine Mingus – *superradchristianwriterchick.com*
Candra Fischer
Tiffany Bluhm
Renee Kemper – *thatsjustlife.com*
Janet Kirk – *faithcounts.wordpress.com*

Made in the USA
San Bernardino, CA
01 November 2017